No Sense
of Direction

Eric J. Raff

EPIC ADVENTURES
NEW YORK

No Sense of Direction. Copyright © 2000 by Eric J. Raff

Printed in the United States of America

Epic Adventures
308 West 103rd Street
Suite 2A
New York, NY 10025

Cover design by Bill Naegels
Cover Photo by Lawrence Kimmel

FIRST EPIC ADVENTURES EDITION, October 2001

ISBN 0-9708732-0-4

For my family — you are always there for me,
no matter how far I travel.

"Would you tell me, please, which way I ought to go
from here?" asked Alice.
"That depends a good deal on where you want to go to," said the Cat.
"I don't much care where," Alice replied.
"Then it doesn't matter which way you go," said the Cat.
—*Lewis Carroll, Alice in Wonderland*

Contents

Introduction

A few years ago, I was a vice president with a large, prestigious advertising agency in Manhattan. I had a good job with a good company. A job half the people in New York were waiting in line for. At least, that's what everyone kept telling me. They had absolutely no clue what the other half were waiting for, but somehow, they were sure the first half wanted my job. So, one sunny, spring day, after weighing the pros and cons of my life, I decided to let the first half have it.

I was bored with my job, tired of the Manhattan social scene, and uninspired by my same day-to-day routine. Basically, I felt that my life needed a major overhaul. But it wasn't until I walked home from a depressing dental appointment one evening that I decided on a clear course of action. After giving my future a great deal of thought, I did what any other rational, well-regarded advertising executive, with a good salary and a solid career track would have done—I quit my job and decided to see the world.

Somewhere during this period of soul-searching, I had read that the *Talmud*—the collective works of Jewish laws, customs, and knowledge—states that a person should do three things in life: Plant a tree, have a child, and write a book.

I had planted a tree when I was a kid. (Actually, I paid to have someone plant one in Israel for me, but I think that still counts.) Having a child would have been difficult, since I wasn't dating anyone at the time. But writing a book—that was something I thought I could do. Or at least, something I could do alone. So after quitting my job, buying a one-way ticket to Europe, and packing a thick spiral notebook, I said goodbye to family and friends and ventured off to see the world.

No Sense of Direction recounts my travels with the colorful cast of characters I met while roaming around Eastern Europe and Asia for the better part of a year. It's called *No Sense of Direction* because it reflects the way I traveled—no plan, no itinerary, and no timeframe.

While facing the future without a plan may not be the best way to live, I'm convinced it's the best way to travel. Or, as some wise man, whose name I can't remember, once said: *You don't have to know where you're going to enjoy the road you're on.*

Getting Old

Making Plans

Goodbye New York

I have a new philosophy. I'm only going to dread one day at a time.
—Charles Shultz

"Brrnng . . . Brrnng. . . . Brrnng . . . "

I grabbed the phone from my desk and answered impatiently, "Eric Raff."

"Mr. Raff?" This is Dr. Silverman's office calling to remind you about your five-thirty dental appointment."

The way my day had been going the last thing I needed to worry about was a dental appointment, especially on a Friday night. "Uh, listen . . . would it be possible to—"

"You've already cancelled twice Mr. Raff. If you cancel tonight's appointment I'm afraid we'll have to bill you for the visit."

I looked at the stack of folders on my desk and the two people seated in my office, then checked my watch. Four o'clock. I had a conference call at 4:15 P.M., a meeting with the media department at 4:45 P.M., and needed to review new creative concepts at 5:00 P.M. I glanced out the window and saw it was snowing. Catching a taxi wouldn't be easy, which meant I would have to take the subway at rush hour. My stomach tightened. "No problem. I'll be there."

An hour later I sprinted from the building at Worldwide Plaza and raced down the street. Weaving my way through a mob of people ahead of me I ran toward the subway at 50th street and Broadway. I stood off the curb on the corner of eighth avenue with a pack of other impatient New Yorkers, each of us waiting for the traffic to thin so we could cross the busy intersection without having to wait for the light to change. At the first break in traffic we scrambled into the street in a rush, just a few steps ahead of the next wave of cars.

I darted past the little newsstand on the corner of 50th street and hurried down the steps to the subway platform. Halfway down I held my breath as the smell of urine and warm stale air from the station drifted up to me. I squeezed through the long line of people waiting to buy subway tokens and slipped my token into the thin metal slot near the turnstile.

The train was coming on the uptown track. I was in luck. For once, it looked like I would get to the dentist on time. As the train came to a piercing, grinding stop, a swarm of commuters lunged through the doors in my direction.

I edged my way through the crowd and squeezed onto the train just as the doors banged shut. As the train barreled along towards 59th street I slowly positioned myself where I could grab a handrail to keep from losing my balance. Not that I could have fallen with all the people surrounding me but I felt better knowing I was anchored to something other than the extremely large, unfriendly looking person beside me. There was plenty of room inside the train, but as usual, everyone congregated near the doors so they could make a quick exit. The cold weather made it worse since everyone was bundled up in winter coats, which made a tight squeeze even tighter.

When the train stopped at 66th street I marched slowly through the turnstiles with everyone else and climbed up the stairs on the heels of the people in front of me. I stepped out on the street and gratefully breathed in the cool evening air. I had two blocks to walk. I checked the time on my watch—5:28 P.M. If I hurried, I could just about make it on time.

I arrived at exactly five-thirty, and barely had time to take my coat off before a dental assistant told me to follow her to the examination room. Two minutes later I was flat on my back in a reclining leather chair with a white apron tied around my neck and an overhead lamp glaring into my eyes. Meanwhile, my dentist was sticking a long metal instrument down my throat while attempting to converse with me.

"When was the last time you had your teeth cleaned?" he asked nonchalantly.

"I'm not sure," I mumbled, as he continued to probe around in my mouth. "Sometime last year, I think."

"Well, you've got some problems, my friend," he said with a frown, as he finished his examination and moved the overhead lamp away from my head.

I sat up and wiped the drool from my chin while I tried to remember what kind of dental coverage I had at work before asking nervously, "What kind of problems?"

He placed his instruments on a small round table to his right and sighed. "You have some bone loss in one or two spots on the upper left and lower-right sides of your mouth. You'll most likely need periodontal work at some point to keep it from getting worse. In the meantime, we can do some deep cleanings to try and contain the problem."

I was always a chicken when it came to dental work and the prospect of "deep cleanings" made me cringe. With a frown, I followed the dentist back to the reception desk where he instructed the attendant to set me up for two appointments. With a pleasant smile and a quick handshake, he wished me good night and signaled his dental assistant for his next patient.

When I left his office, I decided to walk the eight blocks home to avoid another encounter with the subway. On my way uptown I thought about what the dentist had told me and felt myself getting a little depressed. "Bone loss" I mumbled aloud, as I walked along thinking about my teeth. "Just last week I noticed some hair loss. Now I've got bone loss. The way things are going, pretty soon I'll have tooth loss. What's going on?" I didn't feel old, and I knew I didn't look old. But time was obviously taking its toll. It was happening slowly, but it was happening. A few hairs here, a few teeth there, and before long I would be an old, bald, toothless man wondering where my life had gone.

As I made my way along the littered streets of New York, I passed an elderly couple who were strolling slowly beside me. I glanced at them and felt a panic rise inside me as I pictured myself as an old man shuffling along the dark, gray, lonely streets of Manhattan on my way back to a small studio apartment—all alone, without a wife or even a dog to greet me when I got home. Life was going by way too fast. And the worst part was that I wasn't even aware it was going by. The only thing I was aware of was that every day seemed just like the one before. The days, weeks and months had become one long blur, each day indistinguishable from the next. And I realized that if I didn't want to wake up one day and find that the better part of my life was behind me, then I needed to do something about it. I needed a change. And the sooner it happened, the better. Hopefully, before my next dental appointment.

As I stood on the curb waiting for the light to change, I noticed my reflection in a store window. I stared at my face in the window and felt a grateful wave of relief. I was still young enough to do the things I wanted to do in life. I could change things before I really did get old. I touched my teeth and hair for reassurance and felt like I had been given a second chance at life. As I continued walking home I thought about all the things I wanted to do while I still had my health and the time to do them.

I reflected on the various dreams I had at one time or another stored away for some future date and like a flash, it became suddenly clear what I wanted to do. I wanted to travel and see the world—instead of waiting until I was too old to do it. Or worse, never getting the chance to do it. With a renewed sense of energy and a sudden clarity of purpose, I walked quickly back to my apartment through the dark, busy streets of Manhattan, and formulated a plan.

Money isn't everything as long as you have enough.
— Malcolm Forbes

When I returned to work on Monday I was a new man—like Ebinezer Scrooge in "*A Christmas Carol*," the day after he was visited by the three spirits who helped him change his miserly ways. The big difference though, was that I was about to become a miser. At least for the next few months.

Over the weekend I had worked out a budget for taking a year off from work. I already had most of what I needed in the bank but decided that, despite the saying, "Sometimes less is more," when it comes to money, more is always better. So I began saving money with a passion.

From the moment I made up my mind to travel, my whole focus was on cutting expenses. Short of stealing, I took advantage of every opportunity I could. Over the next few months I became the coupon king of 76th street, clipping coupons from every local newspaper in the neighborhood. I brought my lunch to work and cooked my own dinners instead of eating out which, given the way I cook, was no pleasure. And I cut out dating completely. So not only did I become a miser, I became a monk.

I picked mid-April as the time I would leave. I had no planned itinerary but it seemed like the right time since the weather would be warmer and it would give me the advantage of traveling for a few months before crowds of tourists hit the road in the summer.

Towards the end of March I told senior management of my plans and formally handed in my resignation, effective three weeks from that date. When I left work that day I felt great. It was springtime, and that alone was usually enough to give me a renewed sense of energy after the winter. But this feeling was even better. For the first

time in a long while I had no idea what was ahead of me, and that
was a terrific feeling in itself. In less than a month I would be leaving
a comfortable, secure life. And what was remarkable to me was how
easy it was to leave it. Save some money, quit the job, buy a ticket
and go.

The last few weeks at work raced by. Surprisingly, I was still included in planning meetings, creative reviews, and new business pre-
sentations as if nothing had changed. It wasn't until I walked into a
surprise farewell party that I realized my job was finally over.

After I said my last good-byes to everyone I went back to my office
to pick up the last of my things. As I packed away the last few personal
items from my desk drawer I noticed a small wooden plaque that I
had placed there a few years before. It showed a picture of a beautiful
sunset with the silhouette of a tall clipper ship gliding across the seas.
Above the ship was written, "*A ship in a harbor is safe, but that is not
what ships are built for.*" Like an omen, that little plaque dispelled any
doubts I had about leaving.

I picked up the box that held my personal things and glanced
around my office to make sure I hadn't forgotten anything. Satisfied
that whatever I left behind wouldn't be missed, I turned off the light
and slipped my nameplate from the wall outside the door into my
pocket. With a nostalgic look at what was officially no longer my
office, I closed the door and walked down the long, red-carpeted hallway to the elevators and left the building for the last time.

Better three hours too soon then a minute too late.
— Shakespeare

The traffic getting out of the city was a mess. To save some money I had decided to take a bus to the airport instead of a taxi, but regretted my decision as soon as we left the terminal. Not that a taxi could have gone much faster. But watching the bus wait in line while every car around us sneaked in front of it made me think we were the only ones who weren't moving. It took half an hour just to get across town from the Port Authority Bus Terminal to Grand Central Station. I cursed myself for not having left earlier.

I opened a book and put on my Walkman to take my mind off the traffic and help me relax. But as the minutes crawled by faster than we did, I began to worry that I would miss my flight. I looked around to see if anyone else seemed concerned, but the rest of the passengers looked totally calm, as if they had all the time in the world.

I wanted to shout at them, *What's the matter with you people? Why didn't you take a later bus if you have so much time to get to the airport!* Then it hit me. This was why they didn't take a later bus—so they wouldn't have to worry about missing their flights because of a little traffic.

Somehow, no matter how much time I had, I was always running to catch a train or plane. And it wasn't because I was unorganized and not ready to leave on time. It was because I hated sitting around train stations and airports. So I always waited until the very last minute to leave. And then, when unplanned things like traffic jams happened, I was screwed.

Just when I started to wonder what I would do if I missed my flight, the traffic broke and we started to move. A hundred yards up the road we passed the cause of the long back up—a two-car accident in the right-hand lane. Once we passed the police cars and tow trucks, traffic returned to normal and the bus began to cruise along at a good speed.

I patted my pocket to make sure I hadn't forgotten the one-way ticket I had bought to Copenhagen earlier in the week. I had a friend in Denmark and thought it might be easier to start my travels in a country where I knew someone. I had no clue where I would go after that but I figured Denmark was as good a place as any to start my journey. I checked my watch and breathed a sigh of relief as I watched the New York City skyline retreat steadily behind us.

The bus arrived at Kennedy airport with about twenty minutes to spare. I dropped my backpack off at the check-in counter and went directly to the gate, where my flight had begun boarding. I stepped off the boarding ramp and glanced down the double aisles of the wide-body 747. A stewardess glanced at my ticket and pointed me in the direction of my seat. Most of the passengers were already seated and buckled in. I spotted my seat about halfway down the aisle, just behind the wing of the plane, and squeezed carefully past a pleasant-looking woman to get to my assigned seat near the window. After the usual short film on safety procedures, which no one paid any attention to, the aircraft began to taxi down the long, gray runway.

I gazed through the window on my left and watched the bright runway lights race by, one by one, until they became one long white blur. As we picked up speed I felt the energy rise inside me along with the sound of the engines, until all of a sudden, almost effortlessly, we were off the ground and climbing steadily.

I leaned back in my seat and watched Manhattan's tall, graceful skyscrapers taper off in the distance. With a contented sigh, I glanced over at the woman seated beside me. She caught me looking at her and smiled. As much by way of introduction, as to convince myself that my trip had begun, I smiled back and said reassuringly, "We're off."

The soul of a journey is liberty, perfect liberty, to think, feel,
do just as one pleases.
— William Hazlitt

"Would you like some more wine?" the stewardess asked pleasantly. I held out my plastic cup for a refill then sank back in my seat to enjoy the small cup of Cabernet Sauvignon. We were three hours into the flight and I was slowly coming to grips with the concept that I was totally free and without a care in the world.

It was an amazing feeling. From that moment on there was absolutely nothing I had to do except find places to eat and sleep. No responsibilities. No work. No schedule. No nothing. I was retired! It wasn't going to be a long retirement, but for the next year or so, I was as free as anyone could ever hope to be.

It was an incredible concept and every time I thought about it— which was a lot at the beginning of the trip, I couldn't keep myself from smiling. Anyone watching me when one of those smiling attacks occurred would have thought I was out of my mind. One minute I was sitting there looking perfectly natural, just eating or reading or doing nothing in particular, and the next, I was grinning away like an idiot. Which was pretty much the way I spent the flight from New York to London's Manchester airport—eating, reading, and grinning like an idiot.

With the time difference, the plane touched down in Manchester around six in the morning. My connecting flight was scheduled to leave from a different gate one hour later. The flight crew had served breakfast just before we landed, so instead of going off to find something to eat I wandered around the airport to stretch my legs.

At 7:00 A.M. I boarded the plane for the onward flight to Copenhagen. When I arrived at the gate I noticed that the passengers looked noticeably different from those on the earlier flight. Most of them had blonde or light-brown hair, and were all fairly tall, good-looking men and women. With my black curly hair and round wire-rim glasses, I was aware of how much I stood out from everyone else. As if to prove the point, the stewardesses greeted each passenger with a warm, "God Morgen" as they stepped on board. But as soon as they saw me they said, "Good morning" in English.

The plane wasn't full so I took a seat near a window and settled back to watch my second take-off of the day. It was early morning and I was starting to feel a little tired since I had been up since 8:00 A.M. the day before. I pulled down the plastic window guard to keep the morning sunlight out of my eyes and browsed through the morning copy of the *International Herald Tribune* until it was time to depart. It wasn't long however, before the steady hum of the engines and the warmth of the early morning sun made me drowsy. I closed my eyes with the hope of catching a few minutes sleep, and after what seemed like only a few seconds, I felt someone gently tapping my shoulder. I looked up and saw a beautiful stewardess with long, silky auburn hair standing over me, her hand resting lightly on my arm. She said softly, "I am sorry to wake you, but we have arrived in Copenhagen." At first, I thought I was dreaming. Then I realized the girls in my dreams were never that beautiful. I thanked her, then grabbed my small daypack from the overhead compartment and lined up behind the other passengers waiting to exit the plane.

After clearing Passport Control, I picked up my backpack from the baggage carousel, changed a few dollars to Danish Krone, and hopped on the airport bus to the city. When the bus arrived at Copenhagen's Central Train Station I found a public phone and called my friend Henrik. Less than twenty minutes later, Henrik came bounding through the front doors of the station.

"Hello Eric! It is very good to see you again. You haven't changed at all!" he beamed.

Neither had he. Which didn't surprise me. Henrik was only 25 years old, so I didn't expect him to look any different from when I had last seen him. Tall, slim, with long, brown hair and green eyes, he still looked like a Danish version of Sting.

I had met Henrik a few years before while on a vacation to Thailand. I had become friendly with a small group of Scandinavians while I was in Bangkok and Henrik was part of their group. During the two weeks we traveled together, Henrik and I had a running competition playing a card game called "Chinese Poker." Instead of playing for money, we played for Snicker's candy bars. Henrik was the main reason I never ran out of Snicker's bars during my stay in Thailand.

With a big grin and a welcoming clap on my back, he said cheerfully, "Come on my friend—first we will drop your bags off at my friend's apartment where we will be staying. After that, I think I will teach you a lesson in Chinese Poker—assuming you still remember how to play!"

Copenhagen is spread out over a fairly wide area, but the center of the city is actually pretty compact. A few minutes walk from the train station brought us to Radhuspladsen, the large square across the street from the Strøget—Copenhagen's busy pedestrian shopping street, and the heart of the city. The apartment was on a side street a few blocks to the left of the Strøget. Henrik's friend lived at his girlfriend's apartment across town and was letting Henrik use his apartment until Henrik, who recently moved to Copenhagen from Århus, could find a place of his own.

We dropped off my things, then went for dinner at a nice little Greek-owned pizza shop near the Strøget before going back to the apartment to relax. The time difference was finally getting to me and I was beginning to run out of energy. I had been on the move for over a day and a half with only a short nap on the plane and I was fading fast.

Before I went to bed Henrik informed me that some friends of his were coming by in the morning to take us sightseeing in the countryside. One of his friends had a car and Henrik had arranged for him to take us on a long drive up the coast so I could see some sights outside of the city.

"I don't know what time they're planning to get here, but I'm afraid it might be quite early," Henrik said. "If you're too tired, I can ask them to come later."

I suppressed a yawn and rubbed my bloodshot eyes. "No problem—I'm not really that tired. Wake me whenever they get here." Actually, I was exhausted and didn't realize how tired I was until I turned off the lights and got into bed.

As I looked around the unfamiliar room it was hard to believe it had only been a day and a half since I had left New York. It seemed longer. It also seemed strange that an environment could change so quickly in such a short period of time. The bookshelves that lined the walls near my bed were filled with titles in a language I couldn't read. And outside the window I heard people speaking but couldn't understand what they were saying. I closed my eyes and tried to imagine I was back in my own bed on 76th Street. But somehow, even with my eyes closed, I could sense I was in a different place. Everything around me, even the air, seemed to have a different quality from what I was used to.

I suddenly felt very isolated and disoriented. If I felt out of place in a country where I had friends, I couldn't imagine what the road ahead was going to be like—or how I was going to stay away from home for so long. I started to wonder whether traveling without a plan or a timeframe was such a good idea after all. Then, too tired to give it any more thought, I let myself drift slowly into a deep, sound sleep.

The early morning sun seeped through the window blinds and woke me from a good night's rest. A few minutes later, Henrik knocked lightly on the door to my room. "Eric? Are you awake yet? Come on tired-head, it's time to go. We've been waiting for you."

Squinting from the bright sunlight that filled the room, I crawled out of bed and opened the door. Henrik's friends were sitting in the living room eating breakfast. On my way to the bathroom, I looked back at Henrik and laughed. "By the way, it's 'sleepy-head'." Henrik's English was terrific, but sometimes he mixed up familiar expressions.

Twenty minutes later, after a quick cup of tea and some fresh croissants, Henrik, Stig, Anders, Steffen and I were heading north along Denmark's rocky coast in the smallest car I had ever been in. It was a tiny Fiat, and its small size was made even more ludicrous by the size of its owner. At six-feet four inches tall, Steffen looked like he was driving a toy.

Looking at Steffen crammed behind the steering wheel, I couldn't help laughing. "Steffen, why did you buy such a small car?"

He moved his knee away from his mouth so I could hear him. "It was all I could afford. Certain things like cars are considered luxury items in Denmark. They are very heavily taxed and are incredibly expensive here. Much more so than in the States."

A sleek, green Jaguar sped by on the other side of the road. "How much would it be for a car like that in the U.S.?" he asked me.

"Around sixty or seventy thousand, I guess."

"That car probably costs $200,000 U.S. dollars over here. That guy must have a lot of money to want a car like that in Denmark."

We drove along the coast for about an hour, the waves sparkling in the sea off to our right. As we drove along, Henrik pointed out houses of interest and locations of famous castles down various side roads. We pretty much spent the day touring around at random, eventually stopping at Helsingør at the northern end of the coast to see Elsinor Castle, reputed to be the castle from Shakespeare's "*Hamlet.*" After a quick lunch at a small restaurant along the beach, we drove inland for awhile on a desolate country road through beautiful woods filled with Beech trees that had the most incredible yellow-green leaves I had ever seen. Eventually, we made our way back to the coastal road and drove back towards Copenhagen in time to see the sun dip into the North Sea at the end of the day.

Later that evening we went for drinks at a place called *Sømmerskø*, a popular local pub packed with Danish yuppies. Anders, Stig, and Henrik grabbed some stools at a table in the corner while Steffen and I went off to buy a round of beers.

When it was my turn at the bar, the bartender asked me something in Danish. I pointed to a bottle of beer on the counter and said, "Four of these." My English response drew a curious look from an attractive blonde on my right, which Steffen noted with a wink in my direction.

With two beers in each hand we worked our way through the crowd back to our table. When we sat down, Steffen smacked the table with his hand and said with delight, "I think our American friend may have already found himself a pretty Danish girl!"

Stig and Anders laughed loudly and quickly chimed in, "Go for it! Danish girls love Americans."

Not to be outdone by his friends, Henrik reached into his pocket and threw me his keys. With a wide grin he said with amusement, "Here—you can have the keys to the apartment."

"Not so fast!" I said with a laugh, hoping to put an end to their teasing. "He's only kidding—I didn't say a word to her." Steffen laughed, clearly enjoying his little prank. "You didn't have to—didn't you see the look she gave you?" With a playful punch on my arm he added, "Actually, you will be better off if you don't meet any Danish women while you're here because if you do, you will surely change your mind about wanting to leave Denmark to go off traveling."

A few hours and God knows how many drinks later, we sang our way out of the bar and down the street. The four Danes knew more English songs than I did and were still going strong long after they walked Henrik and me back to the apartment, their voices echoing in the deserted, narrow streets of the Strøget as they walked off to find Steffen's little Fiat.

The next morning I woke up with a hangover and cursed myself for drinking so much. Henrik was also feeling the effects of the previous night and sat motionless on the couch with his eyes closed, too tired to get up and make breakfast.

When my brain was functioning almost normally again, I went out to explore the city. Henrik had to study for a German language test he was scheduled to take that week. He had completed his MBA program a few months before but hadn't satisfied the language requirement. If he failed the German test he would need to take the class over again so I thought it best to leave him alone and let him study.

I returned to the apartment later that afternoon and found Henrik in the same spot as when I had left. He was busy scribbling away in his German notebook and repeating German phrases aloud to himself as he worked through the exercises. When he saw me walk in, he closed his book and tossed down his pen.

"That's enough studying for today I think!" he exclaimed.

"So? Are you ready for your test?"

"No problem. It will be a piece of pie."

"Cake."

"Excuse me?" Henrik was always very polite.

"Cake. A piece of cake. You said pie."

"Yes, you're right. Sometimes these English expressions don't translate so well from Danish." Then, with a big grin he looked up and said, "Enough of these German and English lessons, my friend. Now it is time for a *Chinese* lesson! Chinese Poker that is—if you think *you* are ready!" Before I had time to answer, Henrik shoved his books to the side and pulled a deck of cards out from the shelf beneath the coffee table.

It had been so long since I had played the game, that it took me a little while to get going. To Henrik's increasing delight I lost the first few rounds pretty badly. But then, slowly, I began to dig my way out of the hole, and with each passing round, started to turn the score around.

Two hours later, I tallied the score of the final game and stood up triumphantly. "Chinese Poker doesn't seem to be your game Henrik—I think you should stick with your German lessons!"

He tossed his cards on the table with a sigh. "I'm afraid you may be right, my friend—my German lessons were much more successful."

There's no limit to how complicated things can get,
on account of one thing always leading to another.
— E.B. White

Monday. The start of a new week. By the time I woke up Henrik had already left for work. So it seemed had everyone else. Except for a few people buying groceries in the shops across the square, the streets were empty. I opened the shades to let the sun in the apartment, then got dressed, fully rested and ready to start the day.

For most people it was a whole new week of phone calls, meetings, and business decisions. But I had dropped out of the real world and was happy to let everyone else worry about being productive. The biggest decisions I had to make were what to have for breakfast and where to go when I left Denmark.

After a light breakfast of two-day old croissants and a fresh pot of tea, I sat in the living room and thought about where I wanted to travel next. I moved Henrik's German books to the side and spread my map on the table to survey the world.

I studied the map awhile and considered the possibilities. I had been to Europe before but never to Eastern Europe and I eventually settled on Poland as my next destination as it seemed the most logical place to start. Poland was close to Denmark and offered easy access to the other Eastern European countries. From there I could go south to Czechoslovakia and Hungary or east to Russia. Satisfied with my destination, I looked up the names of some inexpensive travel services in my guidebook and found a place called "*Kilroy*," just a few blocks from the Strøget. I grabbed my daypack, stuffed a croissant in my pocket for later, and left the apartment.

When I arrived at the travel agency I was surprised at how busy it was. I took a number from a little red ticket machine on the counter and sat along the back wall in an unoccupied plastic chair, beneath a row of colorful travel posters.

Kilroy was a student travel service, and although you didn't need to be a student to use it, most of the customers looked like students. Even the staff looked like students. When my number flashed on the electronic sign over the counter I walked up and presented my number to a ticket agent named Anna, a small blonde with light green eyes and a friendly smile.

"How may I help you?" she asked politely.

"I'm thinking about going to Poland and would like to know the cheapest way of getting there," I replied.

She flipped open a thick black binder on top of the counter and spent the next ten minutes showing me prices and time schedules for going to Poland by train and boat. I ruled out the boat right away. I wanted to go directly to Warsaw and the boat involved train transfers with long waiting periods between connections at odd times of the day and night. We reviewed a couple of train schedules and decided that the best train for me to take to arrive in Warsaw at a reasonable hour was one leaving the following night at 10:23 P.M.

"The train leaves Copenhagen tomorrow night and arrives at Berlin's Lichtenberg station at 7:10 the following morning," she explained. "From there you will have to transfer to Berlin Hauptbonhoff station to take an 8:03 A.M. train. You will arrive in Warsaw early afternoon."

I shook my head doubtfully. "Anna, I probably have the worst sense of direction in Copenhagen—maybe all of Europe, come to think of it. So I'm a little worried I'll get lost going from Lichtenberg Station to Hauptbonhoff Station. It took me almost half an hour to find *this* place and you're only four blocks from where I'm staying."

She ran her finger down the railway timetable and re-checked the departure times. "The stations are not far from each other," she assured me. "You will have almost an hour to get to Hauptbonhoff station—more than enough time to make the 8:03 train."

Satisfied with her explanation, I counted out my money and paid for the ticket. She entered my reservation in her computer and walked to the printer in the rear of the office. A minute later she returned to the counter empty-handed. "I am sorry, but there seems to be some difficulty with this printer right now. If you don't mind waiting I will print them out on a different machine."

"No problem," I replied, hoping the other printer wasn't also having problems.

After a short wait, Anna strolled happily back to the counter and handed me two tickets. "Here you are. This one is for your train ticket. And this one is for your couchette." I tucked the tickets safely away in the money belt around my waist.

Before I left the counter I asked, "There's one last thing you may be able to help me with before I go. I know I don't need visas for Poland, Czechoslovokia or Hungary. But I'll need one if I decide to go to Russia. Do you know where I can get a Russian visa?"

"Do you have hotel accommodations in Russia?"

"No. I'm not even sure I'm going there yet."

"Well, I'm afraid that without an itinerary of where you want to go in Russia, and where you will stay if you do go, the Russian Consulate will not issue a visa to you."

"But how am I supposed to know where I'm going to stay before I even get there?"

She shrugged and said, "You could go with a tour if you'd like. They would arrange the hotels and visa for you. Or Intourist, the Russian Travel Service, can make reservations for you at one of their hotels. Then it will be no problem for you to get a visa."

"How much are the rooms through Intourist?"

"I don't know exactly. But they are not inexpensive. Maybe $80 U.S. dollars a night. Perhaps more."

I was shocked by the price. "To stay in Russia?" I blurted. "I don't want to buy the hotel—I just want to rent a room in it."

She frowned sympathetically. "The only other way I know is to get a transit visa. Many people take the Trans-Siberian train from Moscow to Beijing. When you buy the train ticket you are given a one-day transit visa to enter Moscow the day before the train departs. A second-class ticket costs around $750 U.S. dollars. The price includes visas for Russia, Mongolia and China, and one night's accommodation in a Russian hotel in Moscow the day before you leave."

"What if I want to spend more than one day in Moscow—can I take a later train?"

"No. The ticket is purchased for a specific date and you are not allowed into Moscow until the day before the train is scheduled to depart."

"I thought trains in Russia were supposed to be inexpensive? Seven-hundred and fifty dollars sounds like a lot of money for a Russian train."

"The tickets are more expensive when they are purchased outside of Russia," she explained. "This is actually a very good price—much lower than you will pay in many other countries. It would be much cheaper if you were to buy the ticket in Russia, of course. But outside of Russia, it is a good price."

Totally confused, I tried to make sense of everything she had just told me. "Let me see if I've got all this straight. Without a visa, I can't get into Russia to buy a cheap train ticket. And I can't get a visa without spending a small fortune on Russian hotels—or buying an expensive train ticket *before* I get to Russia. Did I miss anything?"

She shook her head and laughed. "No, that is correct," she said.

The Trans-Siberian train seemed like a great way to get across Russia. But buying a ticket in advance meant locking myself into a departure date. It also meant I would only be given a one-day visa for Moscow, which didn't appeal to me. If I was going to go to Russia I wanted to spend more than one day there. There had to be an easier way around the problem and I figured I would find it sooner or later. Meanwhile, I had my ticket to Poland and would worry about getting a Russian visa when and if I needed one. I thanked her for her help and walked back to the Strøget to find something to eat.

When I returned to the apartment that afternoon, I found Henrik in the kitchen cooking dinner. I told him of my plans to leave Copenhagen the next day.

"You're leaving tomorrow?" he asked with surprise.

"Yes, I can't believe it."

"Why don't you stay longer—you haven't even been here a week?"

"I know. But if I don't take tomorrow night's train, I'll have to wait another week to catch the next one."

Henrik stirred the pasta then poured us each a glass of wine. He handed me some bowls and forks to help set the table and said, "Since tomorrow will be your last day here we should go to a nice restaurant for dinner. I know—we'll go to the Mongolian Barbecue place. You'll like it, I'm sure."

If you're there before it's over, you're on time.
    —James J. Walker

Early the next morning I went to the train station and stored my bags in a locker so I wouldn't have to return to the apartment for them after dinner. I planned to get to the station with plenty of time to spare so I wouldn't be running to catch the train like I always did.

This was the new me. The one who promised himself on the bus to JFK Airport less than a week before that he would never again have to run for a plane or train.

For once, I would be the one casually waiting on the train, totally relaxed and on time, watching some other poor jerk race to get on board before the doors closed. And all because he didn't have the foresight that I had to leave his bags ready and waiting at the train station.

I checked a few lockers until I found one big enough to hold my backpack and daypack. After shoving both packs in the empty compartment, I dropped a token in the slot and turned the key. The token fell into the coin-box with a thud and was quickly followed by a click in the door of the locker. I removed the key and tested the door. Satisfied that my bags would be safe until I returned from dinner, I placed the key in my pocket and strolled calmly out of the station to spend my last day wandering around Copenhagen.

When I returned to the apartment that evening I noticed Steffen's tiny Fiat parked up the street. On my way up the stairs I heard his deep voice from behind the apartment door, followed by the voices and laughter of Henrik, Anders and Stig.

When I walked in, Steffen was in the middle of one of his outrageous stories, his arms flailing the air and his long legs stomping the ground as he acted out the action. I couldn't understand a thing he was saying since he was speaking in Danish, but it must have been hilarious from the shouts of laughter coming from the rest of the guys.

When he saw me come in, Henrik called out, "Eric, you're missing it. Steffen is telling us about another one of his famous dates—this time about a girl half his height."

"Most girls are half his height," I remarked. "I'm practically half his height."

Henrik searched for the best way to explain Steffen's story, then shook his head and laughed. "Yes, but this girl. . . . well, it would be easier to explain in Danish, I'm afraid."

Stig slid over on the coach to make room for me. "Each of us has girlfriends, so we're always with the same girl," he explained. Then added with a grin, "That's why we like hearing Steffen tell us about his escapades!"

An hour later, after exhausting Steffen's most recent adventures, we finished the last of the beers and decided to head over to the Mongolian Barbecue restaurant before it got too late. There was a large crowd inside the restaurant when we arrived but we didn't have long to wait before we were seated. Meals were served cafeteria-style from a counter in the rear, so after we placed our drink orders at the table, we got on line to order our food. Customers selected what they wanted from an assortment of meat and noodle dishes in front of the counter then gave their requests to the cooks behind the food bar. The line moved past a selection of salads and cheeses while the cooks stir-fried the meals. The process was fast and efficient, and ten minutes after we got on line we were back at our table loaded with food trays.

The meal was terrific—especially the spicy dishes. But the best part was being able to re-visit the food bar for unlimited helpings. An hour and a half later, stuffed to capacity and exhausted from eating so much, we staggered out of the restaurant like fattened calves.

Henrik and I walked Stig, Anders and Steffan back to the car to see them off. Crouched behind the wheel of his tiny Fiat, Stefan rolled down his window and shook my hand. "Where will you go after Poland?"

"East."

He laughed and shook his head. "East? How far east?"

"No idea," I replied.

"How long will you be gone?"

"Until the money runs out or I get tired of traveling, I guess."

Steffan nodded his head and smiled. "Sounds like an interesting way to travel. I would like to try it sometime. If you get tired of going east, come back and visit us in Denmark." He cranked the motor and honked the horn goodbye as they waved and drove off. Henrik and I still had plenty of time for me to make my 10:23 P.M. train, so we walked over to the harbor shops at the Nyhavn marina for an ice-cream before heading over to the station to collect my bags.

At 10:10 P.M. I stepped up to the locker where I had left my packs that morning. I pulled the long brass key from my pocket and slipped it into locker 205. I turned the key and waited for the door to pop open. Nothing happened. I read the instructions on the locker again to make sure I had turned the key the right way, then tried it a second time. Still nothing.

Thinking I might have put the key in the wrong locker, I tried to remove it but it wouldn't turn. I glanced over at the big clock on the wall of the station. 10:12 P.M. I had eleven minutes to go. "*Why do these things always happen to me*," I mumbled to myself, as I attempted in vain to yank the key from the lock.

I looked around for Henrik but couldn't see him. I ran to the next aisle and spotted him helping a woman who couldn't figure out how to work the token machine for the lockers. I told myself not to panic. I stood patiently by and calmly took stock of my situation while I waited for Henrik to finish helping the lady.

After all, what was the worst that could happen? I would miss the train and have to spend another week in Copenhagen, that's all. And maybe pay for a new locker after they smashed it open to free my bags. No big deal. What could that cost—a few hundred dollars at the most.

Nothing I couldn't handle. And certainly nothing to get all worked up about.

Keeping my problem in its proper perspective was having a tremendous calming influence on me. I was in complete control of the situation—like a Zen master in total control of his emotions.

"*I like this new relaxed way of thinking*," I thought, as I calmly watched Henrik explain how to operate the token machine to the woman. "*It's really amazing how relaxed I am*," I told myself, knowing I had less than ten minutes to make my train, as I continued to watch Henrik explain to that *stupid* woman how to operate a simple, idiotic token machine. *"What is her problem? A monkey could have figured it out by now,"* I fumed, feeling myself starting to panic.

Unable to maintain my new Zen-like attitude any longer, I shoved the woman aside and blurted to Henrik, "I'm screwed! The key's stuck. I can't get my bags out of the locker and I'm going to miss the train. Hurry!"

Henrik stared at me with a blank expression for a second or two, trying to make sense of my outburst, then calmly said, "No problem. The time is probably expired on the locker. We'll put another token in and then it should open."

His explanation made perfect sense. I took a deep breath and felt myself relax. "Good idea. Do you have 10 Krone for a token?"

"No, don't you?" he asked. I shook my head and frowned. Henrik ran off to get change from one of the concession stands in the station. I apologized to the woman for my ungentlemanly conduct, then ran off to my locker with Henrik a few feet behind me.

At 10:16 P.M. Henrik slipped another token in the locker and turned the key. No go. This time it was Henrik who looked panicked.

"What time is your train?" he asked anxiously.

"Leaves in seven minutes."

Henrik raced down the aisle. Before he turned the corner he yelled back, "Wait here. I'll find the manager of the luggage room."

At 10:20 P.M. Henrik came running back towards the lockers with a stocky man in his late forties puffing behind him, a chain of keys jangling from the man's belt as he ran.

Henrik said something in Danish then pointed to my locker. The luggage man reached up and tried to turn the key. When that didn't work, he put a coin in the locker and tried the key again. Nothing happened.

Instead of breaking the locker open he took a key from his chain and inserted it into a little round hole in the coin-box beneath the token slot. He turned the key and pulled the long coin-box from the locker. He placed the box on the floor, stuck his arm inside the empty coin compartment and flipped a latch. The locker door sprung open.

I smacked Henrik on the back. "It's open—that's great!" I grabbed my packs from the open locker, thanked the luggage man, and ran off towards track number 7 with Henrik close on my heels.

Henrik stood on the platform while I leaped up the steps of the train and ran down the corridor to drop my bags off in my compartment. I checked my watch. 10:22 P.M. One minute to spare. I caught my breath and walked over to an open window to say goodbye to Henrik before the train pulled out of the station.

A few moments later a train attendant walked down the aisle to check tickets. He was a young man in his mid-twenties with short brown hair and a serious expression. He held a metal ticket puncher in his left hand which he clicked absentmindedly by his side as he walked down the corridor. He checked the tickets in the compartment ahead of mine then stopped at the window next to me. With his right hand extended for my ticket, he glanced up and said in a thick German accent, "Tee-ket." I pulled the ticket envelope from my money belt and handed him my ticket.

He stamped the ticket with his metal puncher. Then, in a tone that was more a demand than a request, he pointed his finger impatiently to the ticket envelope in my hand and said, "Couchette tee-ket."

I had forgotten that a separate ticket had been issued to me for the couchette. I handed him the couchette ticket and continued talking to Henrik. A moment later, the ticket agent tapped my arm to get my attention. Holding the ticket out so I could see it he casually said, "Nicht Gut."

Thinking he was giving me back part of the ticket as my receipt, I nodded my thanks and smiled. This was immediately followed by his jabbing at my ticket with his metal puncher and raising his voice irritably. "Nicht Gut! Nicht Gut!"

I turned to face him, completely bewildered by his sudden outburst. "Look, I have no idea what you're saying—the only German words I know are Heinekin and Lowenbrau. So unless you're ordering a beer, I think we've got a problem."

I suddenly remembered that Henrik had been studying German for his language exam. I pointed out the window to where Henrik was standing on the platform. Seeing me point to Henrik, the ticket agent stepped to the window and fired off something in rapid German. Henrik moved closer to the train so he could hear better and was just about to respond when the train began to pull away from the station. I stepped in front of the ticket clerk and looked anxiously over at Henrik. "Well—what did he say?"

Stepping quickly to keep up with the train, Henrik held his hands out helplessly. "There's a problem with your ticket," he answered.

I shook my head in amazement. "That much I know already—what's the problem?"

Henrik trotted along the platform to keep from falling behind the train. "I don't know. He was speaking too quickly for me to understand."

As the train picked up speed Henrik began to drop back. "Henrik, what do I do?" I yelled helplessly. He looked at me dumbly and shook his head, not knowing what to tell me.

I leaned further out the window so he could hear me as the distance between us increased. "Henrik! When's your German test?" I shouted over the clanking of the rails.

Henrik reached the end of the platform and stopped running. "Tomorrow night!" he called back. "Why?"

I waved goodbye and shouted over the growing noise of the train, "I think you'd better go home and study!"

Henrik was still waving as I watched him shrink smaller and smaller in the distance. When he was no longer visible from the window of the train, I turned back inside the corridor.

To my surprise the ticket clerk hadn't moved. He was still standing next to me with my ticket in his hand. We looked at each other with growing frustration. He tapped the ticket and was about to speak, but before he could open his mouth, I shook my head and said, "I know, I know . . . Nicht Gut."

German Lessons

Videos, Pornos, & Pineapples

The Warsaw Ghetto

The Lady and the Ermine

Only two things are infinite, the universe and human stupidity,
and I'm not sure about the former.

—Albert Einstein

I returned to my compartment and sat on berth 79, the number printed on my ticket, and the one bed of the four that had been made up with sheets and bedding.

I was tired and wanted to wash up and go to bed. Unfortunately, I still had a problem. The ticket clerk had followed me into the compartment. He stood solidly behind me with my ticket in his hand, pointing to the ticket, then to the bed, then back to the ticket again. And the whole time he was busy pointing, he kept rambling away in German.

I sat there listening to the rhythmic clack of the wheels against the tracks, waiting for him to tire himself out. I couldn't believe it. I was on a train bound for Berlin with a ticket collector who had decided to make my lousy ticket his life's work. When he finished his dissertation, he waited for my reply. I didn't know what to say. Feeling pressured to say something, even if it was only in English, I looked at him and frowned. "Look, I'd love to stay up and chat but Henrik's the only friend I know who speaks German. And I'm not too sure about that after tonight's performance. So unless you'd like to head back to Copenhagen, I think we should continue this conversation in the morning after we've each had a good night's sleep." No reply.

"Not thrilled with that suggestion I see. *Wait—I know!* Why don't we just forget this whole thing and meet back on this same train again next year? You know . . . you, me, Henrik—the whole gang. Kind of a little reunion. We can talk about all the fun we had over my *nicht gut* ticket. Okay? Can I go to bed now?" Still no reply.

Finally, I pointed to where berth 79 was printed on my ticket, then pointed to bed 79, and placed my hands together near the side of my head to indicate I wanted to go to sleep.

"Nein! Nein!" he said emphatically, and launched into another German lesson on my behalf.

I contemplated throwing him out of the compartment and locking the door behind him but decided it was too risky. Aside from the fact that he had a set of keys to let himself back in with, he was armed with his little ticket puncher and I didn't feel like getting ticket-punched to death my first night on the train. It was a standoff.

Then, just when I thought I would have to spend the night sitting up, a bearded man with long black hair and round metal glasses peered inside the compartment. "I *thought* I heard an American voice," he said with surprise. When he saw the ticket clerk in my compartment and the frustrated looks on both our faces he asked, "Is everything alright?"

"I've had better days," I sighed.

I invited him into the compartment and explained everything that had happened since I boarded the train. His name was Jim and he was a doctor from California. He had spent a few years living in Germany in the sixties and was on vacation with his two young daughters for a few weeks to show them around Europe.

"My German's a little rusty," he said modestly, "but let me see if I can help you out." He turned to the ticket agent and said something in German.

The clerk did most of the talking after that. Jim listened and nodded his head, occasionally making a comment or asking a question. Every now and then one of them would point to my ticket or to the bed on which I was seated. Once in a while, Jim would point over at me and spread his hands out in a gesture of commiseration.

A few minutes later they both stopped talking and turned to face me. The ticket clerk stood quietly to the side while Jim explained the problem. Stroking his beard with the back of his hand, he let out a sigh. "Okay, here's the story. Your train ticket is fine. It's your couchette ticket that's causing the problem. It appears that there's no price printed on the ticket for the couchette. So he says that if you plan to spend the night in this compartment you'll have to pay him for a bed."

"But I already paid for the couchette," I protested.

"According to him, without the price on the ticket he doesn't have any proof that you paid for it."

I tried to figure out what had happened to my ticket, then suddenly remembered the printer problem at the Kilroy travel bureau. The girl who sold me the ticket had to print my ticket at a different machine when the main printer didn't work. The second printer must have screwed up my ticket.

I thought I saw a way around the problem. I sat up and looked eagerly at Jim. "If I didn't pay for the couchette then why is it that Bed 79—*the same bed number that's on my ticket*—is the only bed in this compartment that was made up in advance of my boarding the train? Okay, so the ticket printer didn't work right and the price never got printed on my ticket. Obviously, the bed was paid for or the train people wouldn't have prepared this bed." I felt like a lawyer who had just finished his closing argument. I was confident I had the case locked up.

"Hmm. Makes perfect sense to me," Jim said. "Let's see if your logic works with him." He translated my argument to the train clerk then turned back to me. "He says your explanation makes sense. And he believes you paid for the bed. However, if there's a problem later on, *he'll* have to pay for the bed since there was no price on the ticket."

"But there won't be a problem—I paid for the bed," I insisted.

"That may be so, but he doesn't want to take the chance. Some nationalities, the Germans in particular, are meticulous when it comes to following rules and regulations. Everything has to be done by the book, believe me."

I knew he was probably right. In any case, the whole affair was taking more time than it was worth. I agreed to pay for the couchette a second time. To add insult to injury though, I had to pay more for the same bed the second time than I had originally paid for it in order to compensate for the difference in exchange rates between the Danish Krone and the German Deutshmark.

When the matter was settled to the clerk's satisfaction he left my compartment and disappeared down the corridor. I thanked Jim for helping me out and locked the sliding metal door to my compartment after he left. When I was finally able to relax in peace, I washed up and went to sleep in the bed I had paid for twice.

The following morning the train pulled in to Berlin's Lichtenberg station right on schedule. After a long screech of the brakes the train came to a halt at a busy outdoor platform packed with commuters on their way to work.

I stepped off the train in the brisk morning air and worked my way through the crowd towards a glass enclosed booth where two uniformed men sat behind what looked like some kind of control panel. I knocked on the door and inquired tentatively, "Hauptbonhoff station?"

A stout, middle-aged man opened the door to the glass enclosure. He didn't speak English so he directed me with his hands to go down the stairs at the far end of the platform and then do something I couldn't quite figure out.

On my way towards the staircase I saw Jim step off the train about twenty feet ahead of me. He was gathering his luggage and waiting for his two young daughters to catch up to him. He told me that if I waited a few minutes he would help me find the track for Hauptbonhoff station.

I had about forty-five minutes to make my 8:03 A.M. connection and was relieved that I wouldn't have to waste time looking for the track—or worse, winding up on the wrong train. I helped Jim and his daughters with their luggage and together the four of us cut a path through the morning commuters to the stairs at the end of the platform.

After locating the correct platform and confirming the time for the next train to Hauptbonhoff station, I said goodbye to Jim and the girls. I thanked him for all his help and said gratefully, "Thanks for playing interpreter Jim. I don't know what I'm going to do without you to help me out. Are you sure you don't want to stick around until I'm safely out of Germany?"

"If I did, your trip wouldn't be as interesting then, would it?" he replied with a smile. I laughed in agreement and waved goodbye as they disappeared into the crowd on the platform.

When I arrived at Hauptbonhoff station I followed the other passengers into the main hall and walked over to an open ticket window to ask about the 8:03 train to Warsaw. The woman behind the counter looked at me curiously and asked to see my ticket. She examined it for a few seconds and then handed it back to me. "There is no 8:03 to Warsaw," she announced. "There was a 7:06 but no 8:03."

"But I was told there was an 8:03," I said irritably. I showed her a copy of the train schedule that Anna had given me at the Kilroy travel agency in Denmark.

She glanced at the schedule and clucked with disapproval. "This is not a recent schedule. The times have changed since this schedule was printed."

Assuming that there would be another train in half an hour or so, I asked patiently, "When's the next train to Warsaw then?"

"There is another train at 15.33 which you can take."

I calculated the time in my head. "15.33? That's—that's 3:33 P.M. *I have to wait seven and a half hours?*" I exclaimed. I had paid for my couchette ticket twice and been given an out-of-date train schedule. I wanted to go back to Copenhagen and strangle that idiot Anna for botching my tickets up so badly.

Watching me stand there mumbling to myself, the ticket woman must have felt sorry for me because as I began to walk off she called me back to the counter. "There is a 10.23 reserved train to Warsaw," she explained helpfully. "If you ask the conductor, perhaps he will let you use your ticket on that train even though you do not have a reservation. The train will arrive at track four at ten o'clock."

"Thanks—it's worth a try!" I said gratefully. I grabbed my packs and wandered off to find something to eat.

At 10:00 A.M., the reserved train was sitting at track four as scheduled. I walked down the platform to find the conductor. On my left, stretching down the platform as far as I could see, was a long, green, solid-looking Russian train with placards on the sides indicating it was headed for Moscow via Berlin and Warsaw. Two men in train uniforms were hanging around the platform near the first train car. I walked over with a big smile, trying to look as friendly as possible.

"Excuse me," I said as I approached, pulling out my train ticket and wondering if they spoke English. "The woman in the station said it might be all right for me to—"

The man to my right held up his hand before I had a chance to finish my sentence. "Nyet," he blurted loudly.

"But I just—"

"Nyet," the other man echoed. Without any further thought to me, they turned their backs and continued their conversation. So much for improved U.S. and Russian relations.

I looked down the platform and noticed two other people in train uniforms speaking with two men at the head of the train. I figured it couldn't hurt to try again. Besides, one of them was a woman and I thought she might be more compassionate. I walked quickly down the platform until I reached the end of the train. When I got within a few feet of them it soon became clear that the Russian woman wasn't talking to the two men. She was arguing with them.

One man looked to be in his early twenties. He was speaking Russian to the woman and translating everything into German for the second man who was older, probably in his early fifties. As I approached the Russian woman I had a sinking feeling that she wasn't going to be too sympathetic to my plea. She was a short, heavy-set woman with an unflattering bowl-shaped haircut and looked about as friendly as a Pit Bull on a bad day. When I walked up, all four of them turned to face me. I held out my ticket. "Excuse me. I have a ticket to Warsaw for the 15.33 train and was wondering if I could get on the 10.23—"

She glanced at the ticket, then at me, and spat out a harsh "Nyet." I was starting to hate that word almost as much as "Nicht gut."

The German-speaking man frowned sympathetically and said in perfect English, "We are also trying to get on this train instead of waiting for the 15.33. This Polish fellow thinks she will let us on. I am not so sure. In any event, you may want to wait, just in case."

I stood quietly by as the Polish man translated the Russian woman's comments from Russian into German. Since the Pole's English was very limited, the German gentleman translated everything for me. The Russian and her male co-worker didn't speak English at all.

The Polish guy was right. The Russian woman was willing to let us on the train. But only if we each paid her 50 Deutschemarks to cover the costs of a bed since it was a reserved train.

Outraged at the amount, the German huffed, "That's ridiculous. Why do we need to pay for beds on a morning train when no one is going to sleep on them? The train is almost empty anyway. She intends to keep the money for herself, no doubt."

It was almost time for the train to leave. The woman looked at us with raised eyebrows as if to say, "This is your last chance—take it or leave it."

The German let out a deep sigh. "I don't want to wait for the 15.33. I will give her the 50 Marks she asks." He picked up his small shoulder bag from the platform and proceeded to board the train.

I also didn't want to wait for the afternoon train but didn't think I had enough Deutschemarks to cover me. I had exchanged some dollars for German marks at the American Express office in Copenhagen, thinking I might need some German currency on the train to Berlin.

I pulled out my wallet and counted. Forty-two Deutschemarks—not enough. With the most pitiful expression I could muster, I held them out to her, hoping she would give me a break.

She leaned her bowl-shaped head toward me, counted the money in my hand with some quick flicks of her finger, and barked, "Nyet." She lifted her head to look at me, then held up eight fingers to tell me I was eight marks short of the fifty she asked for.

Suddenly, the train whistle started to blow. Like a huge snake roused from a deep sleep, the long green train started its slow crawl down the platform. The Russian woman climbed the steep metal steps to the train directly behind the German. Her co-worker and the young Polish man mounted the steps right after her. With no alternative but to return to the waiting room to sit out the next seven hours until 15.33, I lifted my backpack and turned to walk off. The Polish man was standing on the bottom step of the train. When he saw me turn to leave he ushered me aboard with a quick wave of his hand. "But I've only got 42 Deutschemarks," I said. I held out my money so he could see what I had.

"No problem. Please," he urged, waving me to the steps as the train picked up speed. He reached out his hand for my pack. With no time to waste, I swung my backpack up ahead of me and jumped up the steps as the train cleared the platform. When I was safely on board, I followed him and the German down the long narrow corridor to an empty sunlit compartment.

I think crime pays. The hours are good, you travel a lot.
—Woody Allen

The morning sun filled our side of the train with a dusty light that brightened an otherwise stodgy-looking compartment. I sat near the window to take in the passing countryside, sharing the long passenger seat with the German, who was quietly reading his morning newspaper. The Pole sat opposite us on the other seat, stretched out next to one of two huge duffel bags he had lugged on the train with him.

A few minutes after we sat down the Russian woman entered our compartment with a tray of tea. The tea glasses had been inserted into nicely detailed, silver glass-holders which sat securely in the center of the tray next to three small silver spoons and a glass bowl filled with sugar cubes. Just a few minutes before, this woman had made Attila the Hun seem like a Boy Scout. Now all of a sudden she was all smiles and Miss Congeniality. She placed the tray on the small table near the window then said something to our Polish companion and walked out.

The Pole had ordered the tea and began passing the glasses out as if he were hosting a reception at home. The New Yorker in me made me cautious about taking food from strangers so I hesitated to drink the tea. I had heard stories about travelers being drugged on trains after being offered food and drinks from fellow passengers. Hours later they would wake up to find their money and personal belongings long gone. So as not to insult him, I pretended to drink and watched curiously as the German sipped away at his glass while he read his morning paper.

The Pole was clever though. Being street-smart himself, he sensed not only my hesitation, but also the thinking behind it. With a friendly nod of his head to dispel my concerns he said, "Tea is good—is not drug." Realizing I was being overly paranoid, I thanked him and drank the tea, which was excellent.

After settling in awhile, we introduced ourselves. The German gentleman introduced himself as Michael. He was from Switzerland and not Germany as I had originally thought, and was a musician with the Lausanne Chamber Orchestra. Well-dressed, he had a full head of thick, graying black hair which swept back from his forehead in a long mane typical of symphony musicians and conductors.

Our Polish friend introduced himself as "Charlie." He was twenty-two years old but looked ten years older. Big and beefy-looking, with rumpled clothes and unkempt dirty-blond hair that kept falling in his eyes, Charlie looked like a big friendly bear. Constantly fidgeting and shifting around in his seat, he was uncomfortable sitting still for long periods of time. When he wasn't pushing the hair off his face, he was busy drumming his fingers on the leather seat by his side. Happy to have company in the compartment with him, Charlie seemed eager for conversation. And though he and I couldn't converse without having Michael translate for us, that didn't stop Charlie from telling us all about himself.

Four years before, Charlie and his family left Poland for political asylum in West Germany. Not long after his family settled into their new country, he found a job as a mechanic. Looking to find some way to supplement his modest income he began smuggling western-made goods into Poland where he was able to sell them for big profits.

At only twenty-two years old Charlie was an experienced privateer who seemed to know all the tricks of the trade. Happy to share some of his street knowledge with an interested audience, he showed us how to fold $100 bills so they could be carried between the fingers when going through customs checkpoints. He then took some Polish Zlotys from his pocket to demonstrate how to avoid getting ripped off when using Polish currency. When folded a certain way, the 1000 and 100,000 Zloty notes look similar and are easy to mistake for one another. Charlie showed us what to look for and warned us to pay careful attention when changing money on the black market or receiving change from street vendors.

I glanced up at his two huge duffel bags on the luggage rack above his seat and asked him how long he planned to stay in Poland. "Three days," he replied.

"I'd hate to see what he takes when he goes away for a week" I commented to Michael, who also thought it strange that Charlie had brought so much with him for a three day trip. Seeing the curious looks on our faces, Charlie laughed and pulled one of the duffel bags down from the luggage rack.

He held the bag upright between his knees and zipped it open. Michael and I leaned forward and peered inside. The bag was stocked like a mini-warehouse. A stack of pornographic videos and magazines sat above a mountain of beer, food, candies and hand-held computer games. I also noticed several pineapples bulging out from the sides of the bag. Charlie pointed to the second bag on the luggage rack above his head and spoke to Michael in German. Michael nodded and turned to me. "He says the other bag has more of the same."

"Where's he going to sell all this stuff?" I asked curiously.

Michael relayed my question to Charlie and replied, "He intends to sell everything on the street and to people he knows in Poland."

I blinked in amazement. "He's going to sell all this stuff in three days?"

Michael conversed with Charlie, then laughed. "He says everything will be sold in one day. No problem. Except for the pornographic tapes and magazines. They will be sold in one hour."

Charlie glanced up and down the corridor to make sure no one was standing nearby. Leaning forward conspiratorially, he pulled a passport from his jacket pocket and held it out to Michael while speaking in hushed tones.

When Charlie finished talking, Michael scratched his chin and passed Charlie's passport to me. "He says this passport is a fake. As a refugee he is not allowed to have one. When he emigrated to Germany he had to give up his Polish passport in order to be granted refugee status. Whenever he wants to leave Germany he must first obtain permission from the German government. He bought this Polish passport on the black market so he can go back and forth from Germany to Poland whenever he wants to sell western goods there. It is illegal of course, and if he is caught by the German Authorities he will very likely be extradited back to Poland."

Half an hour later, the Russian woman returned to pick up the tea glasses and collect her money. She checked our tickets then spoke in Russian to Charlie, who nodded his head and translated her message for Michael. Michael turned to me and sighed. "She says you must pay her fifty-eight deutschemarks."

"Fifty eight? I thought it was fifty?" I replied with surprise.

Michael raised his hands in resignation. "Charlie is getting out at the border and I am only going as far as Poznan, so she wants fifty marks from us. Since you are going all the way to Warsaw she wants fifty-eight marks from you."

"But I don't have fifty-eight marks," I protested. I pulled the forty-two marks from my pocket and spread it out on the seat. I pointed to the money. "I don't even have the fifty marks she originally wanted."

Michael shrugged as if to say it wasn't his problem. He pulled out his wallet and handed fifty marks to the Russian woman. The woman pointed to my money and said something to Charlie before leaving the compartment. Charlie waved his hands back and forth to get my attention. "No problem, no problem." He took my forty-two marks from the seat and placed them with his own before following the Russian woman down the corridor. I closed the door to the compartment and sat across from Michael. "You think Charlie's getting something out of this?"

"Perhaps. It wouldn't surprise me."

A few minutes later, Charlie returned with another tray of tea. He handed us our glasses and smiled when I sipped my tea without any hesitation this time. I had Michael ask him if the Russian woman would be coming back to get more money from me. Michael was surprised at Charlie's reply. "Charlie says he paid the sixteen marks you owed her."

I didn't know what to say. Since there was no way for me to obtain the additional deutshemarks I needed, I gratefully accepted Charlie's assistance. I thanked him for his help and asked for an address where I could mail him the money I owed him. With a quick wave of his hand he shook his head and smiled. "Is gift. No worry."

We spent the rest of the morning keeping ourselves quietly occupied. Michael read his paper, Charlie thumbed through his girlie magazines, and I gazed out the window at the small houses which lined the flat, grassy countryside in the distance. A short time later, the train began to slow. Charlie jumped up from his seat and stuffed his magazines into one of the duffel bags above his head. "Polish border," he whispered anxiously. He grabbed the larger of his two bags and placed it on the luggage rack above Michael's seat. When he sat down again he looked visibly nervous.

The train pulled to a jerky stop at Kunowice, the border crossing for Germany and Poland. Outside the window, uniformed Passport Police boarded the train up and down the long platform. Within seconds, German and Polish Passport Officers stepped briskly into our compartment. They glanced at the luggage on the overhead racks then asked to see our passports. After a quick look at Michael and me, the German officer handed us back our passports. He held Charlie's passport in his hand and asked him if he lived in Germany. Charlie shook his head and answered, "No."

The officer flipped through Charlie's Passport one more time before handing it back to him. After a quick look around the compartment, both officers walked down the corridor to the next train car. Charlie let out a deep breath and wiped the perspiration from his forehead with the back of his fleshy hand.

As the train moved slowly across the border into Poland we saw a man outside the window being escorted down the platform by two German policemen. He had been caught trying to smuggle goods across the border and was being led back to the station on the German side of the border. Charlie had been lucky. And clever. By placing one of his bags on the rack above Michael's seat, the border police assumed the bag belonged to Michael—a respectable musician from Switzerland. No problem.

At the first stop after the border, Charlie stood up and pulled down his luggage. He slung one bag on his shoulder and dragged the second one behind him down the corridor. He hopped off the train onto the barren platform and waited for Michael to pass the second bag down to him. Michael groaned under the weight of the large duffel bag as he handed it to Charlie. We wished Charlie luck as he trudged off and watched curiously as he walked slowly away under the weight of his bags.

I couldn't imagine where he was going since we didn't seem to be anywhere in particular. There was no city or town in sight. All that was visible from the train was a long dirt road on the other side of the track and a low hill with trees in the distance. Carrying one bag on his shoulder and the other one cradled under his arm, Charlie walked down the road in the direction from which we had just come.

Michael and I stood by the railing near the exit door and watched him walk off. "He can't be going too far with those bags," I remarked. "They must weigh fifty pounds each."

"Most likely he's planning to meet someone on the road," Michael replied.

With a sudden jolt and a loud hiss, the train started to pull away from the station. The Russian woman walked quickly up the platform and waved her arm to a conductor at the far end of the train. When the man signaled back, she huffed up the short metal stairs and stood by the railing next to Michael and me. With a nod of her beefy head and a quick flick of her hand, she waved us brusquely back to our compartment.

The main thing is my life's dream has been realized; I have lived to see Jewish defense in the Ghetto in all its greatness and glory.

—Mordecai Anielewicz, leader of the
April 1943 Warsaw Ghetto Uprising

The long wide avenues, clean streets and tall Western hotels in the commercial part of Warsaw made it hard to believe I was in a former communist country. The streets were busy with European and Japanese made cars and the stores were stocked with Western-made products.

The only major eyesore in an otherwise attractive commercial environment were the electric trams, the sides of which were tastelessly painted with logos of Camel and Marlboro cigarette ads. The part of Warsaw that still had some old-world charm left to it however, was the old city. As soon as I walked into the large, cobblestone Market Square with its small, stone buildings, I felt like I had stepped back in time. I walked down the narrow lanes that led off the square and tried to picture what it must have been like when horses and carriages clip-clopped along the worn, stone streets. I then tried to imagine how those same streets would have looked after the Germans destroyed them in World War II. I didn't have to imagine long however, since a film at the National Museum at the far end of the square showed old film clips of the city before and after the war.

Warsaw was literally reduced to rubble by the Nazis. By 1945, at least two-thirds of the city's residents had been killed and eighty-five percent of the city's standing structures had fallen. By following old blueprints and photos the residents of Warsaw reconstructed the old city area to look exactly the way it had before the war. It wasn't until I saw the film and walked around Warsaw over the next few days, that I realized what an incredible job the Polish people had done rebuilding their city.

On the first Saturday after I arrived, I hooked up with a few people from the hostel to do some sightseeing. Altogether there were six of us, representing four countries—Australia, England, Germany and the U.S.A. Shar and Shane, a young married couple from Australia, were on their way to London to find work after having traveled in Malaysia and Russia the past two months. Peter, also from Australia, had been working up north in Gdansk for the past year with a student travel association and was playing tourist in Warsaw for the weekend.

Michael, a twenty-two year old German, was the youngest of the lot. Perpetually disheveled, with a scraggly beard, long unwashed hair and ragged clothes that he never seemed to clean or change, he was living proof that the spirit of Woodstock lived on in the '90's. The last member of our group was Steve, a clean-cut, twenty-four year old from England. He had been touring with his rugby team in Czechoslovakia for a month and took off to travel around on his own after his team went back to the U.K.

Each of us had already seen the main sights around the city on our own so we decided to head across town to see the former Warsaw ghetto area and the Nozyk Synagogue, one of the few Synagogues reconstructed after World War II that was still in use.

The area where the ghetto once stood had been rebuilt after the war into a residential neighborhood called Muranów—a non-descript housing complex with tree lined streets, tall concrete buildings and fenced-off play areas for children. As I walked around the quiet peaceful neighborhood, it was difficult to imagine it was the former site of the Warsaw ghetto, the place where Warsaw's 400,000 Jews were forced to live in isolation from the rest of the city's non-Jewish population. An impression of the ghetto, as seen from the outside looking in, was printed in a 1941 Underground Polish paper:

> . . . Due to the increasing crowdedness, such undescribably unhealthy conditions were created that cannot be put in writing. Hunger and distress abound. The streets are full of masses of people moving about aimlessly, many are pale and feeble. Alongside the walls, many beggars are sitting or lying around and it is not an uncommon sight to witness people collapsing from starvation. Every day, the asylum gathers up dozens of abandoned babies. Some die in the streets. Contagious disease is rife, particularly tuberculosis.

Before the war, the area had been a thriving Jewish community. Afterwards, only a handful of Jews remained, the majority having been exterminated in concentration camps that the Germans had set up around Eastern Europe.

Other than a monument commemorating the ghetto uprising in 1943 by a small band of heroic Jews who were eventually exterminated along with the rest of the occupants of the ghetto, there was no way to know that this was the area where the ghetto had existed less than fifty years before. But even without physical reminders, the memory of the ghetto lives on as a symbol of Jewish determination to survive against overwhelming odds. In his book, *Resistance, The Warsaw Ghetto Uprising*, Israel Gutman wrote:

> No act of Jewish resistance during the Holocaust fired the imagination quite as much as the Warsaw Ghetto Uprising of April 1943. It was an event of epic proportions, pitting a few poorly armed, starving Jews against the might of Nazi power . . .
> . . . The Warsaw Ghetto Uprising is a historical event, but it also has become a symbol of Jewish resistance and determination, a moment in history that has transformed the self-perception of the Jewish people from passivity to active armed struggle.

Aside from the Ghetto Monument, there was little else of interest to keep us in Muranów so we walked off in the direction of the Nozyk Synagogue, situated a few miles south. When we arrived, the Saturday morning Sabbath service was still in progress but we were hesitant to go inside since none of us was properly dressed. Seeing our hesitation, a woman outside the entrance smiled and waved us up the stairs. Peter and I were the most presentable, so we decided to have a quick look while the rest of the group waited outside.

Peter knew I was Jewish so he immediately looked to me for guidance. Taking the lead, I approached the entrance. The woman flashed a warm smile and handed us Yamulkas to place on our heads before we entered the building. Acting as our guide, she led us down a short, narrow hallway and stopped at a small bookshelf along the wall where she gently lifted two black-covered prayer books and handed one to each of us. Peter tapped my shoulder and pointed to the Hebrew letters on the front of his prayer book.

"What's this say?" he whispered, as we followed the woman down the narrow hallway to our right.

"Beats me. It's in Hebrew," I whispered back.

"But I thought you were Jewish?"

"I am. But I don't know Hebrew. I can read it, but I don't know what I'm reading."

"You're kidding—you don't know any Jewish words?"

"Only the ones you need to know in New York."

"What are those?"

"Bloomingdale's and Zabar's."

I knew Peter had never heard of those two quintessential New York City landmarks, but before he had a chance to question me again, the woman stopped outside the congregation hall and ushered us inside. The high ceilings and bright sunlight coming through the windows from the right side of the room made it seem bigger than it was. But the congregation hall was actually fairly small—much smaller than I had expected. In any case, there was plenty of room for everyone since there were only about a dozen or so elderly men scattered among the first few rows of seats which faced the pulpit at the front of the room.

I didn't see any women, which surprised me, until I glanced up and noticed a small group of elderly women praying from a balcony above the main floor. As is the custom in Orthodox Synagogues, the women prayed separately from the men. I pointed this fact out to Peter and hoped that this little tidbit of Jewish information would make up for my lack of Hebrew language skills. He seemed sufficiently impressed.

I looked at the frail old men with their yellowed prayer shawls draped across their shoulders and their prayer books in their bony hands and felt a certain kinship with them as they recited quietly along with the Rabbi at the front of the room. I hadn't been to a Synagogue in a long time, but the familiar sights and chants coming from my fellow Jews gave me a strange sense of belonging—a feeling of finding long-lost relatives who had never laid eyes on me before but were happy to discover I was related. This sense of belonging was even stronger when I looked over at two old men in the pew closest to where Peter and I stood respectfully in the aisle.

Both men, each in their seventies, shook our hands warmly in welcome and asked where we were from. They spoke English very well, which surprised me, until one of the men told me he had lived in Brooklyn, New York with his family before returning to live in Poland after the war.

We held our conversation in whispers to avoid disturbing the service, but every so often we were hushed by someone for talking too

loudly and we would have to stop speaking for awhile. After a few
minutes the two men asked if we wanted to sit in on their morning
service. We thanked them for their offer but politely declined since
the rest of our group was waiting outside.

As we turned to leave, I took one last look at the elderly men and
women in the congregation hall. These people were living history.
Real-life witnesses to all that had happened to the Jews in Europe—
survivors who had decided to stay on despite all that had happened. I
wondered if they had experienced the Warsaw Ghetto and what the
morning service would have been like if the war had never taken
place—the young men, women and children that would have filled
the seats and raised their young voices in prayer in celebration of the
Sabbath. Along with my feeling of kinship, I felt a deep sadness that
there were only a handful of elderly men and women to represent the
thousands of Jews that used to live, work and pray in Warsaw.

Before we walked off, I leaned towards the two old men who had
befriended us. I smiled at them and whispered, "Shabat Shalom"—
Good Sabbath. They lifted their heads from their prayer books and
nodded warmly at me. "Shabat Shalom," they replied in unison, bow-
ing their heads as a parting gesture before turning their attention back
to their morning service.

I woke early the next morning to pack for a 9:30 A.M. train to Krakow. Shar and Shane—the married couple from Australia, and Steve,
the rugby player from England, were also leaving for Krakow so we
decided to travel together for a few days.

Before we took off, Peter told Steve and me about a party he was
throwing in Gdansk the following weekend. "It's going to be a great
party—loads of Polish girls," he informed us. "I guarantee you guys
will have a good time."

Steve thought Polish girls were beautiful, so a party full of them
was all he needed to hear. He took a pen and a little note pad from his
backpack and handed them to Peter. After jotting down his number in
Gdansk, Peter said, "I wrote down my work number since there's no
phone where I'm staying. Just make sure you call me before 4:30 P.M.
on Thursday. Otherwise, you won't be able to reach me. I'm taking
Friday off to help my friend get everything ready for the party and I
don't know his address off-hand. Try and make it if you can. You
won't regret it—I can promise you that."

Steve said, "Sounds good—count me in." He placed the paper with Peter's work number in his money belt and then pointed to me. "Count him in too."

I shook Peter's hand goodbye and said, "I doubt I'll make it Peter, but thanks anyway." There was no way I was going all the way up north to Gdansk for a party—especially after going south to Krakow from Warsaw.

Steve dismissed my refusal with a laugh and told Peter, "Don't worry, he'll be there."

Before I could reply, Shane and Shar called out from across the room. "Hey guys—we'd better go! The train leaves for Krakow in half an hour."

What one hopes for is often different from what one finds.
     —African Proverb

In many ways, Krakow seemed as different from Warsaw as San Francisco is from New York. Warsaw is a big, concrete metropolis filled with crowds and traffic, while Krakow is compact and tree-lined, with the feel of an important city but the pace of a suburban one. Warsaw also seemed more impersonal and aloof while Krakow felt open and welcoming. But probably the biggest difference between the two, as far as Polish cities were concerned, was that Warsaw was destroyed during World War II while Krakow was left practically untouched by the Germans.

With its old European style buildings, impressive market squares, tall church spires and cobblestone alleys, Krakow was as scenic as any well-preserved Western European city. The only blemish on an otherwise beautiful place was the soot from the smokestacks of Nowa Huta—an industrial complex to the east of Krakow which blackened the outsides of the old stone buildings and could sometimes be smelled in the air, depending on which way the wind was blowing.

When we arrived in Krakow we took a tram from the train station to a hostel Shane had heard about from some other travelers he had met in Warsaw. As usual, the hostel was overflowing with Polish school kids so there weren't many rooms available. The girl behind the desk was helpful though, and found a vacant room with four beds that was big enough for all of us. It was actually a pretty nice room— cheap and clean, with flower-print curtains on the windows, large wooden closets, and solid wood-framed beds.

After we checked in we walked around town awhile and grabbed some lunch at a trendy little pizza place not far from Rynek Glowny, the main market in the heart of the old city. The market square is one of the biggest in Europe and is the focal point for the city's residents. During the day, the square is packed with people strolling around the shops, restaurants and street vendors that line the sides of the square. At night, when the market stalls and the stores close down, it becomes a hangout for teenagers who congregate at the local pubs.

The morning after we arrived, Shane and Shar asked Steve and me if we wanted to go with them to the Zbiory Czartoryskich Museum in the old market square to see a Leonardo da Vinci painting called, "*Lady with the Ermine.*"

"Ever since we left Russia, Shane's been dying to get to Krakow to see this painting," Shar explained over breakfast.

"What's so special about the daVinci painting?" we asked.

"Nothing, really," Shane said with a bit of embarrassment. "It's just that I'd heard there were only ten daVinci's in existence and I thought it would be kind of nice to see them all.* Shar and I saw two of them at the Hermitage Museum in St. Petersburg. This'll make three. When we get to Paris next month we'll look up the Mona Lisa at the Louvre. That'll be four. I'm not sure where the other six are but I imagine they're scattered around Europe and the States. I guess they'll keep till we catch up to them."

I was surprised at Shane's comment that there were only ten da Vinci's in existence and asked, "What are you going to do if some of the last six are in private collections?"

"Good point," Steve agreed. "The Queen has one of the largest private collections in the world. It's a good bet she's got a daVinci or two."

Seeing the disappointed look on Shane's face when he realized he might not get to see all ten Leonardo's, Shar came to his rescue. She

---

*According to a Research Librarian at the New York Public Library, there are twelve Leonardo da Vinci paintings still in existence. For those of you who would like to follow Shane's quest, they are as follows:

France (Louvre Museum in Paris): Mona Lisa; St. John the Baptist; Madonna of the Rocks; St. Anne with Madonna and Child

Italy: Unfinished St. Jerome; Portrait of a Musician; Adoration of the Magi; The Last Supper

Poland (Zbiory Czartoryskich Museum in Krakow): Lady with the Ermine

Russia (Hermitage Museum in St. Petersburg): Benois Madonna; Madonna Litta

Washington, D.C. (National Gallery): Portrait Ginevradebenci

rubbed his shoulders sympathetically and told us, "In that case, we'll just have to be content with seeing all the ones available to the public." We walked to the old city from the hostel and found the museum at the western end of the square. After paying a small entrance fee we scrambled off in search of "*The Lady with the Ermine.*" It wasn't hard to find. The painting was on display behind a small roped off area and was hanging alongside a number of other paintings by artists that none of us had ever heard of before.

If we hadn't known it was a da Vinci, we wouldn't have given it a second look. Or even a first look, for that matter. Basically, it was just a painting of a woman holding an ermine. And not even a great looking woman at that. In fact, the ermine was probably the better looking of the two. If I were Leonardo, I would have named it, "*Ermine with a Lady.*" If there was any particular reason why the painting was considered a masterpiece it was beyond our understanding, so we stood there like four idiots, staring at it until we were content that we had seen what Shane had come to see.

That evening we went for a couple of beers at one of the small pubs near the old market square. It was a relaxing little place with a loft bar, good beer and an upscale local crowd. We sat upstairs at a round wooden table on the loft and talked about what we wanted to see the next day. Shar read from her guidebook and told us about various day trips outside of Krakow that sounded interesting. Steve wanted to visit the salt mines at Wieliczka to see the life-sized statues carved out of salt. Shar wanted to visit a Benedictine abbey at a town called Tyniec, fifteen kilometers southwest of Krakow. And for some reason that was unfathomable to any of us, Shane wanted to have another look at the "*Lady with the Ermine.*"

But there was only one place that I wanted to go and it interested me more than the other places combined. Its Polish name was Oświecim, but it was better known by its German name—Auschwitz.

Auschwitz

A Party in Gdansk

Trouble in Grodno

In spite of everything, I still believe that people are really good at heart.
—Anne Frank, Diary of a Young Girl

Auschwitz, the most notorious of all the Nazi concentration camps, was a mere 60 kilometers west of Krakow. Somehow it didn't seem possible. It was always just a name before. A name from history books, war documentaries and movies about the Holocaust. A name where millions of Jews and other Europeans were exterminated in gas chambers. A name synonymous with death. And now the name was real and I was waiting to board a train in Krakow's Plaszow station to take me there.

It was a perfect spring morning. Almost too perfect for where we were going. A light-yellow sun in a clear, cloudless sky was just starting to melt the shadows on the narrow outdoor platform when we boarded the local train to Oświecim, the Polish town better known the world over as Auschwitz.

The train moved slowly, with the familiar clickety-clack that old trains make on worn tracks that have been around for years. As I listened to the rhythmic click-clack of the rails I tried to imagine what it must have been like for the millions of men, women and children who had been stuffed into cattle cars and transported along these same tracks with no food, water or toilets. Who didn't even know where they were going. Or why they were going there. As I stood near the windows I couldn't help but wonder if they had looked out at the same trees and woods I was looking at.

We arrived at Oświecim station after an hour and a half journey and decided to walk the one and a half kilometers out of town to the site of the former concentration camp. Originally built in 1940 as a holding camp for Polish political prisoners, the camps at Auschwitz soon became a gigantic factory of death where over four million people from twenty-eight countries in Europe, mostly Jews, were sent for mass extermination. Above the main gate to the camp is the cynical inscription, "*Arbeit macht frei*"—work brings freedom.

After passing through the gate, we entered the main building and saw a short film that documented the atrocities committed at the camp. When the film was over, we exited the rear of the building and followed the path outlined in the museum guidebook to the numbered prison blocks with their various exhibits on display in each of their rooms. While the guidebook provided a factual, objective account of the fate of the camp's prisoners, the photographs and personal effects of the victims told their own personal, silent story of the nightmares they were subjected to during their time at Auschwitz.

I looked at the photos of the prisoners, their drawings, and their personal effects and knew it had all happened, but it was too horrible to imagine. It was so overwhelming that it was hard to feel it on a personal level. I felt like I was looking at everything with a detached, almost clinical air in order to keep their pain and suffering at a safe distance. It was only when I walked into the sixth room of Block 6 that I felt an immense sadness I couldn't avoid. This particular room showed the clothes and toys of the children who had suffered under the same conditions and restrictions as the adults.

Along the wall at the back of the room were head shots which showed front and side views of children in their prison uniforms along with their identification numbers. As I glanced from one photo to the next across the vast number of small pictures that lined the wall, my eyes were drawn to a picture of a young girl. She couldn't have been more than nine or ten years old but there was something about her that was different from the others.

I moved closer and felt it even more. And then I realized what it was. It was her eyes. She had tear-filled eyes which looked straight at me. As I stared at her photo I felt an overwhelming sadness for her. She looked so scared. I could feel her fear and confusion and I felt helpless for her. I wanted to reach into the photograph and hold her so she wouldn't be so frightened. I forced myself to look away from her moist, innocent eyes, and hoped that she was one of the lucky ones who survived.

I met up with Shar, Shane and Steve outside the children's prison block, where they were waiting up for me. It felt good to be back outside in the fresh air and sunshine again, away from the haunting accounts of the victims still waiting to be seen inside the other blocks.

We walked along the gravel paths between the rows of buildings and talked about what we had seen, then continued our silent walk through the remaining blocks of the camp. An hour and a half later we returned to the reception building, emotionally drained from the accounts and displays exhibited throughout the prison blocks. We exited the museum through the main gate and left Auschwitz behind us. It was still early afternoon, so we walked towards the village of Brzezinka, three kilometers away, to see Auschwitz II, better known as Birkenau.

It wasn't long before we saw the familiar-looking silhouette of Birkenau beyond the wide open field in front of us. Even from a distance it looked huge and as we continued our approach, I was stunned at how immense it actually was. In fact, the camp was so large that in August 1944, the total number of men and women prisoners numbered close to 100,000. Covering almost 425 acres, the camp contained over 300 buildings. Of those, 45 brick and 22 wooden buildings have survived almost intact. Though the majority of buildings had burned down or were demolished, the outlines of where they stood could still be seen.

The sight of the main watchtower in the distance was chilling. I had seen so many film clips and photographs of the camp in old movies and in books that I felt like I had been there before. The depiction of Birkenau was always the same—railroad tracks leading straight through the main guardhouse, known as "Death Gate," to the unloading ramps where the prisoners were separated for work or death. According to the camp brochure, it was at Birkenau that the Nazis constructed most of their instruments of mass destruction, namely: four crematoria with gas chambers, two makeshift gas chambers in specially converted farmhouses, and cremation pyres and pits.

The camp was pretty much left the way it was found after it was liberated in 1945. We walked freely around the grounds and wandered inside the remaining barracks to see the prisoner's living quarters as they really were—spartan, unsanitary and unheated structures where prisoners were crammed together on long wooden platforms that ran the length of the barracks.

Brick barracks were situated to the left of the unloading ramp and had been built without foundations, directly on the swampy ground. Apart from the compressed earth, most of the barracks didn't even have a floor. When it rained the ground would turn into a quagmire that became a breeding ground for insects and disease. Wooden buildings which had formerly been used as field stables for up to 52 horses, had been modified to accommodate up to 1,000 prisoners packed together in the most uncomfortable conditions imaginable.

With the sun shining over the large, flat, grass-covered grounds and the line of trees at the far end of the camp, it was hard to believe it was ever a place of horror as we strolled around the quiet, peaceful grounds. We walked until we reached the *International Monument to the Victims of Auschwitz*, situated between the ruins of two crematoria. From the monument we could see the unloading ramp in the center of the grounds and the main SS guardhouse at the camp entrance at the opposite end of the camp.

A little further on, through a wooded area off to the right of the monument and past more ruins of crematoria and gas chambers, we found the pond where ashes of the cremated bodies had been deposited. Fifty years later the water was still a murky gray from all the ashes that had been placed there.

It was a long walk back across the camp and we went along in silence, each of us quietly contemplating the sights we had seen. When we reached the unloading ramp I looked back at the railroad track that led directly to the crematoria and felt despair for the whole human race. With so many good people in the world I wondered how a place like this had ever come into existence. And how similar atrocities could still be going on in other parts of the world today. I wondered why God would let man be so cruel?

Before we exited the camp, we returned to the main guardhouse where a small group of people were lined up to record their comments in a visitor's book set up on a table against the wall. I stepped up to the small table. A number of comments had been written in languages I couldn't understand. I skimmed through a few pages and read some of the ones that were written in English. Most were expressions of sadness and appeals for peace. Others stated how we should never forget what took place at the camps at the risk of it happening again.

I stood in front of the visitor's book with a pen in my hand and reflected on the question I had asked myself—why would God let man be so cruel? I then realized I knew the answer to my own question. It's not up to God. It's up to man. I turned to a clean page in the guest book and wrote:

> It's amazing how much good and how much evil man is capable of.
> It's really just a matter of choice, isn't it?

He who hesitates is not only lost, but miles from the next exit.
— Unknown

"He practically guaranteed we'd have a great time. How can we not go?" Steve was doing his best to convince me to go to Gdansk for Peter's party.

"Do you know how far Gdansk is from here? It's an overnight trip," I replied. "Besides, what if the party stinks. Then what? Where do we go from there? I sure don't want to come all the way back down south again when we're already here."

"I'm not sure what part of this you're missing," Steve insisted. "Young, beautiful Polish girls will be there. Lots of them. It'll be worth it."

"Steve, you're 24. When I was your age I was also willing to go anywhere for a good party. Anyway, there probably won't be a Polish girl at the party that's over 19. They're way too young for me."

"All the more reason you should go. How many guys your age get the chance to sleep with a bunch of beautiful 19-year old Polish girls?"

I was convinced. And so, lured by the promise of dozens of young, nubile Polish girls fighting to see who would sleep with me first, I agreed to go to Gdansk—which threw off my original plan completely. I had heard it was possible to get a cheap Trans-Siberian train ticket in Czechoslovakia and Hungary and had intended to go south from Krakow with Shar and Shane to check it out—until Steve convinced me otherwise. Now, Shar and Shane were on their way to Czechoslovakia and I was going north to Gdansk with a British rugby player in search of teenage Polish girls.

That evening, Steve and I went to Krakow station to catch the 11:30 P.M. train to Gdansk. The station was packed—mostly with passengers who sat huddled around their bulky, over-stuffed valises, boxes and bags, but also with people who had nowhere better to go late at night. The hard wooden benches in the center of the waiting hall were occupied so we sat on the floor, suffocating on fumes of cigarette smoke from the people clustered around us until it was time to go.

The train pulled into the station right on time. We grabbed our packs and plunged through the narrow exits onto the dark outdoor platform with the rest of the crowd, hoping to secure a good seat on the train before they were all taken. There weren't any couchettes left when we bought our tickets so we were stuck with the rest of the locals who planned to sleep sitting up in the cramped, crowded seats of the passenger cars.

After an hour of squirming in my seat I gave up trying to get to sleep. Aside from the overhead lights, which I couldn't block out no matter how hard I closed my eyes, the people behind us were smoking, drinking and talking up a storm.

I frowned over at Steve, who was also wide-awake. "Let's see if we can get some beds," I suggested.

"How do you propose to do that?" Steve enquired. "They told us there were no more couchettes left, remember."

"Money talks, right? Let's make an offer."

It was a good thing money talked because the conductor didn't. At least not in English. Eventually, we got him to understand what we wanted and he indicated that we should go to the train car ahead of ours when the train stopped at the next station.

Twenty minutes later, the train pulled into a dark station in the middle of nowhere. Steve and I grabbed our packs and jumped off the train onto the dimly lit platform. We ran to the next train car and began to climb the metal steps up to the compartments when a squat, muscular woman in a blue train uniform blocked our way at the top.

We didn't have to speak Polish to know we weren't getting past her. We tried to explain that the conductor sent us there but she wasn't interested. With a firm grip on the handrail above us, and a dismissive wave of her thick hand, she blocked our way. She had no intention of letting us up. A few seconds later the train whistle sounded. We scrambled back down the stairs and ran along the platform to the next car before the train started to chug out of the station.

Three men in dirt-stained work clothes stood in front of the steps that led into the train car. They were whispering to a train attendant planted on the bottom rung of the carriage who was blocking their way up the steps. One of the men handed the attendant a bottle of liquor. In return, the attendant moved aside and let them mount the steps into the car.

Steve and I hurried over to the attendant. We made a sleeping gesture with our hands and pointed to the rear of the train to indicate we'd been instructed to switch cars. Either we confused him or he just didn't care, because he didn't ask us for liquor, money, or tickets. He simply moved aside so we could squeeze past him with our packs.

We climbed the steps as the train began to move. At the top of the landing I turned to Steve and said with relief, "For a while there I wasn't sure we were going to pull it off."

Steve held the handrail behind me. "Neither did I," he acknowledged. "It was a lot easier to get a couchette than I thought it would be."

I opened the heavy metal door that led into the train car and stopped short. Instead of seeing the usual row of sleeping compartments, there were huge crates and boxes piled on top of passenger seats which lined both sides of the car.

I dropped my pack and leaned against one of the boxes beside me. "I don't believe this. We're in the mail car."

"I should have known it was too good to be true," Steve said despondently.

"Well, at least it's quiet in here."

"Yeah, but where are we going to sleep? At least we had seats in the other car."

The three workers who had gotten on before us were sprawled out on the seats in the rear of the car, their legs tucked between the tall wooden crates around them. They reeked of smoke and alcohol and were fast asleep despite the bright overhead lights. Other than them, there were no other passengers in the compartment except Steve and me.

We moved some crates from some of the seats at the front of the car until there was enough room for us to lay down with our legs up on the opposite seats. It wasn't comfortable but it was better than sitting up all night. I propped my backpack beneath my legs for some support, placed a sweater over my head to block out the overhead lights, then went to sleep.

I woke a few hours later, freezing from the drafts that were seeping through the windows in the carriage. There was no heat in the compartment and the temperature had dropped steadily during the night.

I rummaged through my backpack and put on as many layers of shirts as I could find but it wasn't enough to keep out the cold. I looked over at Steve and noticed that he was wearing a heavy wool sweater. He must have also gotten cold during the night since he wasn't wearing the sweater when we had gotten on the train. I glanced at my watch. It was four-thirty in the morning. I was so cold my teeth were chattering. I cursed myself for not bringing more clothes then huddled against the side of the seat in an attempt to block out as much of the draft from the windows as possible.

Over the next few hours I dozed on and off. I woke up again at six o'clock, still freezing. I couldn't take it any more and decided to go into one of the other cars. I walked to the rear of the corridor and opened the heavy metal door. I stepped across the gap between the cars and went to open the door to the connecting train car when I heard a loud click behind me.

I turned around and saw a bearded train attendant facing me. He was staring at me from inside the mail car I had just exited. I stepped quickly back across the gap of the cars and tried the door. It was locked. I pointed to my seat at the far end of the mail car. He glared at me with a fierce scowl and shouted something through the thick glass window of the door. I banged on the glass but he ignored me and walked quickly down the corridor and exited through the other end of the carriage. I was locked out.

Unable to get back inside the mail car, I crossed over to the connecting carriage. As soon as I opened the door I felt the warmth of the heated car cover me like a thick, wool blanket. People were packed along the narrow corridor of the carriage so I wasn't able to move too far into the car. Rather than shove my way through the corridor, I secured a spot near the door where I could keep an eye out for the train attendant who had locked me out. At least I was warm again. That was my main objective, anyway.

I stood near the door and watched it grow light outside the window of the train while I quietly choked on the cigarette smoke from the passengers around me. An hour later I noticed Steve reading a book by the window of the mail car. I stepped across the carriages and pounded on the door to get his attention but he couldn't hear me. Unsuccessful, I returned to the smoke-filled car.

Seeing my troubled expression, a man next to me who spoke English asked what was wrong. I told him what had happened. When a conductor walked by to collect tickets the man explained my predicament to him then told me, "He says you can go outside train and switch to other car at next station. Outside door to car is not locked."

When the train stopped at the next station I ran up the platform to the mail car and climbed up the steps inside the car, where I made my way back to my seat.

"Where have you been?" Steve asked nonchalantly.

"I've been locked out!" I answered irritably. "Didn't you hear me banging on the door?"

"No. My teeth were chattering so loud I couldn't hear a thing. It was like a fridge in here last night. I'm glad I brought this wool jumper. I had almost decided to leave it home before I went off."

A few minutes later, the attendant who had locked me out came marching down the aisle. He was about my height but broader and heavier, with black, menacing eyes that glared out from beneath the rim of his navy-blue train cap. Beneath his cap, a coarse, brown moustache gave his face a permanent scowl. This was not a pleasant looking person. And when he spotted me back in my seat after having locked me out of his carriage, he looked extremely annoyed.

He strode down the corridor and glowered down at me with an intensity I could almost feel. I stared back at his antagonistic face and sensed he was just waiting for an excuse to throw me off the train. The amazing thing was that I had never laid eyes on the guy until after he had locked me out of the car. But for some reason, he had taken a distinct dislike to me. Maybe I reminded him of someone he hated. He never even looked at Steve. In any case, I was too tired and too cold to get into an argument with him so I kept my mouth shut and quietly read my book until he walked by.

The train pulled into Gdansk at 9:15 A.M. Steve and I hopped off the train with the rest of the passengers and walked into the station to look for a phone. We dumped our packs in a corner where I could keep an eye on them while Steve went off to call Peter for directions to the party. He returned a few minutes later, shaking his head and looking at me with a silly grin on his face.

"Did you get him?" I asked hopefully.

"No. He's not in today. And he won't be back till Monday. They don't know how to reach him."

"He's not in? But . . . it's only nine-thirty in the morning. He told us he would be at work until four o'clock on—Uh Oh . . . what day is it today?"

"Friday."

"We were supposed to call him yesterday, weren't we?"

"Right."

I sat down on the floor next to our bags. "That's just great. You mean to say I came all the way up here to freeze my tail off, get locked out of the train, and as far as I know, be hunted the whole time I'm here by that lunatic train attendant who hates me? I did all that for nothing? Please tell me you're kidding. There's no way to reach Peter? No one in his office knows where this party is?"

Steve spread his hands helplessly. "I asked. They didn't have a clue. Apparently he's throwing it at a friend's house and they don't know who the friend is or where he lives."

It was decision time again. Without Peter we had no party. And without the party we had no Polish girls—at least none who were willing to sleep with us. Too tired to get right back on a train, we decided to spend the rest of the day having a look around the city before moving on. We stored our bags in the luggage room, and after a quick breakfast at the station, went off to wander around the streets and harbor of Gdansk.

After all we had gone through to get there, at least the weather was in our favor. The sun was bright and warm in a deep-blue, cloudless sky, and felt great after the freezing night we had spent in the mail car. We walked along the streets that fronted the harbor and sat on a low wall along the waterfront where we lounged in the sun and relaxed in the cool breezes which drifted off the Gulf of Gdansk.

We returned to the train station later that afternoon to pick up our bags and buy our tickets. Unfortunately, we didn't know where we wanted to go. Neither of us was thrilled with the idea of getting back on a train to go all the way down south again but we didn't seem to have much choice since we were so far north. While discussing our options, we noticed a map of Eastern Europe on the wall near the ticket window. We walked over to have a look, hoping that something might strike our interest.

Steve placed his finger on the map and followed the train line from Poland into Lithuania. "You know, I wouldn't mind checking out the Baltic States now that they're independent from the USSR."

I ran my finger along the Lithuanian border with Russia and glanced over at Steve. "And maybe with a little luck we can sneak across the border to Russia while we're there."

Steve nodded thoughtfully. "It might be worth a try," he agreed. "But that still doesn't answer where we should go from here."

After the lousy train trip from Krakow to Gdansk, we both wanted to get a good night's sleep and rest up for a day or two before traveling into the Baltics. I pointed to a city on the eastern border of Poland. "This place looks as good as any, I guess."

I walked over to the ticket window and asked the woman behind the counter if she spoke English. She shook her head and gave me a blank look. I held up two fingers and a stack of Polish Zlotys. "Bialystock. Two," I said.

We arrived in Bialystock early the following morning. Unfortunately, the city wasn't listed in either of our guidebooks so we didn't have a clue where to go after we left the train station. The only thing I knew about the city was that it was the hometown of Ludwik Zamenhof, the man who developed the language called *Esperanto*. And the only reason I knew that much was because Steve had told me. I didn't bother to ask how he knew.

Basically, Esperanto was based on the Romance languages and was developed to be a simple, easy-to-learn language with universal appeal. However, it never caught on the way Ludwig had hoped, and he died with his dream of an Esperanto speaking world unfulfilled—which was a shame, since it would have been a lot easier asking about hotels in Esperanto than in Polish.

We didn't see a single person for almost half an hour after we left the station and were beginning to wonder whether there were hotels, or people for that matter, in Bialystock. Only after we crossed a bridge a mile or so from the station did we see the first signs of life—a woman waiting to cross the street on the corner ahead of us. Hoping she understood English, we ran over and asked tentatively, "Hotel?"

She glanced curiously at our backpacks then pointed to a bus stop across the road in the opposite direction from which we had been walking. "Hotel Lasńy," she said. We crossed the road and waited at the empty bus stop for the next bus to come along.

Fifteen minutes later we were bouncing along on a nicely paved, two-lane road with a bus-load of Polish commuters. We hadn't gone far however, before we noticed that we were heading away from the

city instead of towards it. Instead of getting closer to city buildings
and car-filled streets, we drove past horses idling in sun-filled meadows and wide, green fields bordered with thick, leafy trees. We had
no clue where we were going but twenty minutes and six bus stops
later, the bus stopped in front of a little bus shelter on a barren, country road. The driver cried out on our behalf, "Hotel Lasńy!"

Across the road, and down a low slope that made it hard to see
from the bus, was a mid-sized brick and glass building that looked like
a motel of sorts. When we walked in we were pleasantly surprised to
see a dining room down a long hallway and a reception desk off to
our left.

For a hotel in the middle of nowhere however, the rooms weren't
cheap. We asked the woman behind the desk if there were less expensive hotels in the area. She frowned sympathetically and told us she
didn't know of any, then added helpfully, "There are some small cabins behind the hotel that are used for camping which are less expensive
than the rooms. Would you care to have a look?" There didn't seem
to be a lot of places in Bialystock for us to choose from so we didn't
have much choice. We left our packs behind the reception desk and
went off to check out the cabins.

We had expected to find run-down, fire-gutted wood huts with
ripped mattresses and outhouses for toilets. But instead, we walked
into a newly built, well-made, two-bed cabin with curtained windows,
clean, comfortable beds and a bathroom with a modern toilet and a
hot water shower. The best thing about it though, was how quiet it
was—like a weekend retreat in the country surrounded by nothing
but grass, trees and birds. We walked back to the reception desk in
the main hotel and paid for two nights in advance.

As we explored the area over the next two days we came to realize
that our cabin was probably the best looking building in Bialystock.
When we rode the bus from the hotel to the city the following morning we watched the scenery change from tranquil rolling fields, with
horses grazing in flowered meadows, to sprawling complexes of ten-
story, concrete-block housing projects.

The city center wasn't any more visually appealing than the surrounding areas. But what it lacked in cultural and architectural charm
it made up for with an unhurried, uncomplicated, semi-modern atmosphere. The small shops and stores, which fronted the sidewalks along
the main road, and the quiet bustle of plainly dressed people on the

provincial-looking streets, reminded me of photographs I had seen of 1950's mid-western American towns.

After two days in Bialystock, we were fully relaxed and ready to move on. None of the ticket agents at the train station spoke English however, so we wrote down the train number and departure time to Vilnius, the capital of Lithuania, on a slip of paper and hoped that the girl behind the ticket window understood what we wanted. The only thing Steve and I weren't sure of was whether we needed a visa to go to Lithuania. We held up our Passports and asked uncertainly, "Visa?" The girl glanced at our Passports and shook her head "No." She then read the paper we had handed her, wrote down the price for the tickets, and waited patiently while Steve and I counted out our Zlotys. After we passed her the money, she re-counted it to make sure it was all there, then slid the tickets across the counter to us.

When we were back outside the station, Steve scratched his head and said, "I'm not quite sure she understood that bit about the visa."

"Sure she did," I replied. "She checked our Passports when we asked her, didn't she?"

"Yes, but I'm not sure she understood what we were asking her."

I looked at him and shrugged. "Well, she wouldn't have sold us the tickets if we needed a visa, would she? "Besides, even if she's wrong, what's the worst that can happen—we'll just get one at the border, right?"

Steve nodded and said uncertainly, "Yeah . . . I guess so."

I don't want the cheese. I just want to get out of the trap.
                                           — Spanish Proverb

"*Passport!*" The guard yanked open the sliding door to the compartment and flicked on the lights.

The sudden outburst in the dark, quiet compartment jolted me awake from a sound sleep. Squinting from the overhead light, I reached for my watch on the little shelf near my berth. It was four o'clock in the morning. Three hours had passed since the last passport check at the Polish border.

Still half asleep, I tried to figure out how we could be arriving in Vilnius so soon. I must have miscalculated the time somehow because I didn't think we were supposed to get there until eight in the morning. I reached under my pillow and pulled my Passport from my money belt then peered down from the top bunk where I had been sleeping to see what was going on.

Two uniformed guards stood in the middle of the small four-bed compartment. One of the guards was checking the Passports of the man and woman in the two bunks across from the ones that Steve and I occupied, while the second guard stood silently by. After finding their documents in order, the guards turned to our side of the compartment. Wordlessly, the taller of the two guards planted himself in front of Steve's berth and held his hand out for Steve's Passport. After a quick check of Steve's photo, he flipped back and forth through the pages. Not finding what he was looking for, he pointed to the Passport with his open hand and asked in a mildly curious tone, "Soviet visa?"

Steve glanced up at me before answering then turned his attention back to the guard and said, "We're going to Lithuania."

"Must have Russian visa," the guard replied. He closed Steve's

Passport and held his hand out for mine. A quick search through my Passport yielded the same result. "Must have Russian visa," he repeated.

I looked over at the two passengers in the other beds. The man in the top bunk opposite mine had rolled over and gone back to sleep but the woman on the bottom bed was watching us from beneath her blanket. Steve looked up at me from the bottom bunk and spread his hands open, waiting for any suggestions that I might have to offer. I propped myself up on an elbow and addressed the guard who held our Passports.

"We're on our way to Vilnius," I said. "We were told we didn't need a visa to go to Lithuania."

The guard glanced up at me from the center of the compartment and arched an eyebrow. "You now in Byelorussia. Need Russian visa."

"*Byelorussia?*" I looked down at Steve from the top bunk. "What's Byelorussia?"

"It was part of the U.S.S.R. They're independent now that the Soviet Union split up. I guess we have to pass through it on the way to Lithuania." It was great traveling with someone who had majored in world history.

I turned back to the guard. "But we asked about visas in Bialystock and were told we didn't need any. Besides, we only want to go to Lithuania—not Byelorussia."

"You must go back to Poland and get Russian visa."

"But we don't want to go to Byelorussia. We're on our way to Lithuania. Can't we just pass through Byelorussia on the way? We won't leave the train till we get to Vilnius—I promise," I added as an after-thought, feeling like an idiot after I said it.

The guard placed our Passports in his pocket. "Need Russian visa," he sighed.

"Can't we buy a transit visa since we're just passing through?" Steve asked hopefully.

The guard frowned and shook his head. "Must go back to Poland, get visa."

It was no use. There was no getting around this guy. What I didn't understand though, was why we were allowed to leave Poland in the first place. When we crossed the border three hours before, the Passport guards stamped us out of the country and let us continue on our way. Why didn't they stop us then instead of making us wait until we were three hours into Byelorussia before telling us we couldn't be there without a Russian visa.

The guards stood outside the compartment while Steve and I got dressed. When my bags were packed I looked at Steve and sighed. "You know, I seem to have lousy luck on trains. Maybe next time I'll book a flight instead."

Before leaving the compartment I glanced over at the woman on the bottom bunk. She looked up at me and pointed to the light. For all she knew, we were being taken off the train to be shot. And all she was worried about was going back to sleep. I wondered if she ever lived in New York. I hit the switch on my way out and slid the heavy door of the compartment until it closed behind me.

Steve and I followed the two guards off the train and down the dark platform like prisoners being led away after an unsuccessful escape attempt. It was dark and cold outside at four in the morning and as we walked alongside the long green train on our way down the platform to the stationhouse, I envied the people still on board who were fast asleep, safe and warm in their little compartments.

As we walked down the platform I heard a woman's voice from one of the carriages at the head of the train. I couldn't make out what she was saying but it sounded like English. Still half asleep, I thought I was imagining things. A few seconds later I knew I wasn't dreaming. Halfway down the platform, a man and woman were being led off the train by an armed border guard. "*This is crazy,*" the woman huffed. "*No one told us we were going through Byelorussia. How were we supposed to know we needed a visa?*"

"I *thought* I heard English!" I remarked, surprised to see we weren't the only foreigners on the train. They were just as shocked to see Steve and me coming down the dark platform in the middle of the night. Relieved to learn they weren't alone in their exodus from the train, they fell into line beside us when we caught up to them.

The four of us walked noisily behind our Russian escorts, joking about how much money we would probably have to pay before we were allowed to get back on the train. "I hope this doesn't take long," the woman said. Then added, "Why couldn't they just tell us how much money they want without making us get off the train?"

"They probably think it makes it more official this way," her husband replied. "You know—official pretenses and all that."

We heard the screech of metal on the track behind us and turned to see the train inching slowly away from the platform. The woman shot a nervous look at her husband as she suddenly realized that no amount of money was going to get them back on board. Instead of moving on to Vilnius with the rest of the passengers we were stuck in a place called Grodno, somewhere in the middle of Byelorussia.

The guards led us into a Passport Control waiting hall packed with over a hundred Russians. I looked around the large hall at all the people squatting on the bare floor with their overstuffed bags of luggage and was amazed at how many people were waiting for trains at four-thirty in the morning.

"You vill vait here for ten o'clock train to Varsaw," the Passport officer informed us when we entered the waiting hall. Without our Passports we didn't have much choice. We stepped carefully through the groups of people and baggage around us and staked out a small area in the back of the waiting hall where we could all sit together.

With over five hours to kill we had plenty of time to get to know one another. David and Deborah were a married couple from Oregon on their way to Lithuania to explore David's family roots, and were a matched pair if ever I had seen one.

With their baggy, tie-dyed clothes they looked like two ex-hippies who had just returned from a Joni Mitchell concert. David had a long scraggly beard, thin, wire-rim glasses, and a floppy Fedora hat. Deborah wore layers of loose-fitting clothes and rows of bracelets on both wrists. In their mid-forties, they were throwbacks to the 1960's and were an odd sight among the drab, plainly dressed Russians around us.

Not long after we sat down, an older man with thick, black framed glasses and a short, fat cigar sticking out of his mouth, came stepping steadily through the crowd in our direction. He was lugging a long suit-bag and a black duffel shoulder bag, both of which bulged at the seams.

"Excuse me," he said in a raspy, slightly accented voice to an old Russian woman as he stepped carefully across her legs. When he reached the spot where we were seated he dropped his bags and pulled his cigar from his mouth. "Are all of you also being sent back to Poland?" he asked.

David looked at him curiously. "Yes. Were you on the same train?"

"I most certainly was—until they told me I needed a Russian visa, which of course I did not have, since I am going to Latvia, not Russia."

"Why don't you come and sit with us?" Deborah offered. We

shifted our packs to make room for him. He introduced himself as 'Vern' and thanked us for letting him join our group. With a grunt and a slight physical effort, he kneeled down and sat beside us.

Vern was a short, mostly bald, heavy-set man in his early sixties, with a potbelly and a round, friendly looking face. He was traveling to Latvia to visit his homeland after thirty-five years away and was loaded down with bags filled with gifts for all the family and friends he hadn't seen since he had left. With the exception of Vern and a brother who lived in Germany, all of his family had died in Siberia where they had been exiled when the Russians took over his country at the end of World War II. After leaving Latvia, Vern lived and worked in a number of different European countries before finally settling down and raising a family in Canada, where he had since became a citizen.

As he got to know us better during the five hours we sat together in the waiting hall, and secure that he was among friends, Vern confided to us that getting taken off the train brought back bad memories and fears he had long forgotten. In his deep, gravelly voice, he leaned forward so no one outside our group could overhear. "I was very nervous when they came to my compartment last night," he whispered. "I do not want trouble with the Russians. They may be different now, but I remember them like they were before. They would take you away somewhere and no one would hear of you again. When I saw them last night on the train, I was scared. It was an instinct from the past. I remembered them with guns and I did not want any trouble."

Vern was worried that if the Russian authorities found out he had been born in Latvia, they might keep him from leaving the country. He cast a nervous look at the guards lounging near the entrance to the waiting hall, then continued his explanation. "The Russians consider anyone born within a Soviet Republic to be a Soviet National. And even though I have a Canadian Passport and am a Canadian citizen, they might try to cause trouble for me."

The time sped by as we listened to each other's stories and before we knew it almost five hours had passed. At nine o'clock a Russian guard opened one of the wide glass doors at the rear of the waiting hall which led to the tracks outside. There was still an hour to go before the train was set to leave but all the people in the room grabbed their possessions and rushed towards the doors to line up. Not knowing when or where we were supposed to go, we stayed where we were, content to avoid the huge line which led halfway down the platform.

A few minutes later a female Russian officer approached us. With a pleasant smile she said in English, "Pleese remain here. I vill come back in a leetle vhile to take you to the train."

"What about our passports?" Deborah asked anxiously. "They haven't been given back to us."

"Your passpoorts vill be returned to you avtar you board the train," the woman replied politely. She paused to address any other questions we might have and when none were asked, she turned and made her way back through the mass of people sprawled along the floor.

Twenty minutes later, our Russian hostess returned and asked us to follow her outside. We grabbed our bags and followed her past the long line of people standing outside the waiting hall. Like a small group of dignitaries receiving preferential treatment, we were escorted to the platform and assigned to a train car before anyone else was allowed to board.

We climbed the steps to the empty train car and settled into a wide, comfortable compartment which faced the long line of people outside the train. A few minutes later, when the rest of the passengers were allowed to board, they quickly broke ranks and made a mad scramble for the train.

At 10:00 A.M., the train pulled sluggishly away from the station in Grodno, Byelorussia. Only an hour away from the Lithuanian border, we found ourselves back on a train. But instead of moving closer to Vilnius, we were on our way back to Warsaw, Poland.

A few hours after we set off, we crossed the Polish border at a place called Kuznica. And since none of us had any intention of going all the way back to Warsaw, when the train stopped at Kuznica station we grabbed our belongings and left the train.

It was now obvious that we needed to find some way to get to Vilnius without going through Byelorussia. Unfortunately, no one at the station spoke English. Vern spoke French, German, Latvian and Russian, so we appointed him team leader and sent him and Steve off to the ticket window for directions out of Kuznica while David, Deborah and I went off in search of food. We found a small cafeteria on the second floor of the train station and returned a few minutes later with Polish hot dogs and cokes. After everyone had eaten their fill, we circled around Vern to hear what he had discovered. Like a general explaining the day's maneuvers to his forces, he pointed to a map of eastern Poland and laid out our plan.

"From Kuznica we take a train north to Suwalki. When we get to Suwalki we take a bus to a town called Ogrodniki. From there we find a bus to take us across the border to Lazdijai in Lithuania." With a quick, dismissive wave of his hand he said lightly, "From Lazdijai it will be a simple matter to find our way to Vilnius."

Vern sat back and looked at each of us in turn to make sure we understood the plan. When we nodded our agreement, he stuck a fresh cigar in his mouth. With a steady hand, he held a match to his cigar and said confidently, "Depending on the train and bus connections, we should be in Vilnius no later than tomorrow evening."

The Challenge

Tickets to Leningrad

Russia or Bust

Do or do not. There is no try.
—Yoda

Lithuania. A month before I couldn't even spell it. And there I was, not even sure why I was there—or where I was going next.

The connections to Vilnius that Vern had mapped out in Kuznica went without a hitch. We bypassed Byelorussia and arrived in Lithuania according to plan. Shortly after our arrival, the five of us booked rooms in a large, old, Russian-built hotel in the center of the city, just a few blocks from the bus station where we had been let off.

David and Deborah planned to hang out in Vilnius for a few days to do some sightseeing before taking off for the countryside to see where David's family had come from. Vern planned to leave for Riga, the capital of Latvia, the following morning in order to spend as much time with his friends and relatives as possible. Steve and I had no plans.

At six o'clock the next morning, with his overstuffed bags slung over his shoulders and his ever-present cigar stuck in his mouth, Vern woke us up to say goodbye. Aside from his loud snoring he had been a perfect travel companion and we were sorry he planned to leave so soon. We wished him luck on his pilgrimage to Latvia then fell immediately back to sleep, exhausted from having been woken up so early.

Because of the rapid changes that had taken place in Lithuania since its independence from the U.S.S.R., there wasn't much reliable info on Vilnius in our guidebooks. Hotels, restaurants, prices and street names were changing too fast for guidebooks to keep up with them. So instead of relying on the sketchy information in our guides, we wandered around Vilnius on our own, idly exploring the narrow winding lanes and pastel-colored buildings in the old part of the city and stopping into local museums and cathedrals whenever we happened upon them. We had no idea what we were looking at but it kept us busy for a few days.

The Parliament building in the modern part of the city was the one building we had heard of. When Lithuania declared its independence from the Soviet Union in March 1990, the local citizens set up barricades to protect the building from being stormed by Soviet tanks. Instead of attacking the Parliament however, the Russians assaulted Vilnius's radio and TV center in an attempt to knock out their communications. Thirteen Lithuanians were killed in the skirmish that followed. After securing their independence, the new government of Lithuania left the barricades in front of the Parliament Building as a symbolic reminder of their country's independence. While we were there a group of people held lit candles and prayed in front of wreaths placed against the side of the building, mourning the thirteen people who had been killed while resisting the Russians.

Vilnius seemed more Eastern European to me than the other cities I had seen in Poland. It was less developed and slower-paced—more of what I expected to find in Eastern Europe. There also weren't too many other Western tourists going to the Baltics at that time, which made it seem more authentic. It was almost as if we had the place to ourselves. But the thing I liked most about Lithuania was its closeness to the Russian border. Ever since the travel agent in Copenhagen had told me how difficult it was to get a Russian visa without spending a lot of money, I had made up my mind to find an alternative way into Russia. It had become a personal challenge and I knew I wasn't going to be happy until I had figured out a way around Russia's bureaucratic regulations.

On the off chance that Russian visas weren't needed from Lithuania I decided to check out the visa requirements at the Hotel Lietuva, the city's towering, 330-room hotel where most business people and well-to-do foreign travelers stayed in Vilnius.

A tall woman in a crisp, red uniform stood confidently behind the reception desk of the hotel. She was recommending a restaurant in the old quarter of the city to a smartly-dressed businessman in front of me. When the gentleman walked off, I stepped up to the counter. I smiled at the woman and asked, "I was wondering if you could tell me whether or not I need a Russian visa to take a train to Russia from Vilnius. I have an American Passport."

"No, I don't think so," she replied. "It should not be a problem."

"Is there any way I can find out for sure?"

"You can telephone the American embassy if you'd like." She handed me the desk phone and looked up the number of the U.S. Embassy in Vilnius for me. I called the embassy and was transferred to a woman in the visa section. "You most definitely need a Russian visa," the embassy official informed me over the phone. "Only citizens from the Soviet Republics don't need visas." I thanked her and handed the phone back to the hotel attendant.

Steve was waiting for me in the lobby of the hotel. I filled him in on what I had found out and remarked, "Well, I guess that takes care of that. It doesn't look like we're getting into Russia from here—at least not legally."

That evening we walked over to the old city to find the restaurant I had overheard the hotel attendant recommending to the smartly dressed businessman. I remembered the name and the street address but we weren't having much luck finding the place. After wandering around aimlessly for awhile we noticed a couple down the lane from us and went over to ask them for directions.

The woman was very helpful and kindly offered to guide us to the restaurant we had been searching for. She had a Ph.D. in Ecology and was fluent in English as a result of working closely with English speaking scientists from the United States and Europe. While we walked along, she asked us where we had traveled before arriving in Vilnius. Steve and I told her about our stay in Poland and how we had decided to come to Lithuania after missing a party in Gdansk. She shook her head and laughed at how casually we made travel plans. "Where will you be traveling next?" she asked curiously.

"We're leaving for Estonia tomorrow," I replied. "After that, we're not sure. I may take off for Czechoslovakia or Hungary." With a nod towards Steve I said, "He's not sure where he'll be going next."

She smiled and asked, "But won't either of you be going to Russia? St. Petersburg is a very beautiful city."

"We'd like to, but neither of us have visas," I replied. I then explained how much bureaucracy was involved in getting a Russian visa. "But it does seem a shame to be so close and not get there, doesn't it?" I said with a shrug.

"Yes, it does." she agreed. "I think you would like it very much."

"We've thought about giving it a go without a visa," Steve chimed in. "But we don't know how easy that would be. We just got booted out of Byelorussia, and we weren't even trying to go there. I would hate to imagine what would happen if we got caught actually trying to sneak into Russia."

We soon reached the street we were looking for and our friendly guide pointed to a narrow stone building halfway down the block. "There is your restaurant," she said. Before she and her friend turned to leave, she handed each of us her business card in the event we needed something while in Vilnius. With a warm smile, she shook our hands and said, "It would be a pity for you not to visit St. Petersburg or Moscow on your journey. Perhaps you will have better luck the next time you try to sneak into Russia." After a thoughtful pause she then added, "Besides, you are young. You are brave. You must try."

With her parting words as a challenge, Steve and I made up our minds. From Estonia we would go to Russia. With or without a visa.

When the cat and mouse agree, the grocer is ruined.
— Persian Proverb

"Have some more tea," Valeri implored, as Steve and I covered our cups to keep him from filling them again. We were already stuffed from the lunch Valeri's wife had made and couldn't eat or drink another thing.

We sat in the living room of their small one-bedroom apartment and relaxed over tea and cakes like old friends who had known each other for years. It was hard to believe we had arrived in Tallinn just three days before, not knowing a soul.

When we first got to Estonia we thought for sure we would have to get back on a train and leave. We had walked around the city for hours trying to find an affordable room but each place we approached wanted from $25 to $50 per night—and they wanted payment in U.S. dollars. Most of the places were small local hotels used by Russians and other East Europeans. And judging by the look of the guests who lounged around the small, cramped lobbies of these hotels it was hard to fathom how they could afford the prices that had been quoted to Steve and me. It soon became obvious to us that there was a separate price list for foreigners.

In desperation, we searched out a small Russian hotel on the other side of the city that was supposed to be inexpensive. As soon as the woman behind the counter glanced at our backpacks however, I knew we were in trouble. She quoted a price of forty U.S. dollars a night for a double-room. Steve was exasperated. "I thought the hotels in these East European countries were supposed to be so inexpensive," he exclaimed in frustration.

I frowned and said loudly enough for the woman to hear, "They are. But only for East Europeans, I guess." With tired sighs, we lifted

our packs for the tenth time that morning and walked towards the
door. Evidently feeling sorry for us, the woman behind the counter
called us over to her desk and told us about a small hotel in the old
part of the city that a friend of hers managed. After giving us directions to the hotel, she wrote a note to her friend and wished us luck
as we left the hotel to trudge back across the city.

The place was perfect—a small hotel on a quiet side street in the
middle of the old city. We climbed up two flights of stairs and walked
down a narrow, carpeted hallway to a room where a middle-aged
woman sat watching television in front of a small desk littered with
papers.

The woman didn't speak English so I handed her the note from
her friend. She put her reading glasses on, gave a short grunt, then
placed a registration book in front of us to record our names and
Passport numbers. When the formalities were completed, she showed
us a clean, sunny room with two beds and a great view of the Market
Square across from the hotel. Steve and I quickly nodded our approval
then followed her back to her office where she wrote down the price
for the room.

"How much do you figure?" Steve asked me as the woman scribbled down the price.

"I'd guess about fifteen dollars each—maybe more," I replied. Especially given this location."

"Well, I'm too tired to look for another place so whatever it is let's
pay it, okay?"

It was a good thing the woman didn't understand English or she
would have increased her price. She handed me the piece of paper
with her price for the room on it and waited for my reaction. I handed
it to Steve and tried not to smile. The price was in rubles and came
to about two dollars each for the room. We paid for three nights in
advance.

After unpacking some things we went for dinner at a small pizza
parlor that we had stumbled onto by chance while wandering in and
out of the twisting, narrow alleyways in the old city earlier that day.
It was a tiny place with three or four small tables on the inside and a
long line going out the door. A minute or so after Steve and I sat
down with our pizzas, Valeri introduced himself from the table where
he and his wife Natasha were seated and asked if we wanted to join
them. We hit it off right away and by the time we had finished our

meal, Valeri and Natasha had become our friends and guides in Tallinn.

Like the other Baltic countries that had declared their independence from the Soviet Union, Estonia wrestled with economic problems that resulted from the switch from Communism to Capitalism. But Estonia had two things in its favor. The first was its proximity to Finland, which brought boatloads of Finnish tourists and Western currency to Tallinn. The second, was that even when it was under Soviet rule, Tallinn was considered one of the most scenic and westernized cities within the U.S.S.R. and was therefore already used to dealing with tourists. The net result was that the shops in Tallinn were filled with Western-made products and looked more like the shops in Helsinki than the shops in a former Soviet Republic.

Not long after obtaining its independence from the Soviet Union, many of the city's 600,000 residents took advantage of the new business opportunities that became available. Valeri and his family were no exception. With the help of a friend from the United States, Valeri started a business selling picture T-shirts. With a good head for business and a lot of hard work, Valeri's business was doing so well in Estonia that he planned to increase distribution to Russia as soon as he could.

When he wasn't selling T-shirts however, Valeri was busy showing Steve and me around the old town of Tallinn. The area comprised by the old town wasn't large, but it was beautiful. Narrow cobblestone streets, dark winding alleys, and shady, tree-filled parks crisscrossed the old city below the tall turrets, spires and steeples of the medieval-looking buildings that had been built along Tallinn's steep hills. The old city looked like it had been lifted from the pages of a storybook—especially at night, when all of Tallinn could be seen in one gulp from the top of Castle Hill, high above the city.

On top of everything else they had already done for us, Valeri and Natasha tried to pay for our drinks one evening at a terrific little café they had taken us to in the old Market Square. Steve and I insisted on paying the check and were able to get Valeri to relent only after we promised to let him pick up the check the next time we went out. Having settled the issue to Valeri's satisfaction, he happily raised his glass in a toast. "To new friends," he said. Then added, "Tomorrow Natasha and I will take you to a nice little restaurant in the old town."

Steve and I clinked glasses with Valeri and Natasha, then followed Valeri's lead by downing our drinks in one gulp. "That little restaurant sounds great, Valeri," I said. "But we're going to have to take a rain-check on it for now since we're leaving for Russia tomorrow."

Valeri looked at Steve and me blankly for a few seconds while the announcement of our departure sank in. "How long will you be there?" he asked.

"We're not sure. However long it takes to have a look around St. Petersburg and Moscow."

"How long are your visas good for?"

"Well, that's where it gets a little tricky."

"You don't have Russian visas?"

"No."

"You don't need visas?"

"Well, yes . . . we do. We just don't have them. But we're planning on going anyway."

Valeri scratched his chin and reflected a moment before responding. "Have you bought the tickets yet?" he asked.

"No, not yet. We figured we would get them in the morning."

Valeri nodded slowly then said, "If you'd like, I will help you buy them. You may find purchasing the tickets at the train station to be difficult without speaking Estonian or Russian."

Steve and I gladly accepted his offer, and after a final round of pastries and coffee laced with liquor, we called it a night. Valeri had an early morning meeting, so we parted company in the Market Square and arranged to meet at the train station at one o'clock the following day.

When Steve and I arrived at the station, Valeri was already waiting for us. "There are no more tickets to St. Petersburg for tonight," he informed us when we approached.

"How about tomorrow?" we asked hopefully. Valeri frowned and gave a shrug. "I can try. But I think they will be sold out for tomorrow also. Today is Friday and many people go to St. Petersburg for the weekend."

Steve and I waited in the corridor while Valeri returned to the ticket window. When he reached the front of the line, we saw the woman behind the counter shake her head at him and wave the next person to the counter as Valeri moved aside. Valeri strolled slowly back to where Steve and I were waiting and said, "She says there are no more tickets until Monday. Do you still want to go tonight?"

Steve looked at Valeri with surprise. "How can we go tonight? You just said the tickets were sold out until Monday."

"Yes, at the ticket window. But that is not a problem—there are other ways to get tickets." Seeing our bemused expressions, Valeri laughed and said, "Follow me."

Valeri pointed to a small ticket window along the side wall of the station. "Sometimes people can't use their tickets. If they want to return them, they bring them to that window for a refund—usually for about seventy-five percent of the ticket price." He motioned us to stay behind while he went to the window to see if any tickets had been returned for the night train to St. Petersburg. When he came back he said with a frown, "No returns." A few seconds later, two people walked over to the window. "Wait here a moment," Valeri said, as he walked quickly towards the people before they could reach the return window. Steve and I watched curiously as Valeri motioned them over to the side of the station.

A few minutes later, Valeri returned with a ticket in his hand. With a smile he said, "That man was going to return this ticket. I bought it from him for full value—105 rubles. Is the price all right for you?" Valeri asked.

"*Are you kidding?*" I replied, amazed at how cheap the ticket was. The overnight ticket from Tallinn to St. Petersburg had cost less than one U.S. dollar—including a couchette for the night.

Valeri then nodded towards a group of shady-looking characters huddled near the money-exchange windows at the rear of the station. "To get a second ticket I think we will have to talk to those people," he quietly informed us. "They are the reason it is so difficult to buy tickets at the ticket windows. They buy all the desirable tickets up and sell them at higher prices."

"If that's true, why is it that they're allowed to get away with it?" Steve asked.

Valeri looked at Steve and explained patiently, "You have to understand the Communist system. They pay off the right people. Everything depends on who you know. When you see empty stores it doesn't mean that there are no products. You have to know where to go and who to pay to get the products. It is very corrupt. But it is the way people learned to survive within the Communist system. Communism may be over but the system is still the same."

Steve nodded and asked, "How much do guys like that charge for a ticket?"

"If you buy the ticket at the window it is 105 rubles to St. Petersburg—the same price we just paid for the ticket you have now. The privateers would sell that same ticket to the locals for 200 rubles. From a foreigner they will take whatever they can get—probably five U.S. dollars."

"That's still incredibly cheap," I remarked.

"For you, yes," Valeri replied. "But it is good money for them."

One of the privateers, a dark-skinned man around thirty years old who looked to be middle-eastern, eyed us from the back of the station with his friends. He had watched Valeri approach the people at the return ticket window, and sensing that there was still business to be had, sauntered slowly over to where we were standing. With a nod towards Steve and me, he faced Valeri and said something in Estonian. After a minute or so, Valeri said, "He says he has two tickets to St. Petersburg for tonight and will sell them for eight U.S. dollars. I told him it is too much money but he knows they are for you and will not lower the price."

"The price is okay," I said. "But we only need one more ticket. Will he sell us just one of the tickets?"

Valeri questioned the man then replied, "He says he would rather not sell just one ticket. If he sells only one it may be difficult for him to get rid of the other one."

Steve and I talked it over while Valeri and the privateer waited for our decision.

"Does this guy understand English?" I asked, hoping to save Valeri the effort of translating everything we said.

Valeri questioned him and turned back to us. "No English. Only Russian and Estonian."

"Okay, I've got an idea," I said. "Tell him we'll give him six dollars for one of his tickets. But only if he lets us exchange his second ticket for the one we already have. That way we'll have two tickets in the same compartment instead of being separated on the train. And he'll make six dollars *plus* whatever he makes on the other ticket he still gets to sell."

Valeri translated our offer and waited while the man thought over our deal. After some deliberation, the man spoke quietly to Valeri. "He says he will do it," Valeri informed us. "He wants us to wait here while he gets the tickets."

Even Valeri was surprised at what happened next. Instead of heading back to his group of friends to get the tickets, the privateer walked quickly towards the back door of the ticket agent's office. He tapped on the door a few times with the back of his hand and waited. A few seconds later, the top half of the door opened. Standing in front of the door was the woman who had previously told Valeri there were no tickets available until Monday. She conferred with the privateer for a few seconds and then walked off. A minute later she returned and handed two tickets to the privateer. She then closed the door and returned to her seat at the ticket window.

"Do you believe that?" Steve blurted with surprise. Valeri scratched his head and shrugged. Two minutes later we walked out of the train station with two reserved tickets on the eleven o'clock night train to St. Petersburg.

At ten forty-five that evening we met Valeri back at the station. We told him he didn't need to see us off, but like a nervous mother sending her two kids to school for the first time, he insisted on escorting us to the train to make sure there were no problems with the tickets. It wouldn't have surprised me if he had shown up with lunch boxes for the trip.

We followed him through the station to the platforms out back and walked beside the massive green train ahead of us until we located our carriage. Steve and I climbed on board with Valeri right behind us. The three of us walked single-file down the narrow, carpeted corridor until we located our compartment a third of the way up the aisle.

Only after Valeri checked the compartment and was fully satisfied that the beds were all right, did he feel comfortable enough to leave us alone on the train. We thanked him for all his help and told him we would probably be back in about ten days—assuming we didn't get kicked off the train during the night or thrown into Lubyanka prison as spies for trying to sneak into Russia without a visa.

At eleven o'clock, exactly on schedule, the train jerked a few times and then started its slow creep away from the station. Valeri waved to us from the platform. We stuck our heads out the window and waved in return. Steve looked over at me and said with a laugh, "Valeri looks nervous." We waved to Valeri one last time as the train pulled away from the platform and flashed him a thumbs up sign to let him know everything was fine.

As we turned back inside the train and closed the window behind us, I glanced down the corridor at the other passengers as they made their way to their compartments. A bit more anxiously than I had intended, I said to Steve, "What's Valeri got to be nervous about— we're the ones sneaking into Russia."

If we don't change direction soon, we'll end up where we're going.
— Prof. Irwin Corey

The yellow glow from the night-lights that lined the ceiling of the corridor gave an eerie look to the interior of the train. I was tired but didn't feel like going to bed just yet, so I stood in the aisle near the windows and watched the lights of Tallinn disappear in the distance as we neared the outskirts of the city. It was black outside the windows, and other than an occasional shape of a house or building, there wasn't much to see as we sped along towards the Russian border.

Along the corridor at both ends of the car, small groups of Russian men in gray trousers and sleeveless T-shirts stood in the aisles and smoked their final cigarettes of the day before going off to bed. Glancing furtively down the aisle to make sure no one could overhear him, Steve whispered, "Do you think we'll get stopped at the border?"

I shrugged and said jokingly, "I sure hope not. I'd hate to spend another night in a Russian waiting hall. Maybe we can convince them to just shoot us instead. Or torture us by making us drink borscht. Listen, if it comes down to the borscht or the shooting, take the bullet. I've had borscht and it's not a pleasant experience."

"Funny," he said with a frown and a slightly worried look.

Surrounded by Russians, and seeing the concerned look on Steve's face, I thought about the visa requirements that were outlined in my guidebook:

> All foreigners visiting the Soviet Union need visas. To get one you must usually have confirmed accommodation for every night you'll be in the country, and the visa is only for those cities where you have the accommodation. . . . At each night's stop you surrender passport and visa so the hotel can register you with the police . . . .

The Police. Maybe getting on a train to Russia without a visa wasn't such a bright idea after all, I thought. Trying to sound more confident than I felt, I said to Steve, "Look, if we get caught we get caught. It's too late to worry about it now anyway. We'll find out soon enough, I guess."

Looking forward to a good night's sleep, we turned from the window and started back to our compartment. But just as we pulled open the heavy sliding door, we were almost blown back into the corridor by the blast of an enormous belch. When we walked in, a heavy-set man in his mid-thirties stared up at us with glazed eyes from the bottom bunk of the compartment. On a tray directly in front of him were three unopened bottles of beer. Three empty bottles rocked slowly back and forth on the floor beneath his bunk.

"Wow—either this guy's thirsty or we walked into the bar car by mistake," I remarked. When our fat friend popped open his fourth bottle of beer, we knew he was thirsty.

I leaned against the door and sighed. "Just once I'd like to walk into a compartment and find a beautiful girl sitting on the bottom bunk. Is that too much to ask?"

We decided to make the best of it. We stepped inside and introduced ourselves to our inebriated bunkmate. His name was Serge, and his English was only slightly better than our Russian, which was limited to about four words.

Other than a dazed look in our direction every now and then, our conversation with Serge didn't get much past the, "Hi, I'm Eric, he's Steve," stage. We covered every topic we could think of, hoping he would eventually relate to something, but it seemed hopeless. In response to each of our questions, Serge would look at us, shrug his shoulders, and then take another drink from his growing beer collection. We were about to give up when Steve hit Serge's hot button.

"Serge, do you like music?"

"Music good!" Serge blurted, followed by a loud burp.

"Which groups do you like?" No answer.

"U2? Phil Collins? Madonna?" Steve prompted.

"Yes! Yes! U2 good! Phil Collins good! No like Madonna!" Serge took a swig of his beer and rolled his head sleepily. Then, with an excitement that made me jump, he bellowed, "You know Zappa?"

"Frank Zappa?" I asked.

"*Yes! Yes! I love Zappa!*" he exclaimed. Serge shifted his overweight frame on the bunk and knocked over two beer bottles. Having pegged his taste in music into the Zappa era, the rest was easy. We spent the next hour and a half covering everything from *The Doors, Pink Floyd* and *Cream*, to *Yes* and *Jimmy Hendrix*, all of which Serge loved.

Steve and I eventually ran out of groups at about the same time Serge ran out of beer. With nothing else to talk about, he placed his last empty bottle with the others strewn across the floor beneath his bed, and rolled over on his side. Drunk and content, he pulled his blanket up to his shoulders and belched out, "Goodnight my friends!" Seconds later, Serge was happily snoring away.

As usual, passport control took place around three in the morning. The door to the compartment slid open with a thud, followed by a flick of the lights and the shout of *"Passport!"* as three uniformed policemen entered the room.

The men stood in the middle of our narrow compartment and waited for us to wake up. Steve cast a questioning look at me from the bottom bunk as we each tried to determine from the insignias on their uniforms whether they were Estonian or Russian border police.

Steve handed his passport to one of the men as I fumbled in my money belt to pull mine out. We watched in silence as the guard thumbed the pages of Steve's passport. A few seconds later he handed it back to Steve and reached his hand up for mine. I felt myself relax. They were Estonian border police. No problem. After a quick look through my passport the guard handed it back to me and stepped over to the bottom bunk across the room where Serge was still sound asleep.

"Passport," the customs officer said, shaking Serge's shoulder a few times to rouse him. Serge kept right on snoring, oblivious to everything going on.

"Passport!" the officer said, more loudly this time. When Serge didn't respond, the officer shook him even harder than before.

To everyone's amazement, instead of waking up, Serge rolled over on his stomach, and still fast asleep, blasted a loud fart in the direction of the passport officer. The officer looked over at me and shook his head impatiently. With a smile mixed with amusement and disgust he reached down a third time and shook Serge so hard that the whole bunk bed started to shake.

Like an old car that suddenly fires up after being jump-started over and over again, Serge finally sprang to life. If you could call the dazed look in his eyes life. But at least he was awake. Rubbing his eyes and babbling in Russian to no one in particular, Serge looked around the room to see what all the commotion was. The officer said something to Serge and held his hand out, waiting for Serge to hand over his passport.

Serge fumbled around in a little brown leather bag, dumping its contents on the small table near the window that previously held his beers. Scattered on the table were little bits of paper, crumpled-up Russian rubles, and three or four U.S. twenty-dollar bills, which Serge kept pushing around the table. But no passport.

Serge continued spewing the contents of his little bag on the table while pushing the money around every now and then. I wasn't sure what he was up to, but if he was trying to bribe the police it wasn't working. The officer kept repeating "Passport" and Serge kept babbling away in Russian, all the while digging through the rest of his bags under his bed.

Just when I thought Serge was a goner, he reached for a jacket that was hanging on the wall near the door. He rummaged around the various pockets of his coat and broke into a wide grin as he pulled out his passport from an inside coat pocket. The officer checked it out and handed it back to Serge with a frown. Then, just as quickly as they had entered, the three men walked out, sliding the door of our compartment closed behind them.

Serge tossed his passport on the table alongside the rest of the junk he had dumped there. With a slow, lazy turn of his amorphous body, he looked at Steve and me with tired eyes, then belched contentedly before rolling over and going back to sleep. I reached over and turned out the lights for the second time that night.

"Steve—are you still up?" I whispered in the dark.

"Yeah."

"You think we'll get checked again on the Russian side?"

"Maybe. Last time they waited until we were three hours into Byelorussia before they stopped us, remember?"

"Yeah, that's right." We weren't in the clear just yet.

I laid in my bunk with my eyes open in the dark and wondered whether we would get stopped again. I tried to stay awake, wanting to be alert if we got checked a second time, but the steady rocking of the train and the rhythmic beating of the wheels lulled me slowly back to sleep.

The next morning I woke from a sound, uninterrupted sleep to a sun-filled compartment. I dug my watch out from my sneaker to check the time. Seven-forty in the morning. Serge was still asleep in the same position in which he had passed out, and Steve was sitting up on his bunk, fully dressed, reading Tom Clancy's *Patriot Games*. Outside the window, blocks of tall, concrete residential buildings spoiled the skyline while large, squat factories spewed thick streams of foul-looking smoke into the bright morning sky.

I glanced at my watch again and bolted up. Seven-forty. The one hour time difference from Estonia to Russia meant it was really eight-forty—we were less than an hour away from St. Petersburg. I jumped down from the top bunk and began to get dressed.

I whispered to Steve so as not to wake Serge. "I thought for sure there was going to be another passport check last night, didn't you?" I asked. Then added, "We made it!"

Steve looked up from his book. "We're still not there yet," he said pessimistically. "I don't imagine anything will go wrong now, but I'll feel a whole lot better when we're off the train and out of the station."

"Yeah, me too," I agreed. "But still, sneaking in was easier than I thought it would be."

Steve nodded and added cautiously, "I just hope getting out will be as easy."

When I returned to the compartment from the washroom, Serge was at the window lazily shoving his stuff back into his little leather bag. He looked totally wasted—almost like a bear that's been roused from hibernation too soon. He grunted a greeting of sorts when I walked in and watched us with sleepy eyes as Steve and I packed our things.

An hour later, the train began to slow as it approached Varshavsky station, a small, provincial station in the southern part of St. Petersburg where trains from the Baltics terminated. Energetic passengers lined up in the corridor outside our compartment, bumping into each other with their luggage, as the train rocked from side to side through the train yards.

With a piercing, high-pitched squeal of its brakes, the train jerked forward a few times, then hissed and came to a final stop. Steve and I lifted our packs and waited for the line in the corridor to thin before leaving the compartment. Serge had to wait for a connecting train to his hometown of Minsk, so we said goodbye and followed the passengers ahead of us down the corrugated metal steps of the train to the wide platform below.

Steve and I merged with the crowd of Russians who flowed around us, following them down the long platform through a big open yard filled with street vendors busy selling food and drinks to the arriving passengers. When we reached the station, the crowd veered down a wide passage off to the right and dispersed on the street outside.

Wide avenues filled with early morning traffic fanned out in all directions ahead of us. Behind us, on the grass to our left, a large bronze statue of Lenin faced the intersection. We stood there, frozen like Lenin, not knowing which way to go. A thin golden spire gleamed in the sun a few miles away from the station. We decided to head towards it, hoping it would lead us to the center of the city.

Before we crossed the intersection, Steve and I turned to look at Lenin one more time. With big, happy grins, we looked at each other and shook hands. We'd done it—we had snuck into Russia.

Leonardo and Leningrad

Golden Arches

Personal Bankers

What I don't like about politics is that no matter who wins, you lose.
—Alan King

With the hope of eventually finding my way into Russia, I had asked Shar and Shane back in Krakow for the names of people who had rented them rooms when they had traveled through Russia. They gave me some names and phone numbers of the Russian people they had stayed with and told me that the local people who rented rooms to travelers did it off the books and didn't care where you came from or how you got there. The only requirement was that you had to pay with U.S. dollars—which was fine with Steve and me, since without visas we couldn't stay at any legitimate hotels anyway.

The name I was given to call in St. Petersburg was a woman named Svetlana. I contacted her the day we arrived and told her my friend and I both needed a place to stay. She gave us bus directions from the city and forty-five minutes later Steve and I were set up in the spare room of her two-bedroom apartment that she shared with her husband and young son.

Given the stories I had heard about government-limited living space per person, the apartment was larger than I had thought it would be. And though it was a long commute from the center of the city, it was a very comfortable room. Besides, at five dollars a night we weren't going to complain.

Steve and I spent our first evening in St. Petersburg sitting around the small kitchen table in Svetlana's apartment, discussing politics with her and her husband. A few years before, a conversation like the one we were having would have been risky for them. At that time, it wasn't even safe to talk to foreigners, let alone provide accommodation to them. But now, to openly discuss Russian politics and have foreigners stay in their home was as interesting an experience for Svetlana and her husband as it was for Steve and me.

"Most of the people did not like Gorbachev very much," Svetlana said.

"But in the West he was given the credit for the downfall of Communism," Steve replied. "Don't the Russian people think he was responsible for all the positive changes that have taken place?"

Svetlana sighed patiently. "Gorbachev did not make it happen." She pointed to the kettle whistling on the stove behind her. "Russia was like a water kettle ready to boil over. He couldn't stop it. He knew he had to open the top to let out the steam. If not him, it would have happened anyway."

"But it was him," Steve said. "So how come the people wanted him out?"

Svetlana's husband spoke up before she could answer. "The Russian people do not believe that someone who has had a Communist ideology his whole life can change his way of thinking. Yeltsin also came up through the Communist system. He, too, has found it very difficult to change the old system."

Trying not to sound too much like a reporter from CNN, I asked, "With all the tough times everyone's going through now with unemployment and inflation, do you think the changes were worth it?"

"Yes, most definitely" he asserted. "But it will take time—maybe ten or fifteen years for real changes to take place in Russia. The new government is still being run by people from the old system and there is too much corruption. The Communist party may no longer exist but the same people are doing the same jobs. It will be difficult to change this. But yes, it is better than before."

It was hard for Westerners like Steve and me to understand Svetlana's and her husband's optimism after seeing the lines they had to wait on to buy everything. One line to buy meat, another to buy cheese, and another for bread. It was hard to imagine living like that every day. I got annoyed if I had to wait more than two minutes for a slice of pizza in New York. But to them, it wasn't that big a deal. After a lifetime of waiting on lines they had become used to it. The big difference seemed to be that they finally had things worth waiting on line for. That alone seemed to give them hope for the future.

Originally conceived to be Russia's "Window on Europe," Peter the Great built St. Petersburg on the marshes of the Neva River and named it after his patron saint, "St. Peter." In keeping with his plan to make St. Petersburg a Western-style city, Peter and his heirs brought Italian and French architects to Russia to design the city's buildings. The influence of their various architectural styles could be seen in the huge baroque palaces, landscaped parks, well-planned canals and sweeping boulevards around St. Petersburg.

One of the nicest things about the way the city was laid out though, was that for a metropolitan city with almost five million people, it didn't feel crowded. Surrounded by water, the city spread across nineteen islands and was linked by almost 300 bridges. With its narrow canals winding past old stately buildings and pastel-colored palaces, it was easy to see why St. Petersburg was called the Venice of the North. But despite all the bridges and islands that crisscrossed the city, an efficient public transportation system made it easy to get around. By the end of the week we were using public transport like pros and could shuttle our way back and forth from Svetlana's place blindfolded if we had to.

One of the first places we visited was the Fortress of Peter and Paul on the north side of the Neva River. With its long golden spire rising four hundred feet in the air above the cathedral, the fortress was probably the most recognizable landmark in St. Petersburg, and had been the spire Steve and I first noticed from the train station when we arrived. The fortress had been built to provide protection against the Swedes but it was never used for that purpose. Instead, it became one of the most notorious prisons in the Russian Empire, its cells and dungeons occupied by well-known Russian revolutionaries.

"Hey, listen to this," Steve said, reading aloud from his guidebook. "One of the prison's earliest victims was Peter the Great's own son. He was beaten to death in 1718—supposedly with the active participation of Peter himself."

"See what happens when you forget to send a Father's Day card in Russia?" I joked. Unfazed by my historical commentary, he continued. "Leon Trotsky was also imprisoned in the fortress in the wake of the 1905 revolution. Even Fyodor Dostoyevsky was held there for a time."

"You don't say. Hey, what's that building over there, Einstein?"

Steve lifted his head from his book. "That," he answered, as if it was the most obvious thing in the world, "is the Hermitage Museum."

On the south side of the river, across from the fortress, was the Hermitage Museum—a long beautiful building with pastel-colored green and white walls. Made up of four connecting buildings, with over twelve miles of galleries and three million exhibits, the Hermitage is the largest museum in Russia and holds some of the most important collections of art in the world. The oldest and most important of the four buildings is the Winter Palace, the opulent, former residence of the Imperial family. A tour of the palace made it easy to see why the peasants, living in poverty and starving at the beginning of the twentieth century, decided to revolt and overthrow the royal family.

I spent two days in the museum, gazing in awe at hundreds of years' worth of incredible masterpieces. But it wasn't until I entered a small gallery in the Western European art collection that I found what I was looking for—two Leonardo da Vinci paintings: the *Benois Madonna* and the *Madonna Litta*. Like da Vinci's *Lady with the Ermine* in Krakow, I wasn't enthralled with either of them, but I was extremely happy to add two more da Vinci's to my list. Including the *Mona Lisa* in the Louvre and the *Lady with the Ermine* in Krakow, the two in the Hermitage brought my total to four. I was one da Vinci ahead of Shane.

Behind the museum was the Palace Square, a huge area with the Winter Palace on the north side and the semi-circular General Staff building on the southern end. The 156-foot Alexander Column, a monument to Russia's victory over Napoleon, stands in the center of the square. Cut from a single block of granite, the column is surmounted by the figure of an angel that supports a twenty foot cross—an impressive sight and a lot more inspiring, in my opinion, than the two da Vinci's in the museum.

The Palace Square was the site of the 1905 incident that became known as "Bloody Sunday," after a group of demonstrators who had gathered in the square to present a petition to the Tsar had been gunned down by soldiers. The massacre sparked the revolution that took place later that same year. Twelve years later, the Bolsheviks assaulted the Winter Palace from the same place, which led to the revolution of 1917. Fortunately, the only yelling and screaming going on in the square while we were there came from street vendors selling sodas and ice cream, and several hawkers with megaphones who were soliciting tourists for guided bus tours of the city.

Not far from Palace Square was Nevsky Prospekt, St. Petersburg's main shopping street. Almost three miles long, Nevsky Prospect was the best place to shop, eat, watch sidewalk artists at work and change money on the black market. The *Dom Knigi*—"House of books," at no. 28 Nevsky Prospekt—was the former site of the Singer Sewing

Machine Company of America. A few blocks down from there, at no. 13 Nevsky Prospekt, is the last residence of Tchaikovsky, who died of Cholera after drinking tap water that wasn't boiled—something the city's residents are still supposed to do to avoid the same fate.

Unfortunately, the tap water wasn't the only thing that needed fixing. Seventy-five years of Communism had taken its toll on what was once clearly an elegant, majestic city. Years of neglect, lack of maintenance, and ongoing industrial pollution made it hard to appreciate how beautiful St. Petersburg must have been in its prime. Even so, there were certain times of the day when the "Venice of the North" lived up to its potential—mostly at night, when the sun dipped slowly into the Neva River, hiding the dirt and age of the buildings in the fading light of day.

The worse victims of neglect though, were the people. Under Communism, most people had next to nothing compared to people in most Western countries. With the fall of the old system and no stable economic or political leadership to guide them, most of the people still had very little. Many of them felt they were even worse off than before.

Each day we passed men and women selling things on the streets to bring in extra money. Some women sold homemade pastries and assorted fast foods along the sidewalks, but most didn't have much to offer. Lined up on both sides of the metro entranceways, they held up whatever they thought would fetch a few rubles—a single pack of cigarettes, or a bottle of Pepsi or Coke. One woman held out a pair of shoes. I looked down and was relieved to find she hadn't taken them off her own feet. Seeing those people standing there each day with nothing but despair in their eyes was a saddening, pitiful sight. And it wasn't any better inside the station. Most of the business that went on in the large underground passageways was typical of most stations in major cities around the world—little makeshift stands and tables where people sold books, posters, magazines, and small electronic gadgets and toys. But aside from them, the other people in the station were a desperate lot. Huddled along the station's walls, lines of impoverished people sold the same dismal items being offered outside the station.

One man was even selling newborn puppies. I peered into the cardboard box and saw the tiny puppies sprawled along the bottom of the box, weak and listless from the heat in the station. I wondered if they would make it through the day. I wondered the same thing about the local people. Freedom was hard-won in Russia and a lot of people I spoke with felt it would get worse before it got better. From what I saw, they were probably right.

After almost a week in St. Petersburg we were ready to move on. Hoping to avoid the crowds at the railway station, we got up early one morning and went to the Intourist Booking Office near Nevsky Prospekt to buy our tickets. A few minutes later, we walked out with reserved sleepers on the next night's train to Moscow. Each ticket cost less than two dollars.

The following night we said goodbye to Svetlana and her husband. Steve and I jumped on a bus to Palace Square then took a second bus to the railway station a few miles down Nevsky Prospekt. Familiar by then with the routines on Russian night trains, we grabbed the best pillows and blankets from the available bunks and paid the conductor his twenty-five rubles for clean linen without his having to ask us. Steve and I were the only two people in our compartment, so we each took a bottom bunk. "It's hard to believe we're actually going to get a whole night's sleep on a train without getting woken up in the middle of the night," Steve said happily.

"I was thinking the same thing," I replied. "I just hope I can handle it. I'm so used to going to bed nervous on these trains that I'm not sure I'll be able to get to sleep without any border crossings or passport checks to worry about." I didn't have to worry though. After I flicked off the lights and climbed between the sheets of my narrow berth I was so tired I could have slept anywhere.

I closed my eyes and listened to the sound of the train wheels as they rumbled unendingly over the tracks. Clik-Clak. Clik-Clak. Clik-Clak. I loved that sound. It was the sound of travel and meant I was going somewhere. But it was more than that. The steady, rhythmic pace implied a sense of purpose—a destination to move towards. And total freedom to come and go as I pleased. I didn't know where I would be sleeping the next night or what country I would be in a week from then—and I really didn't care. Simply moving in the direction of a place I had never been to before was exhilarating enough.

I stretched out in my bunk and smiled to myself in the dark. If I were home, I would be fast asleep in my small studio apartment, waking up the following morning to go to work. Instead, I was being whisked along on a comfortable train through the countryside of Russia, anxious to open my eyes in the morning and wake up in Moscow.

Over one billion served
—McDonald's Slogan

The train screeched to a stop at a big, busy outdoor station at seven-thirty in the morning. I looked over at Steve. "Is this Moscow?"

He peered out the window to see where we were. "I'm not sure. All the signs are in Russian. We'd better ask someone," he replied, as he slid the door to the compartment open.

The corridor was packed with people lined up to exit the train. I pulled my pack down from the top bunk. "This has got to be it," I said, as I slipped my pack on my back.

Steve stuck his head in the corridor and stopped an elderly man outside our door. "*Moscow?*" Steve asked.

"Moscow! Moscow!" the man replied enthusiastically, pointing to the platform and shaking his head up and down so we would understand.

"This is it," Steve confirmed. He grabbed his pack and stepped into the corridor behind me.

We followed the crowd down the platform into the large station ahead of us and walked directly over to some public phones off to the right. I dropped my pack on the ground and took out my note pad with my contact numbers in Moscow. "We've got three names," I told Steve. "I'll try the first one—Vladimir." I slipped a ten-kopek coin into the phone box and dialed the number. "Come on Vladimir—be home," I mumbled to myself when I finished dialing.

It was hard to tell from the short quick beeps on the line whether the number was ringing or busy. I waited a minute then hung up and tried the next name on the list—Nikolai. I heard the same quick beeps as before. This time though, after the fourth or fifth beep, a man answered.

"Da?" (Yes?)

"Hello! Is Nikolai there?" I replied, hoping whoever had answered spoke English.

"This is Nikolai."

"Nikolai—I got your number from some friends who stayed at your place about a month ago. My friend and I just got to Moscow and need somewhere to stay. Do you have any rooms available?"

"Yes. For how many nights will you stay?"

"Probably four, maybe five nights. How much a night?"

"Five dollars a night for each of you."

"That's great. How do we get there?" I flipped Steve a thumbs-up sign.

"Do you know the metro system?" Nikolai asked.

"No—it's our first time in Moscow. We just came in from St. Petersburg about ten minutes ago."

"Then I think it will be easier if I meet you and take you to my apartment. Where are you now?"

"I think we're at Leningradsky station."

"Good. There is a metro there. Take the red line to Prospekt Marksa and go to Red Square. I will meet you by the monument in front of St. Basil's Cathedral at nine-thirty. That is the soonest I can be there because I have to meet someone before then."

"No problem. We'll see you at nine-thirty. Thanks!"

I hung up the phone and walked over to where Steve was waiting. "Well, that's one less thing we have to worry about," I said.

We stopped a friendly looking man in a gray polyester coat who was passing by and asked him for directions to the metro.

"*Mee-tro?*" he asked uncertainly.

"Yes, *mee-tro*," I repeated, copying his pronunciation.

He pointed to a large, square, concrete structure with tall, glass-paneled doors about fifty feet away where a crowd of people were streaming out in a steady rush in our direction. As Steve and I worked our way through the crowd, I felt like a fish fighting to go upstream against the current. While we edged our way past the swarm of commuters, several people gave us curious looks. I assumed we were drawing stares because of our backpacks so I ignored them and kept moving toward the doors.

We entered the station and waited for the few remaining people to step through the line of stalls ahead of us as they made their way out the doors. When the stalls were clear, I took a quick step forward. But before I could walk through, a thick, wooden slat shot like lightning from each side of the stall and slammed shut with a loud crash in front of me, smashing against my right knee before I could jump out of the way.

The sudden appearance of the barricades scared the wits out of me. I cursed out loud at the pain on my knee, then leaped backwards from the stall as quickly as I could. As soon as I was clear, the wooden doors slid back into their compartments, hidden from view.

I limped back to where Steve was standing. He looked almost as surprised as I was at what had happened.

"Are you alright?" he asked, seeing the pained look on my face.

"I'm not sure," I said, still holding my knee. "That thing is dangerous—it almost took my leg off. No wonder we got those strange looks on the way in here. We came in the wrong way. But what set the damn thing off?" I asked, looking back at the innocent-looking stalls.

"Those lights down there," Steve replied. He pointed to a thin beam of light about a foot off the ground that crossed the space between the walls of each stall. "When you walked through the stall you blocked the light. That must have set off the closing mechanism."

"Sounds right," I agreed. "Actually, it's funny when you think about it," I added, as I continued to rub my sore knee. "It's harder to sneak into the metro than into the country."

We left the station and walked around the corner to the entrance on the other side of the building. I passed a two-ruble note to an old woman who was perched behind the window of the token booth and scooped up my tokens from the worn wooden tray on the counter. With my token in hand, I walked up to the entrance stalls and stopped. This time I wasn't taking any chances. I held my hand out and smiled at Steve, allowing him to go first.

Steve slipped his token into the slot and stepped through the stall unmolested. I inserted my token and walked very slowly through the barricade, staring at the sides of the stall the whole way through, ready to leap if the doors slammed shut again. Safely on the other side, we stepped onto an escalator that sped us down an incredibly steep tunnel until we reached the platform below.

"Wow! Would you look at this place—it's amazing!" Steve exclaimed, as we stepped off the escalator into the most beautiful underground station either of us had ever seen. 'Amazing' was an understatement. Phenomenal was more like it. Even luxurious. It was as if we had walked into a palace. We were speechless and stared wide-eyed at the huge chandeliers that hung from the center of a magnificent ceiling of marble, gold, and stucco.

Commuter trains arrived with a quiet swish on both sides of the platform, spitting out swarms of people like bees from a nest that has been disturbed. I glanced around the platform in awe. "This place is unbelievable," I remarked.

"Probably reminds you of New York's subway, huh?" Steve said sarcastically.

"Yeah, right," I laughed. "If they ever built a place like this in Manhattan the chandeliers would be gone by morning. Maybe sooner."

Opened in May 1935, the metro was designed to meet two objectives. The first was to be functional. The second was to offer art for the enjoyment of passengers. With over 200 kilometers of track and 141 stations, it was certainly functional, serving close to ten million Russians every day. It was also very efficient. At the end of each platform a large timer counted off the seconds until the next train arrived, which usually occurred at fifty-second intervals during rush hour. When the timer hit 0:00, you weren't waiting for a train—you were on it and speeding off to the next stop.

Aside from being spotlessly clean, each station's artwork was related to a different theme. Depending on the station, the artwork ranged from heroic sculptures, mosaics, paintings and carvings, to majestic chandeliers and beautiful stained-glass windows.

Steve and I stood on the platform admiring the view as passengers bolted from the trains around us. When it was time to get going we looked at the station signs and tried to figure out which train would get us to Prospekt Marksa. Everything was in Russian however, so we had no clue what we were looking at. I pulled out my compass. "I don't know if this will work down here," I said, "but I know we've got to go sort of south so . . . my guess is we've got to take a train going in that direction." I pointed to the track behind us.

"Sounds good to me," Steve replied. We jumped on the next train that pulled up.

Each train had a recorded announcement that called out the name of each station stop, as well as the next station stop to come. When we heard what sounded like 'Prospekt Marksa,' we got out. We had guessed correctly and after riding the escalators back to the surface asked someone to point us in the direction of Red Square. Neither Steve nor I was too good at following directions, so shortly after leaving the station we got lost.

"Where are you going?" I asked as he veered left.

Steve pointed to a street that branched off from the one we were on. "That man we asked said to go down there."

"No he didn't. He pointed down *that* way."

"Are you sure?"

"Well, no . . . not really. Are you?"

As it turned out, we were both wrong. We walked down a hill, made a left, and walked toward some spires directly ahead of us. We made another left a few blocks down the street and saw the unmistakable onion-shaped domes of St. Basil's Cathedral off to our right. A little further on, and straight ahead of us, spread out like a huge cobblestone blanket in front of St. Basil's, was Red Square.

It was an awesome sight walking into Red Square for the first time. It was early Sunday morning, and other than two or three other tourists and an old babushka in layered clothes and a kerchief on her head who was sweeping the stones with a straw broom, we had the huge square all to ourselves.

Steve read his guidebook and pointed to our left where a large complex of yellow-walled buildings loomed behind an imposing red brick wall on the western side of the square. "That's the Kremlin," he informed me. He then pointed to a low, red and black marble building along the Kremlin Wall. "And that's the Lenin mausoleum. His body is preserved in a glass coffin inside an air-conditioned vault and can be viewed by the public on set days and times of the week. It says here that after Lenin died Stalin had his brain removed so Russian scientists could study how great communist minds think."

"What'd they learn?" I asked.

"Doesn't say."

"They probably didn't learn much."

At the northern end of the square across from St. Basil's is the Historical Museum, a large red building with a white-capped roof and turrets that look like snow. Opposite the Kremlin Wall on the square's east end is GUM, the state department store—a Victorian structure with three stories of ornate gangways and bridges that houses 150 shops under a high-domed, glass ceiling.

When it was time to meet Nikolai, we walked back over to St.

Basil's Cathedral. We were there at nine-thirty, right on schedule, but were surprised to find a guy with a large backpack waiting there ahead of us. We had no idea what Nikolai looked like but it was obvious this person wasn't him. Dressed in drawstring, loose-fitting pants, a faded, yellow tank top, and sandals on his bare feet, he looked like he had just stepped off a beach in southern California. The only accessory that didn't fit with his beach look was a black, flat-topped, Russian military hat, which covered most of his long blonde hair.

When Steve and I walked over, he slid his backpack to the side to make room for us to sit down. With a hint of a European accent, he asked curiously, "Just arrive?"

"We just came in from St. Petersburg" Steve replied. "How about you?"

"I flew in from Nepal this morning. I'm on my way back to Denmark and had a chance to stop over in Moscow for two days on my way home so I decided to do it. I just hope it's not too expensive to stay here because I don't have much money left. My name's Fleming." He extended his hand to each of us in turn.

"Hey, where'd you get the Russian hat?" Steve asked.

"Some Russian guy on the street. I told him I didn't want to buy anything but he kept following me. He had all kinds of military hats and belts, and a lot of watches and medals. And the more I said 'no,' the lower his prices got. He wanted ten dollars for the hat, which was too much, I think. Finally, I gave him eight dollars for the hat and belt." He showed us the belt he was wearing. It was wide and black and had a red Russian star on a bright silver buckle. "I think I got a good price," he said uncertainly.

"That belt is brilliant!" Steve said. "Where can I find this guy?"

Fleming laughed. "They're all over the city. There's also supposed to be some place called 'The Arbat' where tons of this stuff is sold to tourists."

We told Fleming about Nikolai's place and invited him to come along if there was enough room for the three of us. Before long we were telling each other about our travels and were so wrapped up in our stories that we didn't notice Nikolai standing next to us.

"Eric?" Nikolai asked tentatively, looking at each of us in turn.

"Nikolai!" I stood up and shook his hand. After introducing Steve and Fleming, I asked him if he had enough room in his apartment for a third person.

He nodded his head. "It is not a problem. I have an apartment that I rent out when I stay at my girlfriend's place, so there is enough room for four people at a time, if necessary."

With Nikolai guiding the way, we grabbed our backpacks and walked off toward the metro station across from Red Square. We rode the metro for twenty minutes and exited at a stop called Kolomenskaya. A ten minute walk from the station brought us to Nikolai's apartment, situated in a pleasant, three-story, garden-style apartment complex.

The place was perfect—two bedrooms, a large kitchen, and a bathroom with unlimited hot water. Best of all, we had the whole place to ourselves.

Nikolai showed us how to work the locks and handed us a set of keys. We paid him for two nights up front and bought some rubles from him since we were running a little low. After leaving a phone number where he could be reached if we needed anything, he took off to go about his business.

When we had finished unpacking our bags, Fleming said, "I hear there's a McDonald's in Moscow—supposed to be the biggest in the world."

"I know where I'm eating!" Steve said happily. "I never thought I'd hear myself say it, but after traveling in Eastern Europe I'm dying for a Big Mac, some chips and a chocolate shake."

I felt the same way. The toughest part about traveling through Poland, the Baltics and St. Petersburg, was finding decent food. Actually, in St. Petersburg, the biggest problem was finding food, let alone decent food. Not that I considered McDonald's decent food. But at least it tasted good and filled you up when you were through eating.

We took the metro to Pushkin Square and asked around for directions. Everyone knew how to get to McDonalds. When I saw those familiar golden arches down the street, I smiled—until I saw the line waiting to get in.

Hundreds of hungry Russians shuffled behind long metal barricades that stretched halfway down the street and back again before ending up at the entrance to the restaurant. The line moved pretty quickly though, and a few minutes later, we stepped inside the biggest McDonald's I had ever seen.

Outside, I was just another foreigner in a strange city. But once I stepped through those doors I was on home turf. I looked around at all the Russians still lined up outside and laughed to myself. Forget freedom. Forget Democracy. What the Russians really wanted was a Big Mac.

To most Russians, eating at McDonald's was a meal out on the town. Though the prices were incredibly cheap by American standards—less than a dollar for a Big Mac, fries and soda—it was still expensive for most of them. Even so, the place was always packed, and like Fleming said, served more people than any McDonald's in the world.

When it was Fleming's turn at the counter, he ordered two Big Macs, French fries, a chocolate shake and a Coke. He hadn't eaten since dinner on the plane the night before and looked like he was trying to make up for it all in one meal.

After Steve and I ordered, we grabbed our trays and looked around the main floor for Fleming. The place was packed and it took us awhile before we found him. All the booths were occupied, so he had found some places for us at one of the tall round tables near the entrance.

Before I got my Big Mac out of its package, Fleming had already finished his meal. It didn't take long before Steve had also wolfed his food down. When they were through eating they sat there grinning across their littered red trays like two gourmets who had just finished the best meal of their lives.

Stuffing his mouth with the few remaining French fries that had fallen onto my tray, Steve looked over at Fleming and smiled. "I just love American food, don't you?"

Business is a good game. Lots of competition and a minimum of rules
— Nolan Bushnell

"I'm almost out of rubles," I told Steve. "How much have you got left?"

"About eight pounds worth. Fleming didn't want to get stuck with rubles in Denmark so he gave me a good rate before he left for the airport this morning."

"How much is that in dollars?"

"Around twelve dollars, I think."

"That won't cover both of us till Nikolai comes back, whenever that is."

Nikolai's rate wasn't as good as what we could get on the street but it was a lot higher than the rates at the banks and safer than trading on the Black Market. When no one answered the phone number Nikolai had left us, I decided to try my luck on the streets.

Our first stop was the Arbat, one of Moscow's oldest streets and the city's most popular pedestrian shopping area for tourists looking for Russian souvenirs. The Arbat was also supposed to be a good place to change money since most of the vendors along the street wanted U.S. dollars.

Steve checked out the souvenirs while I went off in search of rubles. When we met up again at the end of the street, he had found what he came for—a Russian belt like the one Fleming had bought. I wasn't as lucky. No one had asked me if I wanted to change money, so I was still short of rubles.

After lunching at McDonald's for the third time that week, we decided to split up for the afternoon and meet back at the apartment in the evening. I wanted to mail a few postcards at the Central Telegraph Office and thought it might be a good place to buy rubles since it was a popular hang out for foreign students who studied in Moscow—mainly Africans, Turks and Arabs from the Mid-East. Every other time I had gone there, three or four people had asked me if I wanted to change money, so I thought it was worth a try.

I walked down Tverskaya street towards the semicircular entrance and large, revolving globe of the telegraph office. As usual, there were groups of foreign students loitering in front of the building. I went inside to post my mail then hung around the lobby inside the entrance to see if anyone would approach me. Nothing happened.

I walked outside and strolled slowly past the foreigners who were standing out front. Still nothing. I pulled out my map to make it obvious I was a tourist. No one even looked at me.

Maybe I look too desperate, I thought. I tried to look casual. After ten minutes of looking casual, I gave up. I took the underpass to the other side of Tverskaya and walked towards the metro station. I had no alternative but to go back to Nikolai's place and hope he would stop by the apartment so I could buy rubles from him.

When I reached the entrance to the metro, I noticed two guys sitting on the ledge near the steps. They had dark complexions and looked like they were middle-eastern. The one closest to me couldn't have been more than nineteen or twenty, if that. The other one was older, in his late twenties or early thirties. The reason they caught my eye was that the younger one was holding a small cardboard sign with a dollar sign scrawled on it. It seemed awfully odd to me that they would be advertising to change money on the street outside a metro station—especially since it was illegal. Out of curiosity, I walked up to the young one who held the sign.

"You change money?" I asked skeptically.

"How much you want to change?"

"Depends on the rate."

"You want to change one hundred dollars?"

"Maybe. How many rubles for each dollar?"

"For one hundred dollars—140 rubles each dollar. It's a good price."

"How about for less than one hundred?"

"Fifty dollars?"

"Less."

"How much less?"

"Twenty dollars."

"*Twenty dollars?*" he said with surprise and a hint of arrogance.

That really irked me. Here were two guys sitting on a ledge—with a cardboard sign no less—who should have been thrilled that anyone was willing to do business with them. But instead, they were acting like big bankers. I felt like I was being rejected for a mortgage because the bank didn't handle such small transactions.

"So?" I asked patiently. "Will you change twenty dollars?"

"130 rubles for each dollar," he replied. "It's still a good price." He looked at me and waited for my answer.

"Okay," I said finally, happy he was willing to do business with me.

The older one was the money man. He pulled a folded stack of rubles from his pocket and counted out the bills. When he was done counting, he held the stack of notes in one hand and reached for my twenty dollars with his other hand.

The younger one was watching me closely. I looked at the money man and smiled. "I'd like to count it first," I said. He handed the bills to me and watched carefully as I counted. Sure enough, there weren't enough rubles in the stack he had given me.

I turned to the young one. "I count 2,400 rubles. There should be 2,600."

"You are missing two hundred rubles? Let me count," he replied with feigned surprise. When he finished counting he nodded and said, "Yes, that's right." He shook his head with disbelief and handed the bills back to his friend, who then pulled two one hundred ruble bills from his pocket. While the young one and I watched him, he carefully placed them with the other bills, folded the stack of rubles in half and handed them back to me. Holding his other hand out for my money again he nodded and said, "Okay?"

I had heard that money changers on the black market were adept at ripping travelers off through a variety of scams, the most common being the palming of bills when exchanging money. Which was why I insisted on counting the rubles before I handed over my cash. What surprised me though, was how poorly he did it. I turned to the young one and laughed.

"What's he got in his hand?" I asked.

"There's nothing in his hand," he replied calmly. They looked at each other and shrugged, as if they had no idea what I was talking about.

I smiled, amused by their pretense of innocence. "I saw him," I insisted good-naturedly. "Okay. We'll play it your way," I said with a sigh. I counted the bills out loud. "2,200 . . . 2,300 . . . 2,400. Gee, I wonder where those other two-hundred rubles went?" I said naively.

"2,400—how is it possible!" the young one exclaimed in mock amazement.

I pointed to his friend's right hand. "Maybe it's because he's got the other two hundred in his hand."

The older one looked embarrassed at having been caught. "Okay. Okay. We give 2,600," he said. He reached over for the rubles in my hand.

I held the money out of his reach and said, "That's okay. I'll hold onto these." I held out my other hand for the two hundred rubles they still owed me.

That confused them. Now they had to give me the rest of the money or call off the deal and take back their 2,400 rubles. To my surprise, the young one laughed and tapped his friend's hand. His friend opened his hand and held out the two hundred rubles that he had palmed.

The young one took the bills and gave them to me with a shrug as if to say, What the hell. You win some you lose some. I counted the money one last time to make sure it was all there. Satisfied that I had 2,600 rubles, I pulled a twenty-dollar bill from my pocket and handed it to them.

The whole deal took place in broad daylight in the middle of the street but no one around us seemed to take any notice of what was going on. I placed the rubles in my wallet and turned to go down the steps to the metro. On my way down the steps, the young one called out to me, "You come back when you need more rubles?"

"Of course!" I laughed. "Where else would I find two honest guys like you?"

I Get By With a Little Help from My Friends

The Hotel Savoy

Oh No, Not Again

It's not what you know, it's who you know that counts.
— Variously Ascribed

The week in Moscow flew by and when we had seen everything we had set out to see, there was no putting off the inevitable. It was time to sneak back out of Russia.

We decided to go out the same way we came in—by train from St. Petersburg across the border to Estonia. Our biggest problem though, was getting back to St. Petersburg. Earlier in the week, two British girls who were working in Moscow told us that foreigners in Moscow had to show visas to buy train tickets.

"They'll confiscate your passports if you don't have a visa," they warned, after we confided that we had snuck into Russia from Estonia.

Taking a bus or hitch-hiking to St. Petersburg seemed just as risky, so we decided to go to the ticket office and see if there was some way to buy tickets without having to show visas.

The Intourist Booking Office was on Petrovsky Ulica, a few blocks from the Bolshoi Theater. Situated in a courtyard off the main street, it wasn't an easy building to find. Only after asking for directions did we see the small sign near the arched entranceway to the courtyard, which pointed to the booking office inside.

We crossed the courtyard to the ticket building and walked up the stairs to the second floor. The booking office was to the left of the stairwell in a corner of the hall. A huge line wound around the small room and spilled out the doorway into the main hall. As if the long line wasn't bad enough, we also saw that everyone held passports and visas as they waited for their turn at the ticket window.

Seeing the long line ahead of us, Steve asked, "Well, what's the plan?"

I considered our options. "Let's try this," I said. "When we get to the ticket window we'll ask for two tickets to St. Petersburg. If they ask for visas we'll tell them we left our passports at the hotel. Maybe they'll sell us the tickets anyway. If not, there's no risk of having our passports confiscated. If it turns out we can't get the tickets without a visa, we'll see if Nikolai can get the tickets for us. What do you think?"

Steve shrugged as we approached the end of the line. "It's worth a try, I guess. I just hope we don't have to wait on this bloody queue all day long only to find out we can't get the tickets."

But wait we did. The line moved slowly and two hours later we still hadn't reached the one available ticket window. Part of the problem was that the line stopped whenever the girl at the window took a break. No one replaced her and everything stopped dead until she returned fifteen to twenty minutes later.

The line moved at a snail's pace even when she was working, since she had to fill out tedious forms for every ticket issued and give each person a hand-written receipt. Each person then had to take their receipt to a second line in the main hall and pay for their ticket in rubles before getting on a third line to pay an additional "foreigner fee" in U.S. dollars.

Only after all the necessary receipts were obtained could you return to the first window to pick up your ticket. It was a bureaucratic nightmare and I felt almost as sorry for the girl behind the ticket window as for the people waiting to buy the tickets. But at least she got to sit down.

As it turned out, we were lucky that the line moved so slowly. By some amazing stroke of good fortune—after standing on line for over two hours—a college acquaintance of Steve's from Birmingham University in England walked into the ticket office.

"Peter! I don't believe it!" Steve shouted across the room. "What are you doing here?"

Steve's friend had a degree in Russian studies and had moved to Russia to practice his language skills. He had been living and working in Moscow for almost two years. When we explained our problem he told us not to worry. "I buy tickets here all the time," he said. "I'll use my passport to get your tickets when I get mine. I'll say I'm picking up two tickets for some friends who couldn't make it here today. There shouldn't be a problem."

He was right. He handed his passport to the ticket girl and made some small talk in Russian while she filled out the paperwork. A few minutes later, she handed him the receipts for our tickets. We followed him to the cashier lines and waited with him while he paid the necessary fees. An hour later we left the booking office with two tickets to St. Petersburg for the following night.

Nikolai stopped by the apartment later that evening to pick up the keys since it was our last night in Moscow. "Hopefully I'll be needing those keys again," I said, as I handed him the keys to his apartment. "If I can pick up a cheap Trans-Siberian Express ticket somewhere in Europe I'll need a place to stay when I get back to Moscow. So don't be surprised if I call you in a few weeks."

"How much are the tickets in Europe?" he asked curiously.

"It's hard to say," I replied. "They seem to range anywhere from about four hundred to twelve hundred dollars, depending on the country you buy them in. I heard Hungary and Czechoslovakia are two of the cheapest—around four hundred dollars."

Nikolai looked surprised. "That's still very expensive," he said.

"Do you know where I can get one cheaper?"

"Certainly. In Moscow."

"How much?"

He converted the prices from rubles to dollars in his head. "For Russians it is cheap. Perhaps fifty American dollars. The price for foreigners is around one hundred and fifty."

"One hundred and fifty dollars—that's all? Where do I go to buy one?"

"Without the proper connections, it would be very difficult for you to buy the ticket on your own. I know some people who can get a ticket for you, but you will need to tell me the date you plan to leave since the tickets are only sold for specific dates."

This presented a problem. The Trans-Siberian train crossed the border from Russia to China, so there was no way I could get on the train without a Russian visa. The Passport Officers checked passports and visas before the train even left Moscow. Without a visa there wasn't much sense in my buying a ticket. I also had no idea what date I could leave since I wasn't sure I would even be able to obtain a visa.

Once I left Russia, there would only be two ways for me to get a visa from the Russian Embassy. The first way would be to provide an itinerary and proof of officially recognized accommodations in Russia—hotels that were very expensive. The second way would be to obtain a Trans-Siberian ticket outside of Russia—which defeated the whole point of having Nikolai buy a cheap ticket for me.

"How much time will you need to get me a ticket?" I asked.

"Less than a week."

"Are you sure you can get one that quickly? Because I'm not sure how long the visa will be good for—assuming I can even get one."

"It will not be a problem," he said confidently. "I have bought tickets for other foreigners and it has never taken longer than a week. Sometimes even less."

"Great. I'll call you as soon as I get back to Moscow."

After Nikolai left, Steve said, "Hey, that would be great if Nikolai could get you a ticket for a hundred and fifty dollars. But what are you going to do about a visa? You'll definitely need one for the train."

"I know. I was wondering about that myself." All of a sudden, I remembered something. "*Wow—I can't believe I didn't think of this before!*"

"What's up?" Steve asked, surprised at my sudden outburst.

I snapped my fingers and laughed out loud. "I've got a great idea!"

The only thing that saves us from the bureaucracy is its inefficiency.
—Eugene McCarthy

At eleven A.M. the next morning I stood outside the entrance to the *Hotel Savoy*, one of the most expensive and luxurious hotels in Moscow.

I rubbed my sneakers against the back of my jeans to clean them up a little, then turned to face Steve. "How do I look?" I asked uncertainly.

"Like someone who can't afford this place."

"You're kidding, right? Tell me you're kidding, because I've got to be confident when I go in there."

Steve grinned, obviously enjoying my anxiety. "Let me put it this way. If you're going inside to apply for a job as a bellhop, you look great. Otherwise, you'd better tell them your luggage got stolen."

"I feel much better now. Thanks." I walked to the door of the hotel. Before going in I took a deep breath and tried to look like I belonged there. With a friendly nod to the doorman, I stepped inside the lobby.

I tried to look as inconspicuous as possible in my polo shirt, blue jeans and sneakers, but it wasn't easy with all the nicely dressed people standing around the carpeted lobby of the hotel. The women looked classy and rich in their fancy dresses and jewelry and the men looked important and rich in their crisp, dark-colored, expensive business suits. I wasn't sure what I looked like, but it wasn't important or rich, that was for sure.

I couldn't understand why I was making such a big deal about being there. I was used to staying in nicer places than the Hotel Savoy when I was on business trips back home. But living on a backpacker's budget and looking like a vagabond the past few months had made me self-conscious—like showing up for a black-tie affair wearing a sports coat.

I spotted the reception desk on the left side of the lobby. With a calm and steady gait, I strode purposefully across the room like I owned the place.

The two receptionists were busy with guests so I waited to the side, calmly rehearsing in my head what I planned to say so I wouldn't screw it up. When the guest ahead of me walked off, the receptionist behind the desk turned her attention to me.

"May I help you?" she asked in perfect English. Her manner conveyed an air of sympathy, as if I was a tourist who had gotten lost and was stopping by the hotel to ask for directions back to the dump across town that I was undoubtedly staying at.

I gave her a nice, friendly smile. As if I had stayed there many times before, I said nonchalantly, "I'd like to make a reservation for early July."

She looked at me curiously. After a short pause, she walked towards the door at the end of the reception desk. "I will get the Reservations Manager," she replied warily.

A few seconds later, a short, pleasant-looking, and well-dressed man walked behind the reception desk and stood across the counter in front of me. With a quick and formal smile he said curtly, "I am the Reservations Manager for the hotel. May I help you?"

I flashed him my best businessman smile. "Hi, how are you?" I replied courteously. I shook his hand to establish some personal contact, then launched into the purpose of my visit.

Trying to sound like a harried executive who had stopped by the hotel on his way to a casual outing, I said, "I'm planning to return to Moscow on business in early July and would like to reserve a single room while I'm here."

He paused, then nodded his head slowly as he considered my request. "Certainly. We will be happy to make a reservation for you." He stepped over to the reservations computer on the desk. "What date are you planning to arrive back in Moscow?" he asked.

"July 1st."

"And how long will you be staying?"

"One week."

"Your name please?"

"Eric Raff . . . R-A-F-F."

He entered the information into his computer then said, "I have reserved a single room for you for one week beginning July 1st. Will there be anything else, Mr. Raff?"

I snapped my fingers absently, as if I had just remembered a minor but necessary detail. "Oh yes—I almost forgot," I replied casually. "I'll need written confirmation of the reservation, if you don't mind. I'll have to present it when I apply for another visa, after I leave Moscow."

He looked at me and hesitated for a second before answering. "Certainly. In that case, a confirmation with the necessary information will need to be written up on hotel stationery. I will need your company name and your business card please."

"Of course," I replied confidently. I pulled an old business card from my wallet and handed it to him.

He glanced at my card. "This will be fine. Please wait here while I see to the paperwork."

A few minutes later he returned with an official-looking envelope. He pulled out the written confirmation and handed the envelope and letter to me. Neatly typed beneath the logo of the Hotel Savoy was all the information for my reservation—a single room reserved in my name for one week, beginning July 1, at a rate of $320.00 a night.

I folded the letter and placed it back in the envelope. "This is fine, thank you," I said. "You've been very helpful. What is your name?"

"Vitali" he replied with a quick nod of his head, happy to have been of service.

"Thank you, Vitali. I'll see you on July 1st," I replied, and turned to leave. "By the way, I'll contact the hotel if my plans should happen to change for any reason," I added, knowing full well they would. The minute I got back to Moscow, I planned to cancel my three hundred and twenty dollar a night room and head over to Nikolai's five dollar a night apartment.

I left the reception desk and crossed the nicely furnished lobby to the front door of the hotel. I nodded to the doorman and stepped outside into the fresh morning air to look for Steve, who was lounging against a car across the street, eating an ice cream.

We walked away from the hotel in the direction of Red Square. Half a block down the street, Steve turned to me impatiently. "Well, how did it go?"

I held up the envelope in answer.

"That's terrific!" he said. "Now you'll be able to get a Russian visa for sure."

"Yeah—assuming we're able to get out of Russia tonight without getting caught."

The trouble with born-again Christians is that they are
an even bigger pain the second time around.

—Aphra Behn

The overnight trip from Moscow to St. Petersburg was uneventful. We arrived back in St. Pete's early in the morning and went straight to the Intourist Booking Office to buy our tickets for the night train back to Estonia.

Compared to the booking office in Moscow, the one in St. Petersburg was a model of efficiency. Five minutes after we went in, we walked out with our tickets. No lines. No receipts. No hassles. And best of all, no visa check.

We spent the rest of the day at the Hermitage Museum to see the exhibits we had missed the first time around, and then went for a late dinner at a small café a few blocks up from the Aeroflot Office, just off of Nevsky Prospect. At ten thirty that evening, we hopped on a bus to Varshavsky station, the same station we had arrived at less than two weeks before.

St. Petersburg was still enjoying the "White Nights" of summer—the long summer days of virtually endless daylight from June 11 until July 20, when it never gets fully dark. When the train pulled away from the station at eleven o'clock, the sun was still shining above the tranquil water of the Neva River. The night air was warm and light and we had clear views of the outlying areas and concrete suburbs of St. Petersburg as the train eased slowly away from the city.

Half an hour later, the housing developments tapered off and were replaced by long stretches of grassy fields and empty farmland. Every now and then we rolled past rows of small, green houses and dilapidated shacks with kids in ragged clothes playing in the dirt yards out front. Life in the Russian countryside looked hard and probably hadn't changed much in years. As I gazed at the small, weather-beaten houses stuck in the middle of nowhere, I recalled what a young Russian man in Moscow had said when I had commented that life in Moscow seemed better than I thought it would be. He shook his head and said, "*Moscow is not Russia, the same like New York is not America, I think.*" I finally understood what he meant.

The sky darkened a little around midnight and I turned from the window to go back to the compartment. Steve and the other two passengers in our bunk were already in bed when I came back from the washroom so I had to make my bed and get undressed in the dark. I threw my money belt on the top bunk and climbed under the blanket, trying not to wake anyone. I placed my head on the pillow and felt the same sense of dread I had felt when we first snuck into Russia. Fortunately, I was too tired to let it keep me awake and a few minutes later, I drifted off into a sound, peaceful sleep.

As usual, the knock on the door came at around three in the morning. This time though, I was awake when they came into the compartment. I had woken up when the train stopped at the border and laid awake in bed while the border police made their way down the corridor.

The lights in the room flickered on and two uniformed men entered the compartment. "*Here we go again,*" I mumbled to myself.

When they walked in, I saw right away that they were Estonians. I peered down at Steve on the bottom bunk and saw him looking nervously up at me. One of the men checked the passports of the two people across from us while the second one held his hand out for our documents. We had nothing to worry about from the Estonian Customs Officials, so we handed over our passports and relaxed, anxious to get the formalities over with and get back to sleep.

The guard opened my passport and scanned the pages. "Visa?" he asked quietly.

It took a few seconds for his comment to register with me and when I didn't reply, he repeated his request. "*Visa?*" He looked up at me, waiting for a response.

"Visa? What kind of visa?" I asked nervously.

"Estonian Visa."

"But I just came from Estonia a few weeks ago," I explained. "I didn't need a visa when I was there before. Here look." I pointed to the page where my passport had been stamped at the border crossing from Latvia to Estonia.

During the short time we had been in Russia, the Estonians had changed their rules. To reinforce their independence from the Soviet Union, they were requiring that all foreigners wishing to enter Estonia—Russians included—needed a visa.

The border guard was a young man and didn't seem anxious to make trouble for us. He said he would speak to his supervisor and see what could be done. When he walked down the corridor, I figured we were in the clear. After all, we had been there before and had the stamps to prove it. He returned to our compartment a few minutes later.

"My chief says without visa you must go back."

"Back? Back where?"

"St. Petersburg."

My jaw dropped open. "*St. Petersburg?*" I blurted with alarm.

I started to get an uncomfortable feeling in the pit of my stomach as the ramifications of what he had said sunk in. We were being denied entry into Estonia because we didn't have a visa, and were going to be sent back to a country we had entered illegally because we couldn't get a visa to go there. And since we shouldn't have been there in the first place, it was highly unlikely the Russian authorities would allow us to re-enter—unless of course they decided to let us in so they could throw us in jail.

I was trying to think of possible alternatives to being deported back to Russia when I heard Steve say to the Customs Official, "Transit Visa? Can we buy a Transit Visa?" He pulled out his wallet and held out some bills, as he said enthusiastically, "U.S. dollars!"

At the mention of money, the young guard's interest perked up. He said he would have to check with his chief again. When he left the compartment the second time I jumped down from the top bunk and sat on the bottom bed with Steve to discuss our options.

"Look, if they send us back to Russia we're screwed!"

"I know. Maybe we can get them to send us someplace else. Like Poland instead," Steve suggested.

"That won't work. With your British passport you need a visa for Poland and yours ran out," I reminded him.

"Right, I forgot. Okay, how about Latvia then?"

"Sounds good to me. Let's just hope they're open for suggestions."

While Steve and I were busy picking places to be deported to, the officer reentered the compartment and informed us, "It is possible to obtain Transit Visa. You must fill out papers in station office. Go now, please."

We grabbed our packs before we left the train just in case they decided to take off without us. Stepping hurriedly across the gravel paths that separated the tracks, we jumped onto the concrete platform that led to the station office. Steve and I filled out the visa forms as quickly as we could, then brought the completed paperwork back to the guard, who was still on the train checking passports.

He checked the forms and took them down the corridor to his chief for approval. When he came back he said, "You must pay for Transit Visa."

"How much?" we asked anxiously. He frowned and went off to check with his chief again.

When he returned to the compartment he said, "Ten U.S. dollars for each."

There were no visa fees listed on the forms so we didn't know if ten dollars was the standard fee or a fee of convenience made up by the chief. Or even if there was a chief. In any case, we didn't care. It was a small price to pay to keep from being sent back to Russia.

On the way back to our compartment, we heard female voices laughing and speaking in English from the front of the corridor. Steve stuck his head inside the compartment and said, "Hey, could you girls keep it down in here—we're trying to get some sleep." They laughed and invited us in, surprised to find two Westerners on the train.

"*They made you pay twenty dollars?*" one of them said with astonishment, after we told them we'd almost gotten sent back to Russia for not having Estonian visas.

The girl on the bottom bunk nearest me said, "They asked us for visas too, but a nice Estonian guy in the next compartment talked to the passport officers and got them to leave us alone."

"They didn't make you buy Transit Visas?" Steve asked.

"No. Our Estonian friend next door told them that we had come all the way from America to see their country and they should leave us alone. And they did. *Isn't that great?*" she gushed, with a cuteness that made me wince.

Steve and I thought about the twenty dollars it had cost us to stay on the train and replied half-heartedly, "Yeah. That's terrific."

One of the girls on the opposite side of the compartment chimed in, "Everyone's just been *sooo friendly and nice*—especially in Russia!"

With only the small night lights over the two top bunks, it was hard to see much in their compartment. Snuggled up in their beds with their sheets pulled up to their shoulders, it was even harder to make out what they looked like. That didn't seem to bother Steve, though. Although it was after four in the morning, he was hoping the night wouldn't be a total loss after all.

He nudged me with his elbow and grinned with delight at the four prospects in front of him. Edging his way in front of me, he asked the girls, "So how long were you in Russia?"

The girl on the top bed propped herself up on her elbow and sighed, "Only two weeks. I wish we had more time."

"You're not going home after Estonia, are you?" he asked hopefully.

"No, we won't be home for another two weeks. We're meeting up with the rest of our group in Estonia before going on to Poland."

"You're traveling with a tour group?" I asked curiously.

"Well, I wouldn't call it a tour group exactly. We're part of a church group from the same Seminary College back home and have been traveling around Eastern Europe giving lectures, concerts, and religious classes and things like that. We're studying to be Missionaries."

Steve almost tripped over me as he backed up towards the door. The disappointed look on his face made me laugh. "Well, I don't know about you girls, but I'm exhausted," he said with a sudden change of heart. "Besides, we should probably let you get to sleep. It's very late."

We walked down the corridor to our compartment and gently slid back the heavy metal door so we wouldn't disturb the other two people sleeping in the compartment. Looking forward to a few uninterrupted hours of sleep before arriving back in Estonia, I got undressed and crawled into bed. The last thing I heard before falling asleep was Steve mumbling under his breath. "Missionaries," he muttered with disappointment, as he climbed into his bunk and went to sleep.

Changing Partners

Waiting for Nikolai

To know the road ahead, ask those who have gone before you.
— Chinese Saying

After a few days visiting Valeri and his family in Tallinn, Steve and I took a ferry across the Gulf of Finland to Helsinki to rest up from our travels in Eastern Europe.

Helsinki was beautiful, an attractive port city that offered everything we had been missing over the past few months. Soft toilet paper. Clean water. English-speaking people. And food. All the food we could want. Salads, cereals, muesli, candy bars—you name it. After the food deprivation in Eastern Europe, we ate everything in sight. We filled up on bananas with muesli for breakfast, pasta and sandwiches for lunch, and chicken and steaks for dinner. And we topped off every meal with delicious cakes and other assorted pastries for dessert.

After stuffing myself non-stop for the first few days, I finally got around to doing what I had come to do—securing a Russian visa from the embassy in Helsinki. My note from the Hotel Savoy in Moscow did its trick, and after a week of total immersion back in a westernized country, I was ready to return to Moscow to buy a ticket for the Trans-Siberian train.

The night before we took the ferry back to Tallinn, Steve and I met a friendly, 18-year-old blonde from Minnesota named Sarah, who was staying at the same hostel as us in Helsinki. She had been touring around Europe the past few months and had two weeks left to travel before having to return home for classes. She told us that she had taken some Russian language classes during her freshman year and was crazy about Russia even though she had never been there. When she mentioned that her one regret was that she had never gotten to Russia, I told her that I was planning to go back there before moving on to China, and asked if she wanted to come along with me as far as Moscow.

Her eyes lit up. "Are you kidding—I'd love to! But I don't have a visa," she sighed.

"No problem," I said. "Neither did we. The border was open from Estonia to Russia so we didn't have any problems getting across. If it's still open, you can get in the same way we did."

"When are you leaving?"

"We're taking the ferry back to Tallinn tomorrow morning. After we get there, Steve's heading south to Poland and I'm going back to Russia. My visa doesn't start till next week but I want to sneak in a week early to give myself some extra time to get a Trans-Siberian ticket in Moscow. The ferry leaves at eight A.M. tomorrow, so you've got until morning to decide."

I could see how badly she wanted to go, but she was nervous about doing it. And with good reason. Aside from the potential risk involved in sneaking over the border, she would be traveling with someone she'd only known for less than an hour. It wasn't like she had a whole lot of time to make up her mind, either. At eight o'clock the next morning Steve and I would be gone and her one chance to get to Russia before going home would be gone with us.

"Think she'll come?" Steve asked, after Sarah went back to her room to think about her decision.

"Probably not," I replied. "She's just a kid. Besides, why would she want to risk it? If something goes wrong on the way in or out, her travel plans home will get all screwed up. On top of that, she'll have to find her own way out of Russia since I'm planning to be on the Trans-Siberian train to China."

Half an hour later, Sarah came bounding into our room. With a nervous, but excited look, she said, "Count me in!"

Valeri was thrilled when Steve and I called from the arrival port to tell him we were back in Tallinn and had brought someone back with us. As soon as he learned we were back in town, he insisted that we meet him and Natasha for dinner so they could meet Sarah. They both took an immediate liking to her and the five of us spent the next two nights eating and drinking in the cafés of the old city like we were old friends who hadn't seen each other for years.

After a few days in Tallinn Sarah and I needed to be moving on. She had less than two weeks left to travel before having to go home and I needed to get to Moscow to get Nikolai started on buying my

Trans-Siberian ticket before my visa became valid the following week. Once again, Valeri took charge of getting our tickets to St. Petersburg. Like before, he escorted us to the station the night we were scheduled to leave in order to make sure everything went smoothly. The only difference was that this time I boarded the train with Sarah instead of Steve.

It was strange leaving Steve on the platform with Valeri. He had been a great travel partner and we had become very good friends. It was hard to believe he wasn't coming with me. We had covered a lot of ground together, and though I knew we'd keep in touch, it was sad to part company after traveling together for so long. I glanced across the seat at Sarah and smiled. Actually, it wasn't such a bad trade. She was definitely better to look at, and probably a lot easier to beat in cards than Steve.

As the train chugged away from the platform, we waved goodbye to Steve and Valeri like two newlyweds going off on our honeymoon. I stuck my head out the window. "Thanks for everything Valeri! I've got one last favor to ask—make sure Steve gets on the right train to Poland. Without me to look after him, who knows where he'll wind up!"

Steve shouted back from the platform, "Don't let him cheat at cards, Sarah! And pay no mind to his windjing (complaining). You'll get used to it!" Sarah laughed and waved happily as the train cleared the platform and sped along the desolate tracks towards the Russian border.

The border crossing was the same as the month before. The Estonians stamped us out in the middle of the night and the next morning we awoke in St. Petersburg.

Sarah was as wide-eyed as Steve and I had been when we had first stepped foot in Russia five weeks before. She followed me down the crowded platform with her mouth open, straining to make sense of all the sights and sounds of the station around us. As we weaved our way through the morning commuters and made our way out of the station, Sarah didn't utter a sound. She hovered near my side like a little kid, mesmerized by everything around her, until we were safely out of the station and onto the street.

Outside the station I was on familiar ground and led Sarah around St. Petersburg like it was my home town. I showed her how to use the metros and buses, explained the basic layout of the city, and pointed out the different sights along the way.

Soon after we arrived, we went to the Intourist Booking Office on Nevsky Prospekt to buy tickets for the overnight train to Moscow. I wanted to get there as quickly as possible in order to get Nikolai moving on my Trans-Siberian ticket, and since Sarah would have time to see the sights of St. Petersburg on her way out of Russia, she opted to go with me. I showed her as much of St. Petersburg as possible before we had to leave for the train station. By the time we boarded the train at 10:30 P.M., we were both exhausted and ready for bed.

Sarah sat by the window of our small compartment and watched the Russian countryside drift slowly by. "So what do you think so far?" I asked curiously.

Her face lit up and her eyes flashed with joy. "It's unbelievable—I love it! My head is spinning . . . I *still* can't believe I'm here!"

I couldn't believe I was there again either. But there I was, taking the same trains, seeing the same sights, and going through the same routines I had gone through before. It was kind of strange. Almost like sitting through the same movie twice.

Sarah left the compartment to get washed up for bed. When she crawled into her bunk a few minutes later, she looked over at me and smiled—a bright, innocent, 18-year old smile. "Thanks for letting me come along," she said.

I flicked off the lights and climbed into the bottom bunk on the other side of the compartment. "I'm glad you came. It's nice to have someone to travel with," I said.

Talking more to herself than to me, she said excitedly, "I can't believe I'm on my way to Moscow. Moscow—wow!" A few minutes later, she was sound asleep.

We arrived at Moscow's Leningradsky station early in the morning. As soon as we left the train, I went straight to a phone to let Nikolai know I was back. I dropped a ten-kopek coin in the narrow slot and dialed his number, listening to the quick, continuous beeps over and over as I waited for him to pick up. No one answered. I tried again. He wasn't home. I looked at Sarah and shrugged. "He must have stepped out for awhile," I said. "We might as well go to his apartment and wait until he returns instead of walking around the city with our backpacks all day."

We left the station and walked to the metro. I explained to Sarah how the metro system worked and wrote out directions to Nikolai's place in case we got split up for some reason along the way. Twenty minutes later, we were out of the metro and crossing the woods to

Nikolai's apartment. He still wasn't home. We sat on the steps in the lobby of his building and waited. Two hours later we were still waiting.

Sarah sat on the bottom step of the stairs that led to Nikolai's apartment, her blonde hair falling over her face, as she quietly read a book which she held in her lap. I had nothing to read and was tired of waiting. I stood up and tapped her on the shoulder to get her attention.

"Sarah, I don't know how long we should wait. We could be here all day for all we know. I'll go look for a telephone to call the other names on my list. I'll be back as soon as I can."

Neither of the phones outside the metro worked. I went inside and waited for a man to finish his call at the one phone station that seemed to be operating. I pulled out my note pad and dialed the phone number for someone named Vladimir. After a few short rings, a man answered the phone.

"Allo?"

"Vladimir?"

"Da." (Yes).

"Do you speak English?"

"Yes."

I explained that I had gotten his number from some friends who had stayed with him and told him that I needed a place to stay. He didn't have any beds available but knew a friend who was willing to rent out his apartment for the week. He told us to meet him and his friend at one o'clock in front of the large mural of Communist workers inside the Prospekt Mira metro station.

I went back to Nikolai's place and found Sarah leaning against the wall of the lobby. She was fast asleep. I shook her shoulder gently. "Sarah, wake up—we've got a place to stay. Come on."

When we arrived at the Prospekt Mira metro station, we waited as close to the mural of Communist Workers as we could, but there were so many people coming through the tunnels on their way out of the metro that it was impossible to stand directly in front of it. In any case, two old men were selling stacks of newspapers from a long table in front of the mural so we couldn't get any closer even if the station wasn't packed with people.

"Do you think they'll be able to spot us with all these people coming through here?" Sarah asked nervously.

"Sure. Our backpacks are a dead give-a-way," I replied, though even with her pack on her shoulders Sarah was still tough to see in a crowd, since she was so small.

A few minutes later, two guys in their early twenties waved to us from the crowd. After introducing himself, Vladimir presented his friend Sergei. Skinny, soft-spoken and introverted, with nerdy glasses and conservative clothes, Sergei reminded me of a Russian Jerry Lewis. Vladimir on the other hand, was the complete opposite. Broad and solid looking, with a head the size of a Rottweiler, he looked like a bull standing next to Sergei.

Vladimir's English was excellent from all the practice he had gotten renting his apartment to travelers. Sergei was less confident in his English but spoke well enough to talk about most things without too much trouble. They were both graduate students at Moscow University and seemed like sharp, intelligent guys.

When the introductions were over, Vladimir left us with Sergei, who led us back to the metro and showed us the way to his apartment, a forty-five minute commute outside downtown Moscow by metro and bus. Almost an hour after we set out, we stepped off a bus in front of a large housing development built along the side of a busy four-lane avenue. Sergei's building was in the middle of the apartment complex, a six-floor walk-up with steep flights of stairs and broken lights on virtually every landing. The apartment was on the third floor, a small studio apartment with a separate kitchen and bathroom. With the exception of a telephone and hot water, the apartment was equipped with everything else we needed to make ourselves comfortable.

"It is small," Serge said apologetically, "but you will have it for yourself."

"Don't you live here?" Sarah asked.

"No. It is my uncle's apartment. When he is away, I sometimes stay here. But usually I stay at the university. There is student housing there."

A short time after we arrived at the apartment, a friend of Sergei's named André stopped by to meet Sarah and me. To our pleasant surprise, he had brought a bottle of Russian champagne and a bag of groceries to welcome our arrival. Sergei popped the cork and pulled a cassette player out from behind the bed. We lifted our glasses in a toast to new friends and spent the rest of the afternoon getting slowly smashed on champagne before sitting down to a nice, home-cooked meal of pasta and vegetables that Sergei and André cooked up for us.

Over the next few days, Sergei became our friend and our guide. Each day, he would stop by the apartment and take us to see things we wouldn't have found on our own. He took us on a tour of Moscow University—an imposing, Gothic building that loomed over the Moscow skyline like a dark menacing tower—escorted us to a Russian performance of Cyrano de Bergerac, which featured some of Moscow's most famous actors, and brought us to the top of the Moscow Television Broadcast Tower for an incredible aerial view of the city.

Sarah was having a blast and couldn't believe her good fortune. And I had to admit, it was great having a comfortable little apartment to ourselves in a suburb of Moscow and seeing the city with a Russian friend to show us around. But as nice as it was, it didn't get me any closer to a ticket on the Trans-Siberian Express.

God gives the nuts, but he does not crack them.
                                        —German Proverb

For two days, Nikolai was nowhere to be found. Each morning at eight A.M., I tip-toed out of the apartment so as not to wake Sarah, then ran down to the public phone across from the bus stop to call Nikolai. When no one answered, I went back to the apartment and slept for another hour until Sarah woke up. I continued to call Nikolai at hourly intervals throughout the day and night with the hope of catching him in, but he was never home.

On my third day back in Moscow, I started to worry. My one-week visa was set to begin in three days. The journey from Moscow to Beijing was supposed to take five or six days. Which didn't leave me much time to buy a ticket and cross the border from Russia to China before the visa ran out. If I couldn't find a ticket before my visa expired, I would have to go back to Estonia. And without Nikolai, I had no idea how to get an inexpensive Trans-Siberian ticket.

After numerous failed attempts to reach Nikolai, I reached two conclusions. The first was that he was either on vacation or dead. Neither of which helped me much. The second was that I needed to take matters into my own hands before it became too late. In any case, I didn't think it could be that difficult to buy a lousy train ticket. If Nikolai could do it, why couldn't I?

I set off early the next morning for the ticket booking office near the Bolshoi Theater that Steve and I had gone to the month before. When I arrived, there was a line of people waiting ahead of me, mostly foreign students living in Moscow. I stood on the rear of the line and pulled a book from my daypack to help pass the time. An African man in front of me smiled when I opened my book. "The way this line's been moving, you probably going to finish that book before you leave here," he grinned.

I laughed and said, "I don't care if it takes all day, as long as I walk out of here with a ticket on the Trans-Siberian Express."

"In that case my friend, you going to be here a long time. The Trans-Siberia ticket is not sold here, mon. Those tickets sold at the Taganskaya booking office."

The Taganskaya booking office was on the other side of the city. I thanked him for the tip and went back to the metro. I was getting pretty good at navigating my way around the Moscow underground and found Taganskaya without much trouble. Finding the booking office was a different story, however. As soon as I left the metro I got lost. After half an hour of wandering around in circles, I decided to ask some people for help. Two different people sent me off in two different directions. Forty minutes later, a third person pointed me towards a long, wide boulevard several blocks away. I trudged up the street in the hot morning sun and prayed he was right. I found the ticket office a mile up the road. It was closed. I wanted to shoot somebody. The first person that came to mind was Nikolai.

A small, handwritten sign with a list of addresses scrawled on it was posted on the door of the ticket office. I stopped a few people on the street until I found a man who could translate the sign for me. Stooping down, with his head a few inches from the sign, he said, "Eet says office is closed. They are reorganizing teeket offices in Moscow." He pointed to the addresses listed below the note. "Eet gives list of new locations here." I thanked him for his help and copied the addresses as carefully as I could so Sergei and Vladimir could help me find the new locations.

I checked my map to see if there was a metro nearby and noticed the address for an American Express Travel Office only a few blocks away. I wondered why I hadn't thought of them before. Instead of knocking myself out running all over town, maybe it would be possible to book a ticket through the local Amex office. I got back on the metro for the third time that morning, and forty-five minutes later, was in the clean, air-conditioned office of American Express. In response to my inquiry, the woman behind the reception desk asked in perfect English, "A ticket for the Trans-Siberian train? When are you planning to leave?"

"As soon as possible. Saturday or Sunday at the latest."

She jerked her head in surprise. "Oh . . . that will be very difficult, I'm afraid. July and August are very busy months for the Trans-Siberian trains. Those tickets are usually booked weeks—sometimes months—in advance. If you can leave in August, perhaps . . . "

"*August?* No—it has to be this week."

She thought for a moment. "Perhaps you would be interested in a flight to Beijing? That would not be a problem for this week."

Without a Trans-Siberian train ticket, the only other way for me to get to China from Moscow would be by plane. Since it seemed to be my only other option, I asked how much a flight would cost. She quoted the cost in rubles then converted the amount to dollars on her desk calculator. When she tilted the calculator toward me so I could see the price I almost choked.

"That's . . . that's almost sixteen-hundred dollars!"

"Yes," she sympathized. "Air travel in Russia is very expensive."

"Thanks anyway," I mumbled, as I ruled out the option of flying to Beijing.

I was tired of running all over Moscow with nothing to show for it but dead ends. I was also hungry since I hadn't eaten anything all morning. I decided to call it a day and took the metro to McDonald's to forget my problems over a Big Mac and a chocolate shake.

Sergei stopped by the apartment that evening while Sarah and I were making dinner. He hadn't eaten yet so we pulled up a chair and convinced him to join us. When dinner was over, I took out the addresses I had copied from the door of the ticket office and asked him to show me where they were on a map. "Yaroslavsky station is the closest," he said, as he scanned the list. "If you like, I will go with you to see if I can help with the ticket. But we must go very early to avoid the lines. I will meet you at 7:45 A.M. tomorrow morning outside the Komsomolskaya metro entrance. The ticket office is very near to the station."

I met Sergei at the metro entrance the following morning and saw a huge crowd huddled outside the ticket office near the Yaroslavsky railway station. It wasn't even eight in the morning and already there were hordes of people waiting to get inside the building. Sergei looked at me and shrugged.

When the doors were unlocked at eight o'clock, all hell broke loose. The crowd rushed the steps and jockeyed for position, swaying back and forth like a tidal wave, until they came to rest in one gigantic line in front of the entrance. When the doors were flung open they shuffled through the doorway in a solid mass, as if they were glued together. As soon as they cleared the entrance, the mass exploded and tore down the long hallway, scrambling for a good position in front of the two available ticket windows.

Sergei and I stood outside and waited for the crowd to settle down before going in. When we walked down the hall to the ticket windows, I knew it would be useless to stay. The lines were too long and were moving too slowly. We would be there for hours.

"Must wait long time," said a voice to the right of me. I turned around and saw a short, dark, Asian man standing on the end of the line next to Sergei and me.

I shook my head in agreement and frowned. "How long do you think it will take to get to the ticket window?" I asked.

He cocked his head. Eyeing the line ahead of him he replied, "Maybe two, three hour. Where you want to go?"

"I'm trying to get a ticket on the Trans-Siberian train."

"*Me too!*" he exclaimed happily. "But is very difficult. All ticket gone early. Yesterday I here *four hours!*" He held up four fingers for emphasis. "No ticket left. Today come back early—seven o'clock. Many people waiting here already. I am from Mongolia. I want to go back to Ulan Bator on train but yesterday was told no tickets for this week. All gone. Today, if lucky, get ticket for next week." He smiled and shrugged his shoulders with resignation.

That settled it. There was no reason to wait or to come back. I wished him luck and left the ticket office to get breakfast with Sergei before going back to the apartment to meet up with Sarah.

The prospects for getting a ticket without Nikolai were getting bleaker every day. I finally realized what he meant when he said I would find it difficult to get a ticket on my own. Out of desperation, I continued to phone his apartment throughout the day and night, but as usual, he was never there.

The one thing that still puzzled me though, was how Nikolai could be so confident that he could get a ticket for me within a week. Either he had a contact in a ticket office or a connection with the black market. I didn't have any contacts in a ticket office. Which meant I had only one option left—the black market.

Almost out of Time

Chinese Roommates

The Favor

When the student is ready the teacher will appear
— Spanish Proverb

Tuesday. The day before the start of my one-week visa. I couldn't believe my rotten luck. I should have known something would go wrong.

Everything had been going too smoothly. I had snuck into Russia twice without a visa, tricked the Hotel Savoy into giving me documentation that enabled me to get a Russian visa in Helsinki, and then found out that Nikolai could get me a Trans-Siberian ticket for only one hundred and fifty dollars. It had all been going too smoothly. And all that good luck was going to be wasted because I couldn't find Nikolai.

Sarah and I left the apartment at noon to go to the city. She wanted to see the one o'clock changing of the guard in front of the Lenin Mausoleum and I wanted to find my black market connection, whoever that might be. On our way to the bus, I stopped at the public phone on the corner to place my hourly call to Nikolai. As usual, there was no answer. I hung up the phone and ran across the street with Sarah to catch the bus just before it pulled away from the curb. Twenty minutes later we were off the bus and back on a crowded metro, speeding along towards Red Square.

When we exited the metro, Sarah wished me luck and walked off towards the Lenin Mausoleum in Red Square. I wasn't sure where to go to buy a ticket on the black market, but figured that since I was looking for a train ticket, a train booking office would be the logical place to start. The one I was most familiar with was the Intourist booking office near the Bolshoi Theater, so I decided to start there. I walked north from Red Square for a few blocks then turned left, in the direction of Petrovsky Ulica. Passing the Bolshoi Theater on my right, I walked up Petrovsky Ulica until I spotted the small blue and white sign for the Intourist booking office above the entrance to the courtyard.

When I stepped through the short, arched walkway into the courtyard, I noticed that the grounds looked vacant. When I had been there before, small groups of people lounged near the walkway, smoking and hanging out, while streams of people flowed in and out from the rear entrance of the courtyard. This time, though, there was no one around. The place looked deserted.

I crossed the yard to the Intourist building and still didn't see a soul. When I went inside the lobby I noticed a guard sitting behind a glass window off to my left. I walked over and asked him if the ticket office was open. He looked at me curiously and said curtly, "Ees closed. No more teekets here." Wanting to check it out for myself, I walked slowly to the staircase ahead of me, half expecting the guard to tell me I couldn't go upstairs. When he didn't stop me, I went up to the foreigner's ticket office on the second floor. It was empty.

Crossing bright beams of dust-speckled sunlight that filtered through dirty, glass windows from the right-hand side of the wall, I walked quickly down the long hallway toward the far end of the floor. I was amazed at how fast they had closed the place down. Just a few days before, business had been going on as usual. And now, it was completely deserted. Aside from a few employees doing paperwork behind some of the ticket windows, there was no one on the floor but me.

As I walked toward the stairs at the end of the hall I noticed two young guys leaning against a counter in front of a ticket window near the stairwell. The ticket windows were closed so it seemed odd that they would be standing there. They weren't talking or doing anything in particular other than just hanging out. The taller of the two looked very Russian, with fair-skin, light-brown hair and Slavic features. The shorter one had dark skin, black hair and Asian eyes. They seemed surprised to see me coming down the hall and shifted their positions slightly to keep me in view as I approached. *These guys have got to be black market*, I thought. When I got close enough to see them clearly, I stopped and smiled. "Hi" I said casually, as if I had expected to find them there.

They stood stone-faced, sizing me up with their eyes. The Russian shifted his weight a little against the counter. He looked me over with a cool and steady gaze, then nodded his head slightly and said, "Hello." The Asian kept his eyes fixed on me but didn't reply.

"How's it going?" I asked.

"Not so good," the Russian replied.

"That's too bad. How come?"

"Business is a little slow today. How are you?"

"Not so good either."

"Why is that?" he asked curiously.

"Well, I need a train ticket and I'm not having much luck."

The Russian nodded slowly but didn't reply. I looked at each of them in turn. Up until that point the Russian was the only one who had said anything. The Asian had stood quietly by, taking in our small talk with an amused look on his face. After a moment or so however, he spoke up. "We sell tickets," he said casually.

"I know," I replied.

The Asian was surprised at my response, and with a wide grin and quick laugh, asked, "How do you know?"

I waved my arm towards the empty hallway. "The place is closed. What else would you be doing here?"

He laughed and nodded his head in approval. Having decided I was legitimate, he decided to get down to business. "What are you looking for?"

"A ticket on the Trans-Siberian to Beijing."

"When do you want to go? Tonight?"

I blinked in disbelief. "You can get me on a train tonight?"

"Sure." He pulled a couple of tickets from his jacket. "I have some tickets with me now if you want one," he said. He thumbed through the tickets and handed one to me that was dated for that evening's train. I looked at the Cyrillic letters and was able to make out, '*From Moscow to Peking*' on the inside page of the ticket.

I couldn't believe it. Over a period of three days, every legitimate method I had tried for getting a ticket had gotten me nowhere. And here were two guys in a closed government booking office—neither of whom worked for the train station or the government—selling tickets on that night's train like it was the simplest request in the world. They were friendly too, especially the Asian, and in a short while were happily explaining their business of buying and selling tickets on the black market.

Basically, what it came down to was that the whole system was corrupt. The reason it was so tough to find tickets through legal channels was that there was a network of guys just like them who bought tickets in bulk to popular destinations in order to re-sell them at a profit.

The black market was rampant throughout the satellite countries of the Soviet Union and had thrived because of oppressive government controls that limited free trade. Every country, including the United States, has a black market. But in Russia, the black market was more the rule than the exception when it came to buying products and services that were in high demand.

A man from India who knew the Russian and Asian came up the stairs and joined our conversation. When he heard the Asian describing the Russian system to me he jerked his thumb at them and laughed. "You think they work for the people selling the tickets behind the windows? Not quite. The people behind the windows work for *them*," he said in complete seriousness.

The Asian laughed and said, "Do you want to leave on tonight's train?"

It was a tough decision. The day before, I had bought a ticket with Sarah and Sergei for a concert in Red Square on Saturday night called *Moscow Invites*. It was a special concert featuring Jose Carreras, the famous opera singer, as the main attraction. It was the first concert of its kind in Red Square and I wanted to go if I could. It was even rumored that Boris Yeltsin might show up for the opening ceremonies.

I was torn between leaving Moscow that evening or staying until Saturday to see the concert. If I left on Saturday I'd have three days to get across the Russian border to China before my Russian visa expired. I didn't know how long it would take to reach the Chinese border but I figured three days would be more than enough time.

"Is there a train on Saturday night after eleven o'clock?" I asked hopefully.

The Asian nodded. "There are three trains a week to Beijing. Tonight, Friday and Saturday. I don't think Saturday should be a problem but I'll need a few days to get the ticket for you because I have to go to another booking office. Some of the places I use now are closing down."

We negotiated a little over prices and settled on a cost of $160.00 for the ticket. After sealing our deal with a handshake, we agreed to meet in front of the booking office on Thursday afternoon at three o'clock.

When Sergei and I arrived at the ticket booking office on Thursday, it was pouring rain. I looked for the Asian and Russian on the second floor of the building but the entire floor was empty. Even the few workers that had been there two days before had deserted the place. We decided to go outside and wait.

We sat on a wooden bench on the front porch of the building and watched the rain turn the dirt courtyard into a growing pool of mud puddles. At 3:45 P.M., I started to wonder if I had been stood up. I walked to the door of the ticket office and spotted the Russian inside the lobby of the building. He nodded his head in recognition when he saw me. In response to my questioning look, he stuck his head outside the door of the ticket office and said reassuringly, "Don't worry, he'll be here."

Sure enough, at around four o'clock the Asian came running through the arched entrance of the courtyard, his head covered by his jacket to protect him from the downpour. With a big grin, he wiped the rain off his face and shook my hand like an old friend.

"I have a ticket for you for Saturday night," he told me. He dried his hands on his jacket and handed me a coupon-size ticket booklet made up of four or five pages. I passed the ticket to Sergei to make sure it was legitimate. When Sergei nodded his approval, I took one hundred and sixty dollars in cash from my money belt. "Here you go—one-hundred and sixty dollars." I handed eight, crisp, twenty-dollar bills to the Asian. He put the bills in his pocket without counting them.

He held out his hand and said, "Let me have your passport." When I hesitated, he laughed and said, "I need to write down some information onto the ticket for it to become valid." I handed over my passport and watched as he scribbled some information in Russian on the front page of the ticket. When he was done, he handed the ticket and the passport back to me. "Now it is official," he grinned.

I placed the ticket inside my passport and tucked it safely away in my money belt. "Is there any chance someone on the train will question the ticket?" I asked.

"No, you will not have a problem. *No problem,*" he insisted. Then added, "And if someone does question it, just tell him to fuck off."

I laughed. "Just like that, huh?"

"Seriously. If one of the conductors asks you where you got your ticket, just tell him you bought it in Moscow. If he has a problem with that, then tell him to take it up with the ticket office in Moscow, because it's their problem, not his. But believe me, there won't be a problem, so don't worry."

"Great—thanks," I said. "By the way, if someone questions those twenty-dollar bills I gave you, don't worry. Just tell them to take it up with someone in Washington, D.C." The Asian shot a quick look at me, trying to figure out if I was serious. I clapped him on the back and laughed. "They're real, don't worry."

He pulled out his wallet and said, "Don't joke. Some Chinese woman gave me a counterfeit one hundred-dollar bill yesterday. Here look." He took out the counterfeit bill and placed it next to a real one to show me the differences.

"What did you do?" I asked curiously.

"Nothing yet. I'll see her tomorrow night before she gets on the train." He nodded his head slowly and smiled. "Don't worry, I'll get my money," he said confidently. I had no doubt he would.

When the rain eased up, he stood up from the bench and signaled to his Russian friend inside the lobby. "I have to go," he told me. Then added, "The train leaves from Yaroslavsky station on Saturday night at 1:00 A.M. I'll be meeting some people at the station to give them their tickets, so I'll see you there." With a quick wave, he walked off and joined the Russian inside the ticket office.

Later that day, just for the hell of it, I decided to call Nikolai's apartment one last time. Nikolai answered the phone on the second ring. I couldn't believe it. When I told him how many times I tried to reach him, he laughed. "I've been away for the week on a business trip to Poland," he explained. "I just returned this morning."

"Well, at least I know you're still alive. Though I have to admit, there were times this week that I wished otherwise," I laughed.

I explained all the trouble I had trying to find a ticket without him and told him I had just bought a ticket for $160.00 that afternoon. Nikolai was surprised to hear I was able to find a ticket on my own. In fact, he was so surprised, that it made me wonder whether I had been ripped off.

When I got back to the apartment, I examined my ticket. From what I could tell, it looked authentic to me. Even Sergei had thought so. But what did we know. If the Asian, with all his experience in scams and illegal activities, could fall for a counterfeit one hundred dollar bill, then Sergei and I could certainly be duped into buying a fake Russian train ticket.

In any case, there was nothing I could do about it. I was either getting on the Trans-Siberian train to China on Saturday night or I wasn't. I'd find out soon enough.

This ain't the Waldorf; If it was, you wouldn't be here.
    — Notice found in Country Hotels, ca. 1900

At eleven-thirty on Saturday night, the large, bright concert lights were clicked off in Red Square. Jose Carreras had finished his performance at eleven o'clock and most of the people who had shown up for the highly touted *Moscow Invites* event had already dispersed.

Judging from the number of seats that were left unoccupied during the performance, it was clear that ticket sales for the big event were far less than expected. Most of the unsold tickets were probably accounted for by the eighty-dollar price tag for foreigners. The only reason Sarah and I were able to attend was because Sergei had gotten tickets for us at the Russian price, which was around five dollars a ticket.

It was actually too bad that the turnout wasn't larger because a lot of work had gone into planning the evening's events. The night was kicked off with a fashion show that featured the designs of popular Russian designers and was brought to a rousing end with a terrific performance by Jose Carreras. The only disappointment was that Boris Yeltsin never showed up for the opening ceremonies, as anticipated.

When the concert ended, Sergei, Sarah and I lingered around the square, enjoying the warm summer night and admiring the beauty of St. Basil's Cathedral. Lit up by huge, red floodlights, St. Basil's was bathed in deep scarlet and glowed like a fiery coal in the dark, black square around us. We walked slowly along the smooth, gray cobblestones and strolled past the Kremlin Wall with its imposing tower gate that rose high above St. Basil's. Passing the Lenin Mausoleum on our left, we made our way over to the white-roofed Historical Museum at the north end of the square. By the time we circled back to St. Basil's, it was time for us to leave. Sarah had a long commute back to the apartment in the suburbs and needed to leave before the public buses stopped running, and Sergei had to return to his University dormitory in the southern part of the city.

At the metro station across from Red Square, I said goodbye to Sergei, then gave Sarah a big hug and wished her luck in getting out of Russia. Sergei would help her buy her ticket, but after that, she would be on her own. To set my mind at ease, I made her promise to send a letter to my brother in Philadelphia so I'd know she got home without any problems. She was tough and gutsy and I knew she would be okay, but I wanted to know for sure. After a last round of handshakes and hugs, I entered the metro and took the subway to Yaroslavsky station. I retrieved my backpack from the luggage locker where I had stored it earlier in the day to avoid carrying it to the concert, and arrived at the train station a few minutes after midnight.

The train yard was packed with people, most of whom were loaded down with all sorts of odd-sized bags and valises as they waited for their trains to depart. The rest of the people were either awaiting the arrival of friends and family or had nowhere better to go, seemingly content to be part of the moving cloud of activity that made up a typical Saturday night at Yaroslavsky Station.

I wandered along the platforms looking for Yuri, the Asian who had sold me my ticket. As I looked at the dense crowds around me, I felt doubtful I would ever find him. As I threaded my way between groups of people and luggage, I suddenly felt a tap on my shoulder. When I turned, I saw Yuri's grinning face behind me. "There are some other Westerners on your train. You want to meet them?" he asked. Before I could answer, he plowed a path through the crowd ahead of us.

We crossed over to the other end of the train yard and stopped in front of three people who stood leaning against a pile of backpacks. They were waiting in front of train #20, the train number on my ticket. Yuri approached them with a big smile. He jerked his thumb toward me and told them, "He is also on your train. He's a good guy—you'll like him." He gave me a friendly slap on the back and then walked off to search for some of his other clients. With an hour to wait until the train was set to leave, the four of us got acquainted.

Martin and Annette were in their early twenties and were traveling as a couple. Martin was about my height, thin and well-built, and carried himself with a quiet air of confidence. Annette had an athletic body, short light-brown hair, and was almost as tall as Martin.

Martin was British and had met Annette, an East German, while traveling through Germany. They had been living together for the past six months and when Martin decided it was time to resume his travels, Annette convinced him to let her come along. Before he knew what hit him, her bags were packed and they were on their way to Moscow to take the train to China.

Annette was as bubbly as a newlywed. "We going to Hong Kong after China!" she told me excitedly, in a heavy German accent. "We hope to find work there. And maybe to make money to go to Australia. I can't wait to go to Australia!" She looked at Martin and beamed with joy at the prospect of making it to Australia. Annette was a little self-conscious about her English but was much more talkative than Martin who sat quietly by, amused by her boundless enthusiasm.

The third member of the group was a thirty-one year old named Flavio—a dark-haired Brazilian, who looked like Ricky Ricardo from the old *I Love Lucy* TV show. Flavio had spent the past four years studying psychology at a university in Poland and was on his way to Beijing to take a course in Chinese acupuncture. He was quiet and introspective and had an accent that was a unique mix of Portuguese and Polish—probably the only one of its kind in Moscow.

At 12:45 A.M., the train doors were opened for boarding. Almost immediately, the platform filled with passengers and baggage. And right in the thick of it was Yuri the Asian, shoving his way through the crowd to see me off. "So when are you coming back to Moscow?" he asked expectantly, as if I was just leaving on a short business trip.

"I don't know. It could be awhile," I replied with a laugh.

He shook my hand and patted me on the back. "If you come back, look me up. I'm always here on Saturday nights. I'll show you around. We'll meet girls, have a good time."

"It's a deal," I said with a laugh, as he turned to walk off.

As he walked down the platform towards the station, I called after him. "Hey Yuri, did you ever find the woman who gave you the counterfeit bill?"

With a sly smile he pulled a bill from his pocket and held it over his head so I could see it. "No problem," he called back. With a final wave of his hand, he turned and drifted into the crowd ahead of him.

Slinging my backpack on my shoulder, I walked down the brightly-lit platform with my three new companions. It was a long train, four-teen cars in total, and we had to pass almost its entire length before we reached our assigned train cars. Through some good fortune, Flavio had been assigned to wagon #13—the same wagon as Martin and Annette. I checked my ticket, hoping that all the Westerners had been assigned to the same carriage. No such luck—I was in wagon #12. Their carriage was ahead of mine, so I followed them onto the train to see what the sleeping compartments looked like.

Each compartment had two bunk beds that stood about three feet apart from each other across a worn, carpeted floor. Recessed storage areas were available for luggage above the top bunks. In addition, metal hooks and small rope-trays for personal items were attached to the walls beside each bed. Between the double bunks, and just below the curtained window of the compartment, hung a small metal table that could be propped up for use whenever it was needed. The com-partments weren't spacious, but they seemed comfortable enough for the long journey to Beijing.

Annette was overjoyed when she saw that she and Martin were the only ones assigned to their compartment. She took one look at the four empty beds and cried out, "It's all ours Martin—I love it! Come, let's go to sleep!" Martin dumped their backpacks in the overhead bins while Annette hurriedly made up the two bottom bunks. When the beds were ready she waved goodnight to Flavio and me, then grabbed Martin and laughed as she locked the door to their compartment.

Flavio's compartment was two doors down the corridor. When we walked in, we noticed two small bags on the bottom right berth. Other than that, it looked like Flavio was the only other passenger in his compartment. The lack of other passengers in their compartments surprised me—especially after seeing all the people on the platform who had lined up to board the train. I hoped I would be as lucky when I reached my own compartment.

As I walked down the corridor to the next train car, I noticed that a lot of the compartments were fully occupied. Most were filled with heavy-set Russians or slim-built Chinese, all of whom were busy mak-ing their berths and stuffing oversized bags in the hide-a-way chests beneath the bottom bunks or overhead bins above the door. Most of the compartments seemed to be grouped by nationality—all Russian or all Chinese. There wasn't a single mixed compartment in the whole car. Except for mine. When I entered the next train car and found my compartment, three Chinese heads turned to look up at me. Seeing me framed in the doorway with my backpack, they stared wordlessly at me and then at each other. They seemed as surprised as I was that I had been assigned to their compartment. I took a deep breath and walked in, smiling at each of my bunkmates, in turn. Still in shock at the sight of me, they bobbed their heads in greeting and continued to stare at me without a sound. I checked the bed number on my ticket and dumped my backpack on the bottom bunk to my left.

"Do any of you speak English?" I asked hopefully, as I looked at each of them.

They shot quick glances at each other to see if anyone understood what I said. No answer. "Well, this should be a fun six days" I mumbled to myself, as I sat on the bottom bunk across from them. They looked petrified when I sat down. Hoping to avoid having to stare at each other until the train left the station, I pulled out a book and made myself comfortable. At 1:00 A.M. the train began to move. After jolting back and forth a few times, it gave a loud hiss, then pulled sluggishly away from the station. With no alternative but to make the best of it, I got undressed and went to bed.

The following morning, I stopped by Flavio's compartment to see if he wanted to head over to the dining car for breakfast. When I told him I was in a compartment with three Chinese guys who didn't speak English, he said, "There ees only me and an old Chinese man in my compartment. Why don't you sweetch beds and come in here?"

Happy to take Flavio up on his invitation, I found the conductor of the train car and requested a change of compartments. The conductor didn't speak English but he understood what I wanted to do. After scanning the sleeping chart of his carriage, he led me back through the train to inform the conductor in my train car that I'd be switching compartments.

My three Chinese bunkmates looked totally confused when they saw me pack up my stuff. When I finished packing, I slung my backpack over my shoulder and waved goodbye. On my way down the corridor, I heard a flurry of rapid Chinese from inside their compartment as they tried to figure out what they had done to run me off.

A few minutes later, I was re-situated in Flavio's compartment. I took the top bunk above the old Chinese man. I slid my backpack in the wide bin above the door and placed my toothbrush and soap dish in the little rope tray that was affixed to the wall next to my bed. After hanging my towel on the metal hook beside the rope tray, I was officially unpacked and ready for breakfast.

When Flavio returned from the washroom, we went to see if Martin and Annette wanted to join us for breakfast in the dining car. Just as we were about to knock on their door, we saw Annette come bounding down the opposite end of the corridor. She had come from the toilets at the end of the carriage and burst excitedly past us, into her compartment. "Martin! There are no showers on the train! And you should see the toilets—ugh!" She made a face, then added, "I had to wash up in a little sink!" She shook her head in disgust then closed the door behind her so she could get dressed. When she opened the door a few seconds later, she was dressed in skin-tight, black spandex shorts and a loose-fitting T-shirt. Racing down the corridor ahead of us, she called back over her shoulder, "Come, let's eat—I'm starving!"

Martin shook his head and sighed. "I have a feeling it's going to be a long trip," he muttered. Flavio and I nodded our agreement as we followed him through the train cars in pursuit of Annette.

Every morning signals a new day in which something can go wrong.

—Bob Uyeda

The six-day train journey had a strange effect on my sense of time. Each day melted into the next, with little to differentiate them. Aside from a definitive beginning and end, the time in-between was like one big blur, marked only by meals and station stops. It was like being in a time warp.

The world outside the windows changed before my eyes, but life inside the train stayed constant day after day.

Each morning I would wake up early to avoid the lines for the washrooms, then go to the dining car in the rear of the train to see what the Russian chef had mutilated during the night for breakfast. That they even called it a dining car was a joke, since the last thing you wanted to do after seeing the food was eat. And it was even worse to look at. Almost every meal was some kind of stew with gray meat, soggy vegetables, and strange-looking things floating at the bottom. And the worst part was that if you didn't get to the dining car early enough, there usually wasn't enough food left for everyone on the train. As bad as it was, everyone raced to the dining car to make sure they would get there before it was all gone. It reminded me of that joke where the elderly lady says to her friend, "The food here is horrible," and her friend replies, "Yeah, and the portions are so small." That pretty much summed up how we felt about our meals in the Russian dining car. We hated what they had but were glad that they had it.

After forcing myself to eat whatever it was I was eating, I would wander through the compartments and spend an hour or so talking to the Chinese and Russian passengers who spoke English. When I got tired of socializing, I would return to my bunk to read a book or write in my journal. At some point in the morning, Flavio and I would then go over to Martin and Annette's compartment to play cards until it was time for lunch. After lunch—and then again after dinner—the whole process would start over again, until it was time for bed. It was a simple life, and I was totally content and relaxed, until I examined the station listings posted on the wall of our carriage.

I went into Martin's compartment for our daily morning card game and sat down with a sigh. Annette was sitting cross-legged on the bottom bunk next to Flavio, shuffling the cards when I walked in. I picked up my cards, then shook my head and frowned. The three of them looked at me curiously. "What's the problem?" Martin asked.

I folded my cards in my lap and explained what I had just found out. "Did you know there are forty-three scheduled station stops on the way to Beijing? They're listed on a sheet down the hall, near the toilet." Seeing their blank looks, I continued my explanation. "Well, *forty* of them are in Russia—*only the last three* are in China."

Flavio looked at me like I was crazy. "So? I no understand. What ees zee problem?"

"The problem," I answered, "is that we don't cross the border at Manzhouli until the fifth day on the train—July ninth. My Russian visa expires on July seventh. But that's not all. What's worse, is that my Chinese visa expires on July eighth—the day *before* we reach the Chinese border."

Martin scratched his head. "How's that possible? Didn't you get a one-month visa?"

"Yes. I got a thirty-day visa from the Chinese embassy in Copenhagen when I was in Denmark a few months ago. But my entry into China is supposed to take place before July eighth—or the visa expires. I don't know why, but for some reason I thought we were going to cross the border into China sooner than that."

Annette pulled at Martin's arm. "What's he saying? He's talking too fast! I didn't understand everything." Martin explained my situation to her in German. Annette looked at me and frowned. "That's *terrible!* What are you going to do?" she asked.

"I don't know," I said with a nervous laugh. "There's not much I can do about it now, so I guess I'll just have to wait and see what happens."

Aside from a handful of other Westerners and a few dozen Russians scattered throughout the train, the majority of passengers were Chinese who had gone to Russia to sell Chinese goods to the product-starved Russians. Having sold all their goods, they were returning to China with large sums of U.S. dollars—dollars they weren't supposed to take out of Russia.

A few of the Chinese passengers in our car spoke English fairly well, and over the course of the trip, Martin, Flavio and I had gotten friendly with several of them. Friendly enough, that on the fourth morning of the journey, one of them came to me for help.

I was sitting in my compartment reading *The Godfather*, when I heard a knock. I slid the door open and saw Chen Li Ping standing in the doorway of my compartment. Chen was a small, mild-mannered man in his mid-thirties from China's Gansu Province, one of China's poorest areas. His compartment was at the end of the corridor, but every day he would stop by my compartment on his way to the washroom and strike up a little conversation to practice his English. He was a funny little guy and had the perpetual air of someone who was always just one step ahead of misfortune—sort of like a Chinese Charlie Brown.

I met Chen the day after we left Moscow. He had a small white bandage on his forehead and told me that a rock had been thrown through the window of his compartment the night before and had hit him on the head. "Now I always keep window closed," he informed me. The following day, Flavio and I heard a loud crack down the corridor and saw Chen come racing down the aisle to tell us a rock had just smashed the window where he had been standing. From that point on, we avoided talking to Chen in front of windows.

When he saw the book in my hand he asked timidly, "Do I bother you?"

"No, not at all," I replied. "Come on in. I was just getting ready to stop reading anyway."

Chen looked troubled. He sat down on the bottom bunk and sighed. Just to play it safe, I leaned over and pulled the window shade down before sitting across from him. "What's up Chen?" I asked curiously.

He fidgeted uncomfortably on the bed before answering. After a moment's hesitation, he looked up. "You my friend, so I want to ask your help," he said. He then proceeded to explain his problem.

Chen had been trained as an engineer in China. After a few years of working hard and making very little money, he decided to try his hand at business. He had heard that a lot of Chinese people took Chinese-made products and food goods to Russia to sell for U.S. dollars. Most of them made good money—some earning thousands of dollars in cash in a matter of weeks. Chen was tempted by the prospect of making large sums of money and decided to give it a try. The only problem was that he'd never done anything like that before and wasn't aware of the pitfalls involved.

The Russian government had no problem with the Chinese bringing needed goods into Russia, but they weren't happy about them taking the hard-earned dollars that they made out of the country. Before allowing them to cross the border back into China, the Russians would confiscate any U.S. dollars that exceeded the amount declared when they first entered Russia. Most of the Chinese got around that problem by declaring an amount of U.S. dollars on their entry form that was larger than the dollar amount they actually had—knowing that the amount of money made in Russia would be less than the amount declared. That way it didn't look like they were taking dollars out of Russia when they were stopped at the border on their way back to China. Chen wasn't aware of that little trick before he went to Moscow. He had declared an amount going in that was less than the dollars he had made while in Russia. So now he had more dollars going out then he had when he went in. Worried that the Russians would find his money and confiscate it at the border, he came to me for help.

"You mean to say they just take the money?" I asked incredulously.

"Russian Customs-Man take what he want if not on declaration paper."

"So why not just tell them you don't have any—or at least, not as much as you've got with you?"

Chen looked at me like *I* was the one who had been hit on the head with a rock. "Customs-Man *search* Chinese at border," he explained.

"Oh," I muttered, finally understanding Chen's concern.

"But they not search Western people," he added quickly. "They don't want make trouble with Western people. You say money is yours, no problem."

Ordinarily, I don't mind helping someone who has a problem. But the last thing I wanted was to get caught smuggling money out of Russia—especially when I wasn't even sure I was going to make it past the border with my expired visas. Plus, I didn't really know Chen all that well. He seemed nice enough, but for all I knew, I was being set up as some sucker in a border scam.

I looked at the little bump on Chen's head and recalled the two incidents he had with the rocks at the windows. Maybe there was a reason he'd had rocks thrown at him. Maybe it wasn't just a strange coincidence that every time Chen stood by a window a rock was thrown at his head. After all, no one else on the train had rocks thrown at their heads. I stood at the windows all the time and didn't have rocks thrown at me. *Maybe somebody is after this guy*, I thought nervously.

I looked at Chen's helpless expression and suddenly felt sorry for him. He was a hapless little guy who had no one else to turn to. How could I not help him out? I sighed and shook my head. "How much money do you want me to hold for you?" I asked.

His face beamed with joy. "Two-thousand dollar." He started to pull his money out from a little black bag under his shirt.

"That's okay," I said, stopping him. "You don't need to give it to me now. You can bring it to me just before we reach the border."

Chen thanked me profusely and walked quickly down the corridor back to his compartment, ducking his head each time he passed an open window.

Sick as a Dog

One Lucky Puppy

A Mac and a Mao

Happiness is a warm puppy.
— Charles Schulz

I heard the puppy yelp and knew without having to look down from my bunk that the old Chinese man was the cause of it. The little dog and the old man had been at odds with each other since they started sharing our cramped living quarters the day before.

For the first two days of the trip, Flavio, the old man, and I had been the only occupants in our compartment. New passengers had been boarding the train daily however, so it was just a matter of time before the remaining bed in our four-bed compartment got taken.

Sure enough, when the train stopped in mid-afternoon at a dusty platform somewhere near Lake Baikal, three young Chinese men in their early twenties boarded our train car. They huffed down the corridor as they dragged their luggage behind them and peered into each compartment in a search for empty beds. Two of the young men found empty berths in the compartment next to ours. The third one noticed the one vacant berth in our compartment and immediately laid claim to it by dumping his bags onto the unmade mattress.

All three of the new arrivals looked unsavory, and the old man in our compartment winced when he first laid eyes on them. It wasn't hard to see why. Dressed in black jeans, pointed leather shoes and half-buttoned shirts, they looked like classic villains from a cheap Kung Fu movie—the kind that always get their butts kicked outside a noodle shop somewhere in a garbage-filled, back alley of Hong Kong.

The member of their trio who joined our compartment took the bed below Flavio's. After sloppily pulling a sheet across the mattress, he sat down next to one of his bulky duffel bags and opened the zipper. To my amazement and pleasant surprise, two puppies popped their small heads up and tried to scramble out of the bag, their tongues and ears flapping wildly, as they crawled over each other in their excitement to be the first one out.

Our new Chinese bunkmate—whom Flavio and I jokingly referred to as the "Young Tough," slid the compartment door shut so the dogs wouldn't run into the corridor. Grabbing both puppies by the scruff of their necks, he then yanked them from the bag and dumped them unceremoniously onto the floor.

They were Cocker Spaniels, very young and very small, and couldn't have been more than six or seven weeks old, at the most. Flavio and I hopped down from our berths to play with the puppies as they explored their new home, happy to have a new distraction to help us pass the time.

The old man was lying on his bed. He watched the dogs from the corner of his eye, but didn't pay much attention to them until one of the puppies started to sniff around under his bed. The old man's hand was dangling from the edge of his bed, and when the puppy scampered over to sniff his fingers, the old man flicked it roughly on the nose to chase it away. The dog gave a quick little backwards flip, then righted itself and proceeded to explore the other side of the compartment as if nothing had happened. The Young Tough wasn't happy about what had just happened however, and shot a cold glance at the old man. The old man set his teeth and stared silently back at him, then rolled over and faced the wall. The line had been drawn and the war between the old man and the puppies had begun.

Over the next few days, without fail, one or the other of the puppies would take a poop or a leak on the rug near the old man's bed. Whenever the old man saw the dogs start to squat, he would give them a quick boot with his slippered foot and send them flying. The Young Tough did the best he could to keep the dogs away from the old man's side of the room, but they were fast. They would trot over to the old man's bed, squat, and be done with it before he could catch them. We would then hear a thump, followed by a yelp, as one or the other of the puppies went sailing across the compartment. This was usually followed by a groan and a disgusted look on the old man's face as he watched the Young Tough clean the mess from the rug beneath his bed.

On the fourth day of our journey, it was clear something was wrong with one of the puppies. The night before, the puppy had been less active than usual but no one thought anything of it. We just assumed that the puppy was tired. But when the Young Tough went to feed it the next morning, it was listless and quiet and had a dull look in its large, brown eyes. The second puppy was as active as ever, but the first one stayed under the Young Tough's bed, unwilling to eat or walk around. The Young Tough continued to place food and water under its nose, but it just lay there, eyeing the meal without much interest.

The Young Tough became more and more concerned as the day wore on. Every half hour or so he would come back to the compartment with his two hoodlum friends to look at the sick puppy and try to determine what was wrong. Flavio and I stood by the door and watched the puppy with concern. The only one not concerned was the old man. If the puppy died, it would be one less annoyance for him to worry about.

"They're too young to be away from their mother," I told Flavio.

"The dog, he ees very seek," he replied, as he shook his head sadly.

"I wish there was something we could do."

"Zee dog needs mediseen."

The Young Tough and his friends didn't speak English but knew we were talking about his dog. The Young Tough turned to us with a questioning look. He spread his hands, soliciting any help we could offer. Flavio looked at me. "What are zee leetle red pills I see you taking each morning?" he asked.

"Vitamins."

"Maybe we geeve some to zee dog. He feeds zee dog bread and water—ees not healthy for a little dog."

Over the next day and a half, Flavio assumed responsibility for the health of the puppy. Crushing little pieces of the vitamins I had given him into cups of water, he gently poured the mixture in the puppy's mouth. At various intervals throughout the day, Flavio would spoon-feed the dog with little bits of food to give it strength. After each meal, he would wrap the puppy in a towel to keep it warm and instruct the Young Tough and his friends to leave the dog alone so it could sleep without being disturbed. Flavio tended his little patient with a dedication that would have made a veterinarian proud.

The following morning after breakfast, Martin, Annette and I went back to my compartment to see how Flavio's little patient was making out. When we walked in, we found Flavio kneeling in front of the puppy, with the Young Tough standing quietly beside him. The dog hadn't improved much since the day before. Flavio then did some-thing that surprised us. He unwrapped the puppy from the towel and stroked its head a few times. Rubbing his hands together very rapidly, he then cupped them a few inches above the dog and moved them slowly along its body from head to foot. After repeating this process for several minutes, he then sat back and peered into the puppy's eyes. Martin, Annette and I exchanged bemused glances at each other and then at Flavio.

"Say, Flav . . . uh, what exactly are you doing there?" Martin asked curiously. I was glad to see I wasn't the only one wondering whether Flavio had gone off the deep end.

Flavio looked at us patiently and replied matter-of-factly, "I am sending my heat and energy to zee dog to give eet strength."

"Ohhh," we uttered in unison, nodding our heads slowly, as if his explanation made perfect sense.

Flavio's hand-cupping technique didn't seem to surprise the Young Tough, however. In fact, it was perfectly natural to him since tradi-tional Chinese medicine used all sorts of techniques to manipulate different energy points in the body. In any case, whatever Flavio did, it seemed to work. The puppy became more alert, and over the course of the afternoon, walked around the compartment on wobbly legs and even ate a little food—all of which seemed like a good sign.

The next day, however, the puppy was weak again. Flavio tried everything—more vitamins, more spoon-feeding, more hand-rub-bing. Nothing seemed to have any effect. After awhile, we convinced Flavio to take a break and join us for dinner in the dining car.

On our way back from dinner, the four of us saw the Young Tough standing in the corridor outside our compartment. He was standing near an open window, holding the puppy in his arms. When he saw us, he shook his head sadly and shrugged his shoulders. The puppy had died while we were at dinner. The Young Tough opened the window of the moving train and tossed the lifeless body outside. With a final shrug, he looked over at Flavio and then walked quietly back into the compartment.

Rule #1: Don't sweat the small stuff.
Rule #2: It's all small stuff.
—Dr. Michael Mantell

The scenery outside the windows was pretty much the same for the first few days of the journey. Other than long stretches of flat country-side, which seemed to go on for miles on both sides of the train, there wasn't much to look at.

After about the third day though, the terrain started to change almost daily. Flat fields gave way to low, gently sloping hills, which were eventually replaced by dense woods and forested mountains as we made our way further east, towards the Chinese border.

Unfortunately, the closer we got to China, the more I worried about the border crossing. Each morning, I would wake up and check the station listings on the wall of the carriage to see if we would reach Manzhouli before my Chinese visa expired. And each day it looked less promising. I needed to know what my options were, if any, and decided to tell my problem to a friendly Chinese man named Lee at the opposite end of my train car.

Lee was the coach of a four-woman sailing team from Qingdao, a city near the Yellow Sea on the eastern coast of China. His team had just completed a month-long international sailing competition in Europe and was on its way home. The young women on his team were tall and athletic looking, and like Lee, spoke excellent English from all the traveling they had done through Europe. When I stuck my head in their compartment, Lee smiled and invited me in.

After patiently listening to my visa situation, Lee leaned back and asked quietly, "You say you are supposed to enter China by July eighth or the visa will expire?"

"Yes. And it doesn't look like we're going to cross the border at Manzhouli till Friday, July ninth," I replied.

Lee scratched his chin. "May I see your visa? Maybe there is something written in Chinese that you are not aware of."

I handed him my passport and waited while he studied the visa. After a minute or so he looked up at me. "I see your problem," he said with a grin.

I knew it. I was in trouble. "So what do you think they're going to do to me when we reach the border?" I asked, bracing myself to hear the worst.

"Nothing."

"But you just said you saw my problem."

"Yes, I see your problem. But it is not with the visa. It is with how you are reading the visa. You see here?" He handed my Passport back to me and pointed to the entry date marked '07–08.' He tapped the date with his finger. "In America, you write the month and then the day, so you read this as July eighth. But because we write the day *before* the month, it is really August seventh. You have until August seventh to enter China."

And just like that, all my worries were over. I had wasted all that time worrying about a problem that didn't even exist. I felt stupid and relieved at the same time. We were scheduled to cross the border at Manzhouli the next day, and for the first time since I had boarded the train, I had absolutely nothing to worry about. I thanked Lee for solving my problem and strolled happily over to the dining car for a beer.

At 11:00 A.M. the following morning, the conductor came to our compartment with departure forms that needed to be filled out. We were due to arrive at the Russian border station at Zabajkal'sk at around four o'clock. Upon our arrival at the border, each passenger would be required to hand in their exit form along with the stamped entry document they had received when they first entered Russia.

Martin, Annette and Flavio reviewed each other's entry forms to see what they had each declared when they had first arrived in Moscow. When Martin asked to see my form, I told him I didn't have one.

"Don't tell me you lost it," he said with alarm.

"Worse. I never got one," I replied.

"How's that possible? They wouldn't have let you into Russia without it."

"Well . . . they didn't actually let me into Russia. I kind of snuck in from Estonia." Seeing the surprised looks on their faces, I explained how I had crossed into Russia before my visa became active so that I would have more time to find a Trans-Siberian ticket in Moscow.

"So what are you going to declare on the exit form?" he asked curiously.

I shrugged and said, "Whatever I've got. It shouldn't be a big deal—I've just a camera, Walkman, Traveler's Checks and some cash. Nothing to worry about, I don't think."

"What about Chen's two thousand dollars?" he asked.

"Whoa—that's right. I'd forgotten about that!"

Chen had stopped by my compartment the night before to give me his money. But now, without an entry form to declare that I had entered Russia with over two thousand dollars in cash, the Russians could confiscate the money. I went off to look for Chen and found him in his compartment, packing his bags. I told him about the risk involved in my holding his cash. He considered it for a moment, then dismissed it with a shake of his head.

"No problem. Americans allowed to have dollars. No need to worry," he assured me.

An hour before we reached the border, Martin and Annette told me they had claimed temporary ownership of an electric guitar that was owned by a friendly Chinese couple in the compartment next to theirs. The couple had bought it on the black market and was afraid the Russians would take it from them, since they didn't have a sales receipt for it.

"But what good will *your* claiming it do?" I asked Martin. "You don't have a receipt for it either."

He shrugged. "What can I say? They figure it's got a better chance with me."

Flavio had also decided to play the Good Samaritan. When he heard that all pets purchased in Russia without proper papers would be confiscated at the Russian border, he offered to assume temporary ownership of the Young Tough's remaining puppy.

With the exception of the old man, everyone in the train car had grown to like the spunky little puppy and no one wanted to see it confiscated at the border—least of all Flavio, who had a soft spot for anything or anyone that needed help. But why Flavio thought a Brazilian who lived in Poland stood a better chance than a Chinese national did to take a dog from Russia into China, was beyond me. But there we were, the three of us, less than an hour away from the

Russian border, heading from a former Communist country towards a confirmed Communist country—each of us committed to smuggling dollars, products and animals across their borders.

We arrived at Zabajkal'sk at four-thirty. The train had barely stopped moving when a uniformed Russian guard stepped into our compartment and demanded to see our passports and customs documents. Before we arrived, we had been instructed to place our belongings on top of our bunks. Though everyone had complied, the guard did a thorough job of checking the overhead storage bins and chests beneath the bottom beds anyway. After examining the documents of the Young Tough and the old man, the guard inspected my passport and departure form.

"Entry declaration?" he asked curtly.

"I was never given one," I replied. I could have lied and told him I had lost it but I decided it might be better if they thought it was their fault that I didn't have it instead of mine. He looked at me for a second, then said, "You must go to customs office in station." He placed my passport and exit form in his coat pocket and turned to Flavio. When Flavio failed to produce the necessary paperwork for the puppy, the Russian pocketed his documents and told him to report to the customs office as well. As it turned out, all the passengers had to exit the train anyway since it had to be refitted with different gauge wheels so it could run on the meter-gauge tracks on the Chinese side of the border.

When the train inspection was completed, four hundred people stepped off the train onto the sunny platform at Zabajkal'sk station. Walking in small groups, we made our way to the large waiting hall inside the main building to sit out the five-hour wait while the wheels were refitted. Most of the passengers went inside the dusty station hall to stretch their legs and look for something to eat. Others wandered up and down the long concrete platform in little groups, talking and smoking in the warm afternoon air.

I went inside the station and asked a uniformed woman where I was supposed to go to collect my passport. She pointed across the lobby to a row of offices which ran along a long, green-walled corridor to the left of the main hall. I passed a number of old, empty offices until I reached a large, windowless room filled with Russian Passport Officers that were seated around a big, square, wooden table in the center of the room. Piled on the table in front of them were stacks of passports and a small mountain of documents that looked as if they would collapse if anyone sneezed. I stepped inside the room and told a man near the door that I needed to see someone in customs about my passport. He said something in Russian to the men seated at the table. One of the officers spoke English and told me to wait outside.

A few minutes later, a pleasant looking man came out to see me. He was holding my documents in his hand. With a serious, official-looking face, he thumbed through my passport and examined my departure form.

"How did you come to Russia?" he asked casually.

"By train from Estonia," I answered truthfully.

"Have you ever been to Russia before?"

"No," I lied.

No one going from Estonia to Russia would have been given a customs form, since Russia hadn't yet set up a border control between the two countries. Since there was no way for the Russians to know I had crossed the border before my visa became valid, I had nothing to worry about. The only thing I dreaded was the prospect of having to fill out tons of paperwork before being able to get my passport back. But to my relief, the officer scribbled something on the departure form and gave my passport and the approved form back to me. That was it. My punishment was over and I was allowed to go back outside and play with the rest of the passengers.

On my way back to the waiting hall, I ran into Flavio. He was standing in the middle of the hallway with the puppy in his arms, the two of them looking very confused. In fact, I wasn't sure who looked more lost—Flavio or the dog. Flavio's English wasn't great and he was having trouble finding out where to get the documentation he needed to take the dog out of the country. "Zey tell me I must go to zee veterinarian to get written authorization for zee dog—but I don't find his office," he said wearily.

"Come on Flav, I'm sure we can find someone who knows where it is," I said encouragingly.

I found someone who spoke English and was told the office was outside the station and to the right of the main building. Thirty yards down the platform, we stopped in front of a long concrete building with an official-looking sign above a narrow doorway. We walked inside and crossed a small, unlit foyer to a room on our left.

Inside the room, behind an old metal desk littered with papers, sat a short-haired, middle-aged man in a faded, yellow shirt. The walls of the room looked like they hadn't been painted in years, there was no examination table, and nothing in the place looked clean. Aside from a small glass cabinet near the door that contained some vials, a few rolls of gauze pads, and some other out-dated, medicinal-looking stuff, the office could have been a storage closet for all we knew. It was the last place in the world I would want to be taken if I were a sick dog—or any animal, for that matter.

The man lifted his head when we entered. In his best broken-English, Flavio made a quiet, soft-spoken request for the authorization papers required to take the puppy out of Russia. Unfortunately, the veterinarian didn't speak English. He knew what Flavio wanted but could only reply in Russian. And from the sounds of it, it didn't look good. Even without knowing Russian, we could tell from his hand motions at the dog, and then at some document he kept waving in the air, that Flavio's request wasn't going to be granted.

Flavio looked at me and frowned. "I think this man, he like to keep zee dog."

"I think you're right," I replied, after watching the way the man kept eyeing the puppy. "We'd better find a Russian who speaks English that can help us out. The customs man who returned my passport to me spoke English and he also seemed like a really good guy. Wait here—I'll see if I can find him," I said, as I left Flavio with the dog and walked back to the station.

Ten minutes later I returned with Alec, the Russian Customs Officer. Alec and the Russian veterinarian spoke for a few minutes while Flavio and I stood quietly by. By the tone of their conversation, it didn't seem like the man was going to change his mind about the puppy. All of a sudden, though, Alec raised his voice and started waving his hands around. He pointed at the man, and then at the puppy, and then at Flavio and me, and finally back at the man again.

When Alec finished speaking, the man mumbled something under his breath and then shook his head in resignation. He thumbed through some papers on his desk and pulled out a wrinkled document. After filling out the form, he signed it, and with a frown, handed it to Flavio. Alec smiled and said something in Russian to the man. The veterinarian let out a tired sigh and looked over at the puppy. With a quick, dismissive wave of his hand towards us, he sat back down in his chair and resumed his paperwork. Alec told Flavio to take the document to the customs office. "Once you pay the required fees, you will then be allowed to take the dog to China." Flavio and I thanked him for his help and walked back to the main building.

The clerk in the customs office informed Flavio that the fees for the dog would be sixty U.S. dollars. I watched the dog while Flavio went off to find the Young Tough to see what he wanted to do. The Young Tough didn't have enough money on him and asked if Flavio would lay it out until they got back on the train. Flavio returned to the customs office and paid the fees.

While everyone else on the train was happily relaxing outside or lounging around the waiting hall over snacks, Flavio was busy running from one office to another, filling out forms, and paying fees with his own money. And Flavio didn't have much money. The only reason he was going to a university in Poland was because he couldn't afford a university in Brazil. He had even brought his own food on the train, eating in the compartment most of the time, while Martin, Annette and I went to the dining car to eat.

Not many people would have given the time or the effort to do what Flavio did to help the Young Tough and his little dog. But Flavio didn't think twice about helping someone in need. Whatever it took to get the dog out of Russia, he was willing to do. At the end of the day, Flavio boarded the train with the little puppy in his arms. He looked tired but content. The dog was a free man and could go to China with the rest of us.

After the passengers were all back on the train, a group of Russian guards went from compartment to compartment in an exhaustive search through everyone's luggage. This was the moment the Chinese passengers feared. And with good reason. When the search was over, the guards left the train loaded down with an assortment of confiscated goods. From our carriage alone, the Russians confiscated a rubber dinghy, a pair of binoculars, five-hundred dollars cash, and several small birds that some of the Chinese passengers had hidden beneath their beds. Martin and I watched from a window as guards carried armfuls of goods down the platform to the stationhouse. Along with several other items, one guard carried two small, white dogs under his arms, confiscated from their owners because proper documentation hadn't been obtained. Martin shook his head and wondered aloud, "What in the world are they going do with all that stuff?"

I shook my head and shrugged. "Probably keep what they want and sell the rest," I guessed.

As far as I could tell, all of the items had been taken from the

Chinese passengers. None of the things in our care had been touched. Flavio gave the puppy back to the Young Tough. I returned Chen Li Ping's two thousand dollars. And Martin handed the electric guitar back to his Chinese neighbors. Unfortunately, some of the other Chinese passengers hadn't fared as well.

When I returned to my compartment, Chen was seated on the bottom bunk next to the Young Tough. The Young Tough wanted to thank Flavio for his help and had asked Chen to act as his translator. When the Young Tough finished speaking, Chen told Flavio, "Because of the dog's good fortune, he has named the puppy "Lucky."

Flavio scratched the puppy's head and laughed. "Ees a good name."

Chen continued. "He says you are a very good person. He wants to thank you for your help and asks me to say you are invited to stay at his home in Beijing if you do not have a place to stay." The Young Tough wrote out his address and phone number and handed it to Flavio. Chen said, "After we cross the border, the Russian dining car will be replaced by a Chinese dining car. Chinese food much better than Russian food. He would like to buy you lunch tomorrow—anything you want!" Chen looked at me and grinned. "I take you to lunch, too!"

I was happy the Young Tough got to keep his dog but was surprised he was willing to pay so much money to take it over the border—especially since he had never shown the dog that much affection. When I mentioned this to Chen, he didn't seem surprised that the Young Tough had paid the fees for the dog's papers.

"In China, a dog like this is worth much money," he explained.

"He's going to sell the dog?" I asked in amazement.

Chen didn't know for sure. I thought of having him ask the Young Tough what he planned to do with the puppy when he got to Beijing but decided I didn't really want to know. I liked the dog and wanted to think it was going to have a nice home and not end up on someone's plate for dinner. As the train moved slowly away from Zabajkal'sk station towards the Chinese border, a Russian guard rode along on the back of the train and hopped off just before we left the Russian side of the border. When the train was officially in Chinese territory, it screeched to a halt in front of a long platform. Within a few short minutes, Chinese immigration officials boarded the train and monitored our departure into the waiting hall across the platform. There was a huge difference between the Russian and Chinese waiting halls. Everything the Russian station lacked in the way of amenities, the Chinese made up for in abundance. In addition to comfortable chairs and benches, there were televisions placed in the hall so passengers could watch Chinese TV programs while they waited for their trains. Passengers who were hungry could buy all sorts of food from the long, glass-covered counters in the middle of the waiting hall or the fully-stocked shelves and counters on each side of the room. There was even a bank where people could exchange foreign dollars for Chinese currency.

It was a major change from the stark, bleak, Russian waiting hall we had recently left. And though we were only a few hundred yards from the Russian border, and still a day and a half away from Beijing, it seemed like we were worlds away. Compared to the Russian way of life, we were.

We arrived in Beijing less than two days later, almost a week after we had set out from Moscow. After saying goodbye to the friends we had made on the train, we walked down the long, wide ramp that led away from the platform, and stepped into the large, unfamiliar surroundings of the Beijing train station. Swarms of dark-haired Chinese passengers raced by us in all directions, while throngs of Chinese men and women flashed their ticket stubs to station attendants at the exits before proceeding through the narrow barricades to the street outside. We walked past the exit barriers with the rest of the crowd and stepped into a large, concrete lot in front of the station.

We planned to stay at the Qiaoyuan Hotel on Dongbinhe Lu, a popular backpacker hotel in the southern part of the city. None of the people that we asked for directions seemed to know any English, so I stuck my guidebook under the nose of a Chinese man beside me. He read the Chinese address of the hotel and pointed us toward a line of red buses across the street. Ten minutes later we were onboard a crowded, dilapidated bus, which rattled noisily and dangerously close to thousands of bicycle-peddling Chinese. The bus traveled west down Fuxing Lu, Beijing's main avenue, then turned south, directly across from the Forbidden City.

"*Martin look!*" Annette tugged Martin's sleeve excitedly as we passed Tiananmen Square. "There's the city from the movie, 'The Last Emperor.' And there's the Square—I forget its name—where the people were run over by the tanks! Oh, *I can't believe* we are finally here!"

Life is an ever elusive, moving target—an adventure
to be relished, mostly for its detours.
—Tom Peters

Beijing is a sprawling, dynamic city filled with eleven million Chinese. As the capital of the People's Republic of China, and the country's political, cultural, and administrative center, Beijing controls the reins that run the rest of the country—reins that have been held for almost 700 years under the Mongols, the Ming, the Manchu, and currently, the Communists.

Despite its enormous size—at 16,800 square kilometers, the city is roughly the size of Belgium—most of the historical sights are centered around Tiananmen Square, in the heart of the city. A few miles south of Tiananmen Square was the *Qiaoyuan Hotel*, a low-budget, backpacker hotel, with over 200 rooms, including five, twenty-bed dormitories. To save money, Flavio and I took beds in a sixteen-bed dorm on the third floor, while Martin and Annette took a double-room for some privacy. Aside from its unfriendly staff, most of whom faithfully lived up to their reputation of being rude and unhelpful to the foreign travelers who stayed there, the *Qiaoyuan* was a convenient place to stay and a great place to meet other travelers.

The morning after we arrived, we rented bicycles from one of the small bicycle stalls behind the hotel. We hopped on our old-fashioned, one-speed bikes and rode past the privately-run laundry shops, food stalls, and restaurants outside the hotel until we reached the bus depot down the road. Rather than follow our maps, we waited for a bus to pull out of the depot then trailed slowly behind it until we reached Tiananmen Square.

Tiananmen Square has been the heart of China since October 1, 1949, when over three million people gathered there to hear Mao Tse Tung proclaim China as the People's Republic. His speech was made from the balcony of Tiananmen Gate, the southernmost gate of the Forbidden City, just across the street from the square.

The Square was named after Tiananmen Gate, the "Gate of Heavenly Peace," but it wasn't peaceful on the night of June 4, 1989, when armed Chinese troops and military tanks crushed a non-violent assembly of protestors that had gathered in the square to demonstrate for greater political freedom in China. The protestors included Chinese people from all levels of society: students, farmers, journalists, factory workers, even Party members—all of them calling for more democracy and an end to government corruption. Official Chinese government reports claimed that 200 to 300 people were killed as a result of their efforts to break up the demonstration. U.S. Government and eyewitness reports estimated much higher numbers of casualties, however—hundreds killed, and thousands wounded in the military assault.

"Just imagine, Martin—the tanks rolled right here where we are standing," Annette said with awe. "Isn't it terrible, what happened?" Before Martin could answer, Annette hopped back on her bicycle and peddled past the tall, stone *Monument to the People's Heroes* in the center of the square and over towards the *Mao Mausoleum*, directly behind the monument. "Come Martin—I want to see Mao!" she called excitedly over her shoulder. Martin looked at Flavio and me and sighed, "I think Annette wants to see all of Beijing in one day."

We parked our bikes against some metal barricades that had been erected at the edge of the square then walked over to a long line of Chinese tourists who were waiting to go inside the mausoleum to view Mao. If it wasn't for a friendly Chinese tour-group leader standing on line ahead of us, we would have been on line for hours. She told us that foreign guests were allowed to bypass the lines since we had less time to see the sights in Beijing than the Chinese. We felt a little awkward cutting to the head of the line, but walked up the steps to the entrance doors of the *Mao Tse Tung Memorial Hall* as she suggested. To our surprise, the Chinese guards at the door let us walk right in.

Soon after we entered, we were led into a dark, red-carpeted room that had a crystal sarcophagus in the middle of the floor. The long line of Chinese people in front of us shuffled slowly and quietly past the coffin, gazing solemnly at Mao Tse Tung's preserved body. His corpse was dressed in the typical blue suit worn during the years of the Cultural Revolution and was covered with a flag of the Communist Party.

The guards in the room kept the line moving, which prevented us from lingering for more than a few seconds as we filed past the coffin. Except for the muffled sound of feet shuffling along the thick red carpet, there wasn't a noise in the mausoleum—until Annette blurted, "Martin, Mao's face looks like plastic!" Martin silenced her with a finger to his lips and hurried her past the coffin towards the exit at the opposite side of the room.

As soon as we exited the mausoluem, Annette was a bundle of energy again. "That was so strange! Imagine being on display like that so everyone can stare at you after you are dead? Ugh! I wouldn't like that at all. Martin, if I die in China, don't let them do that to me!"

Martin turned to Flavio and me and whispered, "There's probably not enough embalming fluid in all of China to keep her still!" When Flavio and I laughed, Annette wagged her finger at Martin and said, "You're making fun of me, aren't you Martin?" With a wink at Flavio and me, Martin placed his arm around Annette and said innocently, "Who, me?"

Having seen the famous Mao Tse Tung, we rode to the corner of Fuxing Lu and Chang An Avenue and parked outside the Beijing McDonald's. It wasn't as impressive as the one in Moscow, but it wasn't bad—especially after our previous week's diet of Russian stew and Chinese noodles on the Trans-Siberian Express.

We spent most of the next day at the Summer Palace, about seven miles northwest of Tiananmen Square. The Palace and its park was originally called *Yiheyuan*—the Garden of Cultivated Harmony—but soon became known as the Summer Palace, after the Empress Dowager Cixi started to bring her royal court there during the summer months to avoid the heat in the Forbidden City. The Palace was surrounded by Lake Kunming, which occupies three-quarters of the park. Nowadays, the lake is used for swimming and boating in the summer months and skating during the winter.

The Summer Palace was impressive, but it was nothing compared to the Forbidden City—an enormous 250-acre complex of palaces, temples, and servants' quarters that housed the imperial emperors of China for over 500 years. Surrounded by a wide moat and 35-foot walls, the Forbidden City was traditionally off-limits to all Chinese who didn't have permission to enter its gates.

Created by Emperor Yongle in 1420, the Forbidden City was home to two dynasties of Chinese Emperors, the Ming and the Qing. It was the center of power of every Chinese Emperor until 1911, when emperor Pu Yi, the "Last Emperor," was forced to abdicate control of China by Yuan Shikai—the Imperial Marshall who assumed control of the government in 1909. The pampered life of a Chinese emperor was recounted in Pu Yi's autobiography when he described a simple walk in a garden:

> " . . . at the head marched a eunuch, a herald whose function was like that of a car horn. He walked twenty or thirty yards in front of the others, constantly hissing 'chi, chi,' to shoo away any other people in the vicinity. He was followed by two of the higher eunuchs walking like crabs on both sides of the path. Behind them came the main group of the procession, the Dowager Empress and me.
>
> If I was carried in my palanquin, two of the younger eunuchs walked at my side, ready to attend to my wishes at any time. If I was walking, they held me under the arms to support me. Behind me followed a eunuch with a great silken canopy. He was accompanied by a great crowd of eunuchs, some of whom carried nothing, others with their hands full of all kinds of paraphernalia—a chair to rest on, a change of clothes, umbrellas and parasols; after the eunuchs who personally served the emperor came the eunuchs from the Imperial Tea Office with boxes of cakes and delicacies, with jugs of hot water and the tea sets; they were followed by the eunuchs from the Imperial Pharmacy . . . at the end of the procession came the eunuchs carrying chamber pots and pulling commodes. If I went on foot, an open or closed palanquin followed, according to the season. This brightly coloured circus parade of several dozen people progressed in complete order and silence."

For better or worse, the imperial life of China's long line of emperors ended forever after Mao Tse Tung and his Communist forces took control of the country in 1949.

Later that week, Martin popped his head into our dorm room one morning after breakfast and called out, "If you two want to get out to the Great Wall, you'd better hurry up and get downstairs. The seats on the mini-bus are filling up fast!"

The hotel ran minibus tours to the Great Wall, and Martin and Annette had signed up for that morning's ride. Flavio had made plans to meet a Polish friend who was studying in Beijing, so he told us to go without him. I ran downstairs with Martin and Annette and grabbed one of the last open seats on the bus. Two hours later the van dropped us off in Badaling, 75-kilometers northwest of Beijing.

The view as we drove towards the wall was staggering—an endless stone barrier that stretched over the green-carpeted mountain ridges of the North China Plain as far as we could see. Parts of the wall were constructed 2,000 years ago, but most of what still stands was built in the 15th century as a line of defense against the invading Mongols in the north of China. The wall took more than 300,000 men ten years to complete and was actually a primitive version of an elevated highway—built wide enough to allow five horses, or ten armed men, to travel abreast between the battlements set up along the northern frontier.

The seemingly endless wall at Badaling was just a tiny section of the Great Wall. Scholars estimate that the wall, with all its fortifications and garrisons that made up the original complex, once stretched for 6,200 miles (10,000 kilometers), from the Yalu River in the northeast of China, to Xinjiang in the northwest. The current remnants of the wall run about 3,750 miles (6,000 kilometers) from the Shanhaiguan Pass near the Bohai Sea to the Jiayuguan Pass in the Gobi Desert. But even in its scaled down version, which is almost half its original size, the Great Wall was the only human construction that could be seen with the naked eye by American astronauts when they made their first flight to the moon.

By the end of the following week, we each made plans to move on from Beijing. We had formed good friendships and promised to keep in touch, but the time had come to go our separate ways. Flavio planned to stay in Beijing for the summer before returning to Poland to complete his university degree. To supplement his coursework during his stay in China, he had signed up for some classes in Chinese medicine at a local university, a few miles west of the Forbidden City. Martin and Annette were ready to head to Hong Kong, where they hoped to earn enough money to go to Australia for a year or so. And for me, the road was open. I planned to head east to the coast and stop at a few places along the way until I reached Shanghai. After that, I wasn't sure. In any case, it didn't really matter. I'd choose my course as I went along—which was exactly the way it was supposed to be.

A Night on a Mountain

A Simple Mistake

Shanghai

From the summit of Tai Shan the earth seems small
— Confucious

The cold wind and rain stung my face and woke me from the restless sleep I had drifted into only minutes before. I felt around in the dark for my flashlight and pointed its thin beam toward the spot where Helena and Andrea slept a few feet away from me. Sheltered from the rain by their heavy overcoats, they were sound asleep. I looked at them and frowned. They looked so warm and comfortable while I was freezing my tail off. And all because they wanted to sleep on top of the mountain. I didn't even want to climb the damn thing, let alone sleep on it. In New York my idea of scaling new heights was taking the elevator to the top of the Empire State Building—not climbing to the top. How I let them talk me into sleeping on top of a mountain was beyond me.

As the wind whipped cold drops of rain against my face, I laid there envying their sleep. I pulled the thick collar of my heavy green Chinese topcoat around my head to block out the wind, and placed my hands in the deep lined pockets to keep them warm. It was dark and cold and I was exhausted from the day-long climb up the mountain. As I stared blankly into the misty darkness, I thought how strange it was that just one week before, the three of us didn't even know each other. And there we were, huddled together on the summit of Tai Shan, the most revered of China's five sacred mountains.

I had met Helena a few days before I left Beijing. She had just flown in from Sweden and had two weeks to travel on her own before meeting up with friends in Shanghai. After she told me her travel plans, I said, "Maybe I'll see you there. I'm leaving in a few days in that direction myself. I plan on stopping at a couple of places along the way, and I'll probably get to Shanghai in about two weeks."

When she heard I was going to Shanghai, her eyes lit up. "I have two weeks before I have to meet my friends, and would like to see as much of China as I can before then. But I don't want to travel by myself. Maybe we can travel together?" she asked tentatively. Since only an idiot would have turned down an offer to travel with a beautiful 26-year old, blonde girl from Sweden, I told her she was welcome to join me, and made train reservations for later in the week.

A few days after we left Beijing, we arrived in Tai'an, a small, rural town at the base of Tai Shan. Exhausted from a 13-hour train trip, we checked half the hotels in town before finding a place with two spare beds in a triple room. Andrea was in the third bed, fast asleep.

A large, broad-shouldered, athletic German in her late twenties, she had been traveling around Europe and parts of Asia for the past six months while earning her keep working on freighters. Taller and stronger than most Western men, she towered over virtually all the Chinese, and didn't seem too concerned about traveling alone as a single woman.

She had been in Tai'an for two days by the time Helena and I got there and had intended to climb Tai Shan as soon as she could, but hadn't been able to do so because of bad weather. The sun broke out the morning after Helena and I arrived, and since Andrea seemed to know quite a bit about the various routes up the mountain, we decided to take advantage of the clear weather and make the climb with her.

She spread a map of the mountain trails across her bed and pointed to the one she wanted to take to the summit. Her main goal was to avoid the soft drink and souvenir vendors along the main path. She also wanted to steer clear of the hordes of Chinese tourists who followed one another in huge packs up the mountain. Her plan sounded fine to us, and after packing an extra shirt and some toiletries, we each grabbed our day packs and started our hike up Tai Shan.

Not long after we set off, we realized Andrea's little tourist map wasn't very accurate. An hour or so up the mountain, the side trail disappeared and we found ourselves lost in a patch of bushes and small woods that led nowhere. Unable to get back to the main walking path, we wound up hiking for hours in the hot sun on an asphalt road that had been built for cars and minivans along the side of the mountain. So much for our nice little nature walk.

The road snaked slowly up the mountain and ended at a parking lot near Zhongtian Gate, the halfway point. From there, the only way to the top was by cable car or by foot—up 7000 incredibly steep steps that had been carved into the rock face of Tai Shan. At 1500 meters in height, about 5000 feet, Tai Shan wasn't that tall. But the long, arduous climb up the narrow stone stairs took patience and endurance—enough endurance that Chinese folklore claimed that anyone who climbed Tai Shan would live to be 100.

After he reached the peak, Confucious supposedly said, "From the summit of Tai Shan, the earth seems small." Not to be outdone, Mao Tse Tung watched the sunrise from the top of the mountain and uttered, "The east is red"—whatever that was supposed to mean. He was probably delirious from the climb. Anyone wishing to record our first words would have heard, "Oh my God, I can't believe we've got to go down all those stairs tomorrow!" Not exactly immortal words, but probably a whole lot closer to what Confucious and Mao really said than what was recorded for posterity.

We finally reached the top in late afternoon. On the plateau above the steps was a large, temple courtyard made of stone where Chinese visitors could pay their respects after their long climb to the summit. There were also dormitory-style guesthouses near the courtyard for people who planned to spend the night. At the far end of the summit, across a long, flat, stone clearing, the plateau ended in a large group of rock formations where pilgrims who had slept on the top of Tai Shan could watch the sunrise.

Famished from the climb, we relaxed over a decent dinner of rice and mixed vegetables at one of the outdoor food stalls near the temple courtyard. It was late in the day when we sat down to eat, and by the time we finished, the sun had dropped quickly towards the horizon. When it finally dipped out of sight, the temperature dropped with it. I had no desire to spend the night freezing outside and did my best to convince Helena and Andrea to check out the beds in the dormitories with me.

"I'm going to sleep outside with the rest of the Chinese," Andrea informed me.

"Yes, me too," Helena said, echoing Andrea's resolve to commune with nature.

The prospect of spending the night outdoors wasn't one I had planned for. "Not all of the Chinese are sleeping outside," I argued.

"Look how many are going into the dormitories." I pointed to the guesthouse across the courtyard where a group of Chinese men and women was lining up to go inside.

Helena sighed. "The beds cost money. Besides, it will be nicer to sleep under the stars."

"But we'll freeze out here. Can't you feel how cold it is already?"

"We can rent those big coats," she replied, pointing to a man across the courtyard who was renting heavy green overcoats to people who had lined up in front of his table.

"Look . . . let's at least check out the dorms," I pleaded. "It can't hurt to look, can it?"

Andrea was set on sleeping under the stars, so she waited outside while Helena and I went into the guesthouse across the courtyard. The Chinese manager ushered us past a large, fully occupied dorm room to a second room with eight beds, six of which had Chinese men in pajamas and heavy shirts sprawled out on them.

When we walked into the room, the men leered at Helena like they had just seen a ghost. She took one look at them and frowned. With a shake of her blonde head, she turned around and strode back to the courtyard. I gave a sheepish grin to the manager as if to say, "*Women! What can you do?*" With a sigh, I turned around and chased after Helena like a hen-pecked husband.

When we were back outside she said, "I don't think it will get that cold. Anyway, it won't be long before we have to wake up for the sunrise. You can stay in the guest house if you like, but I'm going to sleep outside with Andrea."

I was suddenly faced with a dilemma. I could either tough it out and sleep outside with the girls, or be a wimp and sleep in the guesthouse. I didn't mind looking like a wimp in front of Andrea. She was bigger and stronger than me and no doubt thought I was a wimp anyway. But I didn't want to look like a wimp in front of Helena. After all, I was the guy she had asked to escort her safely to Shanghai. Besides, if she could sleep outside in the cold without complaining, then why couldn't I?

"Well, then I guess I'll sleep outside too," I said in resignation, following Andrea and Helena across the stone courtyard to rent an overcoat.

Wrapped up in our long, green, military topcoats we looked like soldiers in the Chinese army. I looked around and noticed that the rest of the Chinese on the mountain were wearing identical coats and felt like we had become part of a huge military operation on the summit of Tai Shan. By the time we rented the coats, it was getting dark and starting to get cold, so we bought a final round of beers and a bottle of awful tasting rice wine to help us warm up, then walked off to find a place to sleep.

A low, stone wall ran down the length of the plateau to an archway that separated the main courtyard from the rock ledge at the edge of the summit. Most of the Chinese had staked out some sleeping space along its base. So many people were lined up in front of the wall, that they took up almost the whole length of the plateau. Some were fast asleep, but others were propped up with their backs against the wall, talking or playing cards in the dim, yellow light of kerosene lanterns. Small groups of Chinese men and women were also scattered around the grassy areas west of the courtyard. They sat huddled together, drinking and laughing next to portable cassette recorders that blasted high-pitched Chinese music into the night. They didn't look tired and probably intended to stay up and party until sunrise.

Helena, Andrea, and I followed a dirt path opposite the temple, hoping to find a secluded area away from the music where we could get some sleep. We walked about fifty yards up a low incline until we came to a gazebo-like structure with large stone pillars which supported a stone slab roof. The floor of the structure was cold and rocky but offered some shelter from the wind. We laid down and made ourselves as comfortable as possible.

Black clouds blocked the moon and stars, and without my pocket flashlight, I couldn't see much beyond the path ahead of our shelter. Other than the drone of Chinese music and occasional squeals of laughter coming from the people squatting near the temple, it was quiet on our end of the mountain. Tired from the climb, and warmed by the liquor, I closed my eyes and went to sleep.

I hadn't been sleeping long when the rain blew against my face and woke me up. I wrapped my coat around my body like a blanket and drifted back to sleep. An hour later, the cold, wet rain whipped across my head and woke me again. I decided to find a new shelter. I turned to check on Helena and Andrea again, but this time they were gone. I assumed they had gone to the temple to find a warm, dry place to sleep, and went off to find them.

It was almost 3:30 A.M. The rain had turned into a steady mist, which was annoying, but bearable. Other than a few isolated groups of people whispering along the perimeter of the courtyard, most of the dark shapes around the pitch-black summit were silent and still. I walked across the courtyard until I reached the tall, wooden archway that separated the temples from the lookout point. My only hope of finding my traveling companions was to spot Helena's blonde hair from among the hundreds of black-haired Chinese who lay sleeping along the ground. But it was way too dark, and there were far too many people to check everyone. Twenty minutes later I gave up and returned to the stone gazebo, hoping they had gone back to our sleeping place. They weren't there. I sat down with my back against one of the pillars and closed my eyes. When I awoke again it was a little after 4:00 A.M. Unable to sleep any more, I decided to get up and wait for the sunrise. I went back down the path to the courtyard and walked east towards the lookout point at the end of the summit.

The wide, yellow beam from my flashlight scattered like shotgun pellets in the thick, misty fog that hung a few feet above the ground and made it hard to see where I was walking. I turned off the light and let my eyes adjust to the darkness. A few moments later, I noticed a horde of black, silent shapes moving slowly around me. I had unknowingly joined part of a growing procession of Chinese pilgrims who were heading towards the edge of the summit. Like soldiers in a long, steady march, we shuffled silently along, our faces hidden by the tall, thick collars of our overcoats.

When we reached the lookout point, the people fanned out quietly in the dark and nestled themselves against the huge, flat slabs of rock that rose in different angles from the top of the plateau. I found a secure spot against a shallow dirt embankment to my left and settled in with the rest of my companions to wait for daybreak.

For the next hour or so there wasn't much to see. The dark clouds continued to spill a light rain down on Tai Shan. Then slowly, as if a heavy, dark curtain was being raised from an enormous stage, the sky began to lighten. With the growing light, the clouds and haze that had covered the summit during the night lifted like a thin veil in a breeze. I moved closer to the edge of the plateau and saw tiny specks of light coming from the homes in the valley below the mountain.

The black sky continued to give way to the morning sun until the last trace of night had disappeared completely. When the sun had risen above the horizon, everyone stood up and walked silently back to the temple courtyard.

I crossed the archway that led back to the temple and saw Helena and Andrea walking through the courtyard looking for me. They told me that the rain had awakened them during the night and they had gone off to find better shelter. I was sleeping when they woke up so they'd decided not to disturb me. They had spent the night in the one dry place I hadn't searched when I went looking for them—beneath the balcony of the cable car platform, less than fifty yards down the hill from the gazebo. Helena looked exhausted, and was no doubt regretting her decision to sleep under the stars. I was dying to say, "I told you so," but thought better of it. Instead, I asked innocently, "So? How was the big night on the mountain?"

Helena frowned. "It was awful. It was cold and wet. I don't think I slept for more than two or three hours."

"And we missed the sunrise as well," Andrea added, dismally.

This was too good to be true. Even Wonder Woman looked tired. I shook my head with feigned disappointment. "That's too bad," I said. "I think you would have really enjoyed it."

"Was it worth getting up for?" they asked hesitantly. Something told me they were both hoping I'd say no.

"Unbelievable."

"It was? What was it like?" they asked with pained looks.

I paused for a moment, searching for exactly the right answer.

"Let me put it this way—" I waved my hand across the horizon from the summit of Tai Shan. "The east is red."

Everybody has a right to pronounce foreign names as he chooses.
— Winston Churchill

"No more hard-sleeper ticket left," the Chinese student told us. He had done his best to get tickets for us at the crowded ticket window and looked disappointed that he was unable to help us out.

Helena and I wanted to take the 9 P.M. train to Suzhou, a city in China famous for its beautiful gardens, but we were having trouble getting beds on the night train since Suzhou was a big tourist spot for the Chinese and sleeper-seats went fast. There was always the option of buying "hard-seat" tickets, but on an overnight trip those seats were unbearable. It was the cheapest way to travel on Chinese trains, and since it was the only class of travel most Chinese could afford, those carriages were crowded beyond belief. Faced with the news that sleeper tickets weren't available, Helena and I discussed our options.

"I don't know if I have the energy to travel hard-seat again," she sighed.

"Me either," I agreed. "But it's probably the only way we're going to get out of here tonight." I sat on my backpack while she thought it over.

We had traveled hard-seat for thirteen hours when we went from Qingdao to Tai'an, and it wasn't fun. Every conceivable spot where a body could fit had been occupied. Seats meant for four passengers had eight or more people squeezed on them. And the aisles were even worse. To reach our seats we had to shove past scores of Chinese who squatted in the aisle from one end of the carriage to the other. Even the transit areas between the carriages were jammed. We couldn't get from one car to the next without stepping over, under, or around scores of people. When we finally did get to our seats, we were stuck in them for thirteen hours straight—hemmed in by the mass of people in the seats and aisles around us.

The heat in the unairconditioned hard-seat carriages was almost as bad as the crowds. The air was stifling, especially with hundreds of people packed into a wagon meant for less than half that number. And all the Chinese men chain-smoked. It was like being in a sauna with smokers. By the end of the trip we were drenched and exhausted and had to fight our way through the crowded aisle twenty minutes before the train stopped at our station to make sure we had time to exit. We swore we wouldn't ride hard-seat on any long trips again. But there we were, faced with the same decision—go hard-seat or hang out another day or two until hard-sleeper tickets became available.

While Helena was considering whether she would have the strength to ride hard-seat all night long, I came up with an alternative plan. "I've got an idea," I said. "Let's buy the hard-seat tickets. That way we'll make sure we're on the night train. Then, after we get on board, we'll see if we can upgrade the tickets to hard-sleeper. Our friend here can write a note for us to give to the conductor. What do you say—do you want to give it a shot?"

"What if it doesn't work?"

"It'll work."

She thought it over. "Well . . . I guess it's worth a try."

I handed Helena a sheet of paper and a pen. "I'll go get the hard-seat tickets while you ask him to write us the note. I'll be back in a little while." I left my bags with Helena and crossed the large station hall to the crowded ticket windows.

When it was my turn at the counter I asked for two tickets to Suzhou for the nine o'clock train. "*SUZHOU*" I repeated, after the ticket girl said something in Chinese that I didn't understand. I held up two fingers—"Er-ga," I said in Chinese. She fired off the price for the tickets. I shook my head, not understanding what she'd said. "Dow show Chien?"—*how much*, I asked. I understood her the second time. I handed her the 34 Yuan she asked for. She counted the money to make sure it was all there, then slid two cardboard stubs across the counter.

Proud of the successful transaction with my limited Chinese language skills, I strode back to where Helena waited with the bags. In answer to her questioning look, I held up the two tickets. "Piece of cake!" I bragged. We lifted our packs and walked off to find our train.

As expected, the hard-seat carriages were swamped with Chinese passengers. To avoid having both of us struggle through the packed aisles with our bags to search for the conductor, Helena happily agreed to wait with our packs near the doors while I waded through the sea of passengers to find him.

I moved unsteadily down the aisles as the train barreled along the tracks, trying not to step on anyone as I made my way from one hard-seat carriage to the next. It was tiring work and I was dripping with sweat and out of breath from the heat and smoke as I fought my way from car to car. When I reached the fourth carriage, I saw a man in a blue uniform at the far end of the corridor. He had his back to the wall and stood on a box, facing a frantic group of passengers who were busy waving tickets and money in his face as they tried to get his attention. The ticket clerk didn't seem distressed by the horde of flailing arms in front of him. He dealt with them calmly, on a random basis, choosing them one at a time as he saw fit. Like me, they were each trying to upgrade to a hard-sleeper for the night.

The aisle was packed with chain-smoking Chinese. I edged my way slowly past them and walked steadily toward the crowd in front of the ticket agent. Most Chinese outside the big cities were unfamiliar with foreigners and usually gave them a lot of leeway. When the mob in front of me saw me coming, they gave me curious looks and parted to let me by. I walked directly up to the ticket clerk and handed him my note. The passengers around me cast confused looks at one another and stood quietly by, trying to read the note over the clerk's shoulder.

When he finished reading my note, he locked his metal box and pushed a path through the crowd around him. He then turned and motioned for me to follow. We walked through three or four train cars until we reached the soft-sleeper carriages. The clerk stopped in front of the first compartment and knocked softly on the door. A few seconds later, the door slid open with a dull thud. Five men in white uniforms were playing cards inside the smoke-filled compartment. The clerk handed my note to the head conductor, a stocky, serious-faced man seated on the bottom berth.

The other men in the compartment signaled for me to step inside and take a seat. The conductor read the note and looked me over. He was the boss. There was no higher authority on the train. He would decide whether Helena and I spent the night sitting up in a crowded, smoke-filled car with overhead lights and music on all night long, or whether we slept in the quiet comfort of a six-bed compartment. I nodded respectfully and said "Nee-how"—*hello*. The men in the compartment were surprised to hear me say something in Chinese and laughed with approval.

The chief continued to scrutinize me. A few seconds later, he stood up and pulled down his sleeping chart. He located two empty berths and began to total up figures from a fare book. He wrote down the amount for the upgrade to hard-sleeper and showed it to me. I paid him for the beds and shook his hand to show my gratitude. I placed the upgraded tickets in my pocket and walked back through the length of the train to find Helena.

When I reached her, I noticed that her face was flushed and fatigued from standing in the hot car for so long. "We've got beds!" I cried jubilantly. She wiped her damp, blonde hair from her face with the back of her hand and let out a deep sigh. "Thank God!" she breathed with relief. She hoisted her pack on her shoulders and followed me to our berths.

When we entered the hard-sleeper car it was like entering a different world. The only people in the aisles were passengers returning to their compartments from the wash rooms at the end of the carriage. The overhead fans kept the air reasonably cool, and even though the compartments were open-ended, there was still a nice sense of privacy from the other passengers in the carriage. In any case, it was a blessing compared to the zoo we had just come from.

Helena took the middle berth below mine. A few minutes after we made up our berths, she was washed up and ready for bed. "Ohhh, this is great," she purred, as she stretched out in her bed. I knew how she felt. I was worn out from clawing my way back and forth through the packed train and couldn't wait to lie down. I climbed up to the top berth and dropped off to sleep as soon as my head hit the small foam pillow.

"Eric! Eric, wake up!" I opened my eyes and saw an arm shaking my mattress in the dimly lit compartment. I peered over the edge of my bed and saw Helena propped up on an elbow, pulling my mattress with her other hand. I looked at my watch. It was almost 1:00 A.M. I glanced out the window and noticed that the train had stopped at a station and was being boarded by passengers lined up on the platform outside. As I turned my attention back inside the compartment, I noticed a female ticket clerk and two Chinese passengers standing by the side of Helena's bunk. I looked down at Helena and asked wearily, "What's going on?"

Helena stuck her head out to face me. She nodded in the direction of the ticket clerk beside her berth and said, "This woman says we are at Suzhou."

"That's impossible. We're not supposed to get there till nine in the morning."

Helena waved her hand towards the window. "Well, she woke me to say this is Suzhou."

I looked at the man and woman standing next to the ticket woman. "Who are they?" I asked curiously.

"I don't know. I think they're waiting for our beds."

I pointed to the platform outside the window and looked at the ticket woman. "Suzhou?" I asked uncertainly.

She shook her head up and down vigorously. "*Xuzhou! Xuzhou!*" she answered.

It sounded like Suzhou but it was hard to tell. Just to make sure, I took my guide book and flipped to the section on Suzhou. I held the book out and pointed to the Chinese characters for Suzhou. I tapped the book and pointed out the window. "*Suzhou?*" I asked again.

The woman waved her hands over the guidebook and shook her head back and forth. Apparently, we weren't at Suzhou. She jabbed her finger toward the platform outside. "*Xuzhou!*" she said adamantly. She displayed the hard-seat tickets we had handed in when we first boarded the train. "*Xuzhou!*" she exclaimed, stabbing her finger at the tickets.

I still couldn't tell the difference between *Su*zhou and "*Xu*zhou," or whatever it was she was saying, but it was clear I had bought tickets to the wrong place—or, to be more precise, I had asked for two tickets to Suzhou, but was sold two tickets to Xuzhou. As far as I was concerned, the woman who had sold me the tickets made the mistake so I had no intention of getting off the train in Xuzhou.

Unable to communicate with us, and seeing that we had no plans to disembark the train, the ticket lady led the two Chinese passengers down the corridor to find other beds for them.

"What will happen now?" Helena asked with a worried look.

"I don't know. I just hope they don't wake us up again before we get to Suzhou."

A few minutes later, the train hiccupped a few times then chugged steadily away from the station. We waited nervously for the ticket woman to come back. Fifteen minutes later she still hadn't returned. We stopped waiting and went back to sleep.

I woke up early the next morning, but not as early as everyone else, apparently, as I had to wait on a long line for my turn in the bathroom. After washing up, Helena and I relaxed on the fold-down chairs near the windows in the corridor to read our books in the warm morning light. Half an hour later, the ticket lady returned. Planting herself in front of us, she chattered away in Chinese about something, then waited patiently for our response.

"What do you think she wants?" Helena asked.

"I have no idea," I replied, as the ticket lady and I exchanged blank-eyed looks.

When we didn't respond, she became even more vocal, aggravated that she wasn't having any more luck getting us to understand her than she had the night before. We looked at her helplessly as she babbled on, her frustration apparent in the rising pitch of her voice.

To our surprise, the other passengers in our compartment were enjoying the show immensely. In fact, everyone in the carriage seemed to be aware of our problem. The toilet was at our end of the train car and everyone who passed by to use it got an earful of the ticket lady. Helena and I seemed to be the only ones who had no idea what she was talking about.

Unable to take any more of the ticket woman's incessant prattling, I looked at her and said, "Wu bu dong"—*I don't understand.* The woman was stunned to hear me say something in Chinese. She stood there with her mouth open, suddenly speechless.

"Wu bu dong!" a skinny old man near the window echoed with pleasure. He shook his bald head up and down and roared with laughter.

By then, a small crowd of people had huddled around our compartment to see what all the commotion was about. The ticket lady was frustrated, we were frustrated, and no one around us could tell us what was going on. Then to everyone's surprise, a pleasant-looking Chinese woman in her late thirties stepped through the crowd of onlookers. "May I help you?" she asked politely. She told us she was an English teacher in Shanghai and wondered if we could use her assistance. It was as if someone had dropped her from heaven to rescue us.

Helena rushed over to her. "Yes—please!" With a nervous glance at the ticket woman, Helena asked, *"What is she talking about?"*

The English teacher smiled and stepped forward to speak with the ticket woman, who looked as relieved to have her help as we were. A few minutes later, the English teacher turned to Helena and me and explained the situation. "She says your tickets were for *Xuzhou* and not *Suzhou*. But you are staying on the train until Suzhou, so you must pay more money for the tickets."

I looked at the English teacher and laughed. *"That's* what this is all about? No problem. How much more do we owe?" I figured it couldn't be more than fifty or sixty Yuan. To show we were willing to settle the matter right on the spot, I pulled some Renminbi from my wallet and held them out. When the ticket lady saw my money, she blurted something to the teacher and pointed to my wallet.

The teacher said gently, "She says you must pay 276 Yuan. And because you are foreigners, you must pay in FEC money—not Renminbi."*

I was stunned. "How can that be? We only paid 34 Yuan for the hard-seat tickets—and I already paid another 120 Yuan last night when we switched from hard-seat to hard-sleeper. How can it be so much more money just to go from Xuzhou to Suzhou? And why do we have to pay in FEC when we paid with Renminbi for the hard-seat tickets?" The teacher translated my questions to the ticket woman.

There was some clucking and head nodding from the gallery of bystanders in the aisle who seemed to feel I had made some good points. After waiting for the ticket woman's reply, the teacher said, "She says you should not have been allowed to pay for the hard-seat tickets with Renminbi. You are foreigners and must pay with FEC."

The old man near the window scratched his chin and frowned as he pondered the facts, while the crowd in the corridor gazed curiously from the ticket lady to Helena and me as they waited for our response. I turned to Helena.

"Two hundred and seventy-six Yuan is way too much money. We

FEC—Foreign Exchange Certificates— the "official" money that all foreigners were supposed to use in China. In addition to looking different from *Renminbi*, the "people's money" used by the local Chinese, FEC was more expensive due to its lower exchange rate against the dollar. (The use of separate currencies for foreigners and locals has since been done away with, *Renminbi* being the only currency presently in use.)

already paid for our tickets up to wherever we were last night. I'm willing to pay them for using the beds from there to Suzhou, which I think is fair. But to all of a sudden start charging us more for the tickets because we're foreigners—and in FEC no less, is outrageous. Besides, the woman who sold me the tickets is really the cause of all this. I asked for *Suzhou* when I bought the tickets. It's not my fault she thought I said *Xuzhou*. What do you think?"

"I don't think it's fair either. In any case, I don't think we have enough FEC to pay them." She was right. We only had about 250 FEC between us. We agreed to hold our ground. I turned to the English teacher. "Please tell her we will be happy to pay the difference in price for the hard-sleeper tickets from Xuzhou to Suzhou—but only at the Chinese ticket price and only in Renminbi, since that's how we paid for our hard-seat tickets. We think this is fair."

The teacher listened patiently to the ticket woman's reply, then looked at Helena and me with concern. "She says you must pay the full price for the tickets—and only with FEC. These are the regulations. She understands what happened but there is nothing she can do. She wants to know—will you pay or not?" She then added, "If you do not pay you will be met by the Public Security Bureau when the train arrives in Suzhou." The Public Security Bureau was the official name for the Chinese Police.

I looked at Helena. "She's bluffing," I said hopefully. "Why would they go to so much trouble just to make us pay in FEC?"

"What if she's not bluffing?"

"Well . . . then what's the worst that can happen? If the police tell us to pay, then we'll pay. Trust me—there won't be any police waiting for us in Suzhou." I glanced at the ticket woman's impassive expression and whispered to Helena, "Look at her—she's definitely bluffing. Besides, how's she going to contact the police before we get to Suzhou. There's no way they have a telephone on this train. I'll bet she backs down and takes the Renminbi. Let's play it out and see what happens."

I smiled at the teacher and shrugged my shoulders like it was no big deal. "Please tell her we will only pay the local price for the tickets. And only with Renminbi."

The teacher translated our response. The Ticket woman blinked in surprise then pulled a walkie-talkie from her back pocket. She barked a few commands into it then turned abruptly on her heals and walked off. *Of course! How could I be so stupid*, I thought. The old walkie-talkie trick. So that's how she was going to contact the police. I hadn't thought of that.

After she left, the little crowd of passengers around us slowly dispersed, satisfied there was nothing more to hear. I turned to the teacher. "Do you think she's serious about the police?"

"Oh, yes. They will be waiting for you in Suzhou," she replied confidently. After a quick glance at her watch, she said, "We will arrive in ten minutes. I must go back to my compartment and pack my things. I wish you good luck and a pleasant stay in China." She smiled and walked back to her compartment at the far end of the carriage.

Helena and I packed our stuff and sat wordlessly by the windows, eating a light breakfast of tea and tangerines. I squinted into the bright sunlight that filled the corridor and savored the sweetness of the small tangerine as I watched the trees speed by the window outside the train.

Ten minutes later, the train began to slow down. We were arriving in Suzhou. All the passengers jumped up at once and grabbed their bags from the overhead luggage racks in the corridor. With their luggage in hand, they shuffled noisily toward the exit doors at both ends of the carriage.

After another minute or two, the train squealed to a stop. Helena and I lifted our backpacks from our beds and followed the other passengers down the corridor. As we approached the exit, we saw the ticket lady standing on the platform next to two uniformed policemen. They were waiting for us. Helena looked nervous. With an apologetic grin, I shrugged and said, "I guess she wasn't bluffing."

The two policemen looked skinny and frail in their oversized, ill-fitting, green uniforms, and were a lot less threatening looking than I had imagined. We stepped off the train and stood in front of the policemen like fugitives who had no choice but to give themselves up.

Satisfied that the matter was in the hands of the Public Security Bureau, the ticket lady climbed back on board and disappeared down the corridor. The policemen looked at each other, then nodded to Helena and me, indicating that we should follow them.

The Public Security Bureau office was inside the station just to the left of the exits. The door was open and we followed the officers inside. Three men and one woman, each dressed in the same shabby uniforms as our escorts, stood around a small, dimly-lit outer office. I whispered to Helena, "If there's a top-ten list of the worst dressed policemen in the world, these people are on it."

The female officer pointed to a corner of the office for us to place our backpacks. One of the men then brought over two chairs so we could sit down. When we were seated, the woman handed Helena and me a cup of tea. To our surprise, we were being treated like guests who had dropped by unexpectedly for a tour of a Chinese police office.

We drank our tea and patiently waited for something to happen. Shortly after helping ourselves to a second serving, another woman instructed us to follow her down a short hallway to an office on the left side of the hall. Both of the women, and one of the policemen who had walked us from the train, stood around a large, wooden desk at the back of the room. No one spoke English. They looked at us and smiled, then spoke among themselves while Helena and I exchanged curious looks, each of us silently wondering what was going on.

"They don't speak English," I whispered to Helena. "How are they going to ask us anything?" Before she could reply, a black telephone on the edge of the desk started to ring. One of the women lifted the receiver from its cradle. After a few brief words and a nod of her head, she held the receiver in our direction. Helena was closest to the desk, so she walked over and took the phone from the woman. She held the receiver to her ear with both hands. "*Hello?*" she asked curiously.

Helena stood in front of the desk and listened to the person at the other end of the line while the rest of us waited. "Yes . . . Yes . . . to Suzhou," Helena said courteously. "No, that will be fine. Okay, hold on. Thank you." She handed the phone to the woman behind the desk. The woman said something in Chinese to the mysterious voice on the other end of the line, then placed the receiver back on its cradle.

Helena sat back down beside me. "Who was that?" I asked curiously.

"I don't know. But she knew why we were here. Her English was very good too. She said we will have to pay 40 Yuan to make up for the difference in price for our tickets from Xuzhou to Suzhou."

"*That's all? Only 40 Yuan? How can it be so little?*"

She shrugged. "I don't know. She asked me if this price was all right and I told her yes. Then she asked to speak to the woman again. That was it."

I was astonished. I thought for sure we were going to have to pay more—a lot more. But they only charged us the local rate for the difference in price from Xuzhou to Suzhou—and only for hard-seat, not hard-sleeper. The thing that surprised me most, though, was that they let us pay the extra 40 Yuan with Renminbi and not FEC.

What we thought was going to be a horrendous bureaucratic mess turned out to be a fairly pleasant experience. We had some tea, saw the inside of a Public Security Bureau Office, and got to meet some friendly Chinese police. Plus, we wound up getting a bargain price for the train to Suzhou. All in all, our little brush with the law was worth it.

We said, "*Shei, Shei*"—thank you, to everyone in the room, retrieved our packs from the outer office, and strolled out of the station to the quiet, tree-lined streets of Suzhou.

This defeat has taught me a lesson, but I'm not sure what it is.
—John McEnroe

We heard the shout before we saw who it came from. "Helena! You made it!"

Before she knew what hit her, Helena was being hugged and twirled around the lobby of the *Pujiang Hotel*, the large, old, majestic building where most backpackers stayed in Shanghai.

As soon as she got her breath back, Helena introduced me to Lars and Britt, the two friends from Sweden that she had planned to meet up with in Shanghai. They had arrived a few days before us and had been waiting for her to show up.

Lars laughed and shook my hand when Helena introduced us. "So *you're* the unlucky bastard who's had to put up with her all this time, eh? Where are you two coming from?"

"Suzhou. We just came in from the train station," I replied to the ebullient Swede in front of me.

"Never heard of the damn place. Nice?"

"Terrific. Great gardens, nice people and a really laid back town. A great place to relax away from the big cities. What's Shanghai like?"

"Bloody hot! My wife doesn't even want to go outside, it's so damn hot." He nodded toward Britt and laughed. Helena and Britt were busy talking a mile a minute about their travels while Lars filled me in on what he and his wife had seen in Shanghai.

Lars was an outgoing, fun-loving guy with a great sense of humor and an infectious laugh. He had shaved his head when he arrived in China, which surprisingly, made him even more likeable. Anyone that unselfconscious had to be a nice guy. His wife, Britt, was an attractive brunette with long, straight hair that reached the middle of her back. She was gentler and more soft-spoken than Lars—the perfect balance to his high-energy nature.

They were a terrific couple and we hit it off right away. From the moment we met, they included me in everything they and Helena did together and we became fast friends during our week together in Shanghai. Taking advantage of a break in Helena's and Britt's conversation, Lars said, "Come on, let's get you two checked in. Then we can go for lunch. I haven't had a thing to eat yet and I'm starved!"

Lars wasn't kidding when he said it was hot. The stifling heat and humidity in Shanghai was exhausting and seemed to get hotter every day. If there hadn't been a huge air-conditioner in the sixteen-bed dorm room I checked into, it would have been an unbearable week.

If the heat wave bothered the locals, though, they didn't show it. Aside from the occasional flick of small paper fans in front of their faces, the thick air didn't seem to slow them down much. They dashed through the busy streets dodging bicycles and push carts and went about their business without breaking a sweat. It was the foreigners who melted on the wide, concrete streets of Shanghai from the oppressive heat and humidity. If it weren't for the line of refreshment stands selling sodas and ice creams along the streets, we wouldn't have lasted more than an hour without collapsing.

By noon, the temperature usually hit 100° Fahrenheit, and often climbed to 104° or higher, before leveling off for the day. It was only at night, when the temperature dipped back down to the mid-80's or low 90's, that it wasn't painful to be outside.

To find relief from their small, sweat-box living quarters, most of the local Chinese put reclining chairs and cots on the sidewalks outside their homes in order to cool off at night. The elderly people sat on the street and listened to their radios or played with their grandchildren. The young, married couples talked amiably with their friends and next-door neighbors, while groups of young men played loud, boisterous card games late into the night. The hot summer evenings in Shanghai were like one huge block party and were a great time to wander around the streets and people-watch.

One evening, after our nightly stroll through the residential neighborhoods of the city, I suggested that we go for drinks at an outdoor bar near the harbor. Lars checked his watch. "We don't have the time, I'm afraid. We're due back at the hotel in half an hour."

I was surprised they'd made plans without me, and asked Lars curiously, "What's going on back at the hotel?" Helena and Britt looked as surprised as I was.

Lars grinned at me. "You and I have plans, my friend. I challenged one of the Chinese blokes who works at the *Pujiang* to a match of Ping-Pong. You and I are going to play doubles against him and his friend."

"Are you out of your mind?" I protested. "The Chinese are born with Ping-Pong paddles in their hands—we'll get killed."

"I hope not," Lars laughed. "The only reason they're willing to play us is because I said we would teach them how the game is supposed to be played."

"I didn't know you were such a good Ping-Pong player," I said with admiration.

"I'm not," Lars grinned. "But I was hoping you were. That's why I challenged them to a game of doubles. You can play, can't you? Because I told them my American friend thinks he can beat anyone in the hotel." Seeing the shocked look on my face, he let out a big laugh.

"Please tell me there's no money riding on this match," I asked nervously.

"Nah, it's just a fun match. Come on," he said, leading the way back.

When we arrived at the hotel, Lars strolled across the lobby to a young Chinese man dressed in a white uniform. When he saw Lars, he smiled and looked around to make sure none of the other staff was around. "Wait here," the Chinese man said quietly, before walking quickly down the hallway and into the kitchen.

A few minutes later, he returned with a friend. The second man was older—in his late forties or early fifties, and didn't speak any English. The younger man whistled to Lars and me. "Come, quickly," he whispered. Lars and I exchanged confused looks and followed them up the stairs. When we reached the second floor, we went down a wide, carpeted hallway to a door halfway down the hall. The door was locked. The young guy said something in Chinese to his friend and then ran down the hall and up the stairs.

Within minutes, he came bounding back down the stairs. In addition to the key, he had brought a young Chinese woman who was dressed in a red hotel uniform with him. "Foreigners not supposed to be up here," he explained, as he unlocked the door. "But is okay. Not worry," he assured us with a smile. When the door was opened, he stepped inside and turned on the lights.

We followed him into a big, square room with heavy, red drapes over the windows. In the center of the room stood a large, rectangular table, covered by a long, green, drop-cloth. The girl closed the door as the two men removed the heavy cloth, revealing a green Ping-Pong table underneath.

The young woman bent down and took a folded Ping-Pong net from beneath the table. Fastening the net's metal hinges on both sides of the table, she made sure the net was straight before tightening the screws to hold it in place. After the net was set up, the young Chinese man looked over at Lars with a big smile and said, "Okay?"

"Looks great!" Lars said. Then added, "I see you brought your girlfriend to help out, eh?"

"No, no. Not girlfriend. She referee."

I looked at Lars. "Referee? Why do we need a referee?" I whispered. "Are you sure there's no money on this match?"

Lars shrugged in answer and picked up one of the paddles that the young woman had placed on the table. Lar's Chinese friend picked up a paddle and tossed Lars an eggshell colored Ping-Pong ball. "First we warm up. Then we play," he said. The older Chinese man and I each took a paddle from the table and got into position on opposite sides of the table.

Lars and I stood across the table from our two Chinese opponents. They were holding their paddles upside down and were crouched in a low stance on the opposite side of the table, waiting for Lars to serve the ball. I shook my head and thought, *Oh God, we're going to get killed.*

Lars served the ball to the older man, who tapped it gently back over the net to me. I hit it to the young guy who then hit it to Lars. We hit the ball back and forth to one another for a few minutes to warm up. After everyone felt ready, we stopped volleying and got set to start the match. I relaxed and thought, *Hey, they're not that good. Maybe we can take these guys. Just because they're Chinese doesn't mean they're good at Ping-Pong.*

Lars tossed the ball in the air and hit the first serve of the game. He served the ball to the older man directly opposite me. *Smack!* The man smashed the little ball back over the net like a bullet. *Whoosh!* Lars and I swung at it and missed. The Chinese girl in the corner held up a finger. One nothing, their favor.

Lars tossed the ball in the air again and hit his second serve. *Whap!* The little ball whizzed by my ear after a solid crack on my end of the table. The Chinese girl held up a second finger.

"We'd better come up with a strategy pretty quickly," Lars remarked.

"How's this for a plan—let's try to get the ball back on their side of the table," I suggested.

"Right!" Lars agreed, as the third return went flying past our heads. Lars frowned. "Any other ideas? That one's not working very well." The girl held up a third finger.

"Maybe we can pay off the referee," I suggested. *Whack!* Fourth finger up in the air.

It was pretty much down hill from there. The young guy wasn't bad, but his older friend was incredible. Neither of us could return his shots. Whenever we served to him, he smashed the ball back over the net with such force that we had to duck to get out of its way. And when he served, the ball would spin wildly off our rackets whenever we were lucky enough to make contact with it. The ball sliced and curved and twisted like it had a mind of its own. And if, by some fluke, we were fortunate enough to return it over the net, one or the other of our Chinese opponents would smash it back across the table for the point.

After an hour's play in the un-airconditioned room, we were all drenched and ready to call it quits. Our two opponents also had to go back to work. Lars and I helped them roll up the net and spread the cloth cover neatly over the table before leaving the room.

"Where did he learn to play like that?" I asked the younger one, as he and his friend escorted us downstairs to the lobby.

He laughed and clapped his friend on the shoulder. "He very good. Play long time." That was a major understatement. He was probably handed a paddle before he was toilet-trained.

Lars and I thanked our friendly opponents for the games and went back to the dorm to shower before going to bed. On our way to the room we passed Helena and Britt in the hallway. When they saw how sweated up we were, Helena asked with a quizzical look, "So, how did you do?"

Lars answered her in English so I could hear his response. "Well, it was pretty close there for awhile, but being guests in their country, you know . . . we thought it was only fair to let them win." With a smile and a knowing look at Britt, Helena laughed and shook her head. "That was nice of you. I'm sure they appreciated it."

Other than some good restaurants, and an appreciation of its Western-style architecture, Shanghai didn't offer much in the way of sights, so by early the following week I was ready to move on. I had been in

China for almost a month and felt I needed a dose of the modern world again so I booked a ticket on a passenger ferry to Japan for that coming weekend.

Lars, Britt, and Helena were also planning to leave. They booked themselves on the next week's ferry to Hong Kong, where they planned to relax for a week or so before traveling on to Malaysia and Indonesia. Helena had signed up for a language course in Indonesia as part of her University studies in Sweden and didn't plan on returning home for another six to nine months, while Lars and Britt were hoping to spend a few months in New Zealand after Malaysia before returning to Sweden.

On the morning of my departure, Helena, Lars and Britt walked me to the International Passenger Terminal to see me off. The modern, white, Japanese ferry was moored behind the Passenger Terminal along the Huangpu River. As soon as we stepped into the small waiting hall I felt like I was re-entering familiar territory. The ticket attendants, customs personnel, and even the atmosphere of the waiting hall itself, seemed different and more modern than the Chinese world just outside the open doorway of the waiting room.

When it was time to board the ship, I said goodbye to Lars and Britt. They gave me the address of a post office in Malaysia where I could contact them if I made it that far, and promised to write me when they had an address in New Zealand. Helena stood quietly by their side and waited for me to say goodbye.

"Lars tells me you have a birthday coming up this week?" I said. "Yes. I'm going to be twenty-seven. I'm getting so old! Not as old as you—but old," she laughed.

When all of the passengers ahead of me had been cleared through customs, I gave Helena a big hug and slung my backpack on my shoulder. "Well, I guess this is it," I said. "Have a great time in Indonesia. And have a great birthday. I'm sorry I won't be here to share it with you."

She smiled and gave me a kiss goodbye. "Take care of yourself," she said.

After a final wave goodbye, she walked out of the passenger terminal with Lars and Britt. I watched the three of them leave the sanctuary of the waiting hall for the brutal heat outside, then lined up behind the other passengers to board the ferry to Japan.

Uno House

Birds of a Feather

An Unhappy Traveler

Laugh and the world laughs with you, snore and you sleep alone.
— Anthony Burgess

"*Uno house!*" snapped a European voice on the phone.

"I was wondering if you've got any beds available?" I asked, surprised at hearing a European answer the phone at a Japanese guesthouse.

"How many people?"

"Just myself."

"Hold on, let me check." A few seconds later, he returned to the phone. "There are some dorm beds still available. Where are you calling from?"

"Kyoto train station. I just got in."

"No problem. Come on by."

Half an hour later, I hopped off a local bus and walked down a quiet lane lined with small, two-story, wooden houses. *Uno House* was halfway up the lane on the left side of the street. I placed my sneakers in an empty wooden cubicle near the door then stepped through a narrow foyer into a small kitchen where several Europeans and Australians were having lunch and watching a Japanese TV program.

"Can someone tell me who to see about getting a bed?" I asked, to no one in particular.

A British girl who was washing dishes at the sink pointed a soapy finger to the hallway outside the kitchen. "Go straight through there and look for a Japanese fellow in a yellow shirt. He'll help you out." Five minutes later, I was set up in a small dorm room at the rear of the house.

Uno House was a typical "Gaijan House," an inexpensive guesthouse for foreigners. Compared to other accommodations in Japan, Gaijan Houses were cheap and a good place to meet other backpackers. But like everything else in life, you get what you pay for. And what I got for thirteen dollars a night was a tatami mat and a pillow in a small dormitory room with five other people—two of whom were lucky enough to have gotten a bunk-bed near the wall. I had paid for the privilege of sharing the hard wooden floor with three other people. And judging by the size of the room, it looked like we were going to be sleeping shoulder to shoulder. What surprised me though, was that it could have been worse. In the main room on our left, fourteen tatami mats were laid out side by side, stretching from one end of the floor to the other.

What concerned me even more than the cramped living quarters, however, were the mosquitoes. When I surveyed the room, I spotted squashed mosquitoes all along the walls and knew right away that the nights in *Uno House* were not going to be pleasant. Fortunately, I had packed a portable mosquito net before I had left New York. It was a little embarrassing to use, however, since it looked like a small igloo when it was assembled. But it was better than being eaten alive all night. I pulled the net from my backpack and tossed it on my tatami mat. I hoped I wouldn't need it, but wanted to have it available just in case.

When I returned to the room that evening, the other four people were fast asleep. Not wanting to wake them, I tiptoed around the room and got undressed in the dark. Just before I stretched out on the floor, I heard a mosquito buzzing around my head. Less than a minute later, it bit me on the leg. I pulled out my pocket flashlight and set up my portable net as fast as I could.

I attached the thin, fiberglass poles together and slipped them through the ends of the net. When the poles were secured I placed the assembled tent on top of the tatami mat, trying not to disturb the two people sleeping on the floor on either side of me.

Before I could slide beneath the net, several aggressive mosquitoes landed on my neck and arms. I swatted at them in the dark and ducked quickly under cover. Fully protected under my little tent, I pitied my poor floormates who slept exposed to the little blood suckers buzzing around their heads. I closed my eyes and smiled in relief, confident I would get a good night's sleep.

Not long after I fell asleep, I felt the floor vibrate heavily beneath me. "BAM! BAM! BAM! BAM!" The floorboards shook on both sides of me, less than two inches from my head. I lurched up and banged my head against the top of my mosquito tent. "Hey, what's going on?" I blurted in a daze.

The room was pitch-black and it was hard to see through the mesh netting around my head. All of a sudden, an enraged voice boomed so close to my head that it vibrated the netting near my ear. In a barely controlled voice that was ready to go berserk at any minute, the person on the left of me seethed, *"You're snoring! It's driving me crazy!"*

I realized what the pounding had been. My floormate had been slamming the floor near my tent to wake me up. "Oh . . . sorry," I said, slightly embarrassed. I took a deep breath and tried to relax as I lay back down on my mat. I turned on my stomach so I wouldn't snore, then closed my eyes and went back to sleep.

"BAM! BAM! BAM! BAM! BAM! BAM!" came the pounding again in the middle of the night. I realized I was on my back again. I turned myself over and waited for the pounding to stop. When the banging stopped, I dozed back off again.

After a fitful night's sleep, I crawled out from my net in the sun-filled room and noticed that the floor around me was empty. I looked around with surprise and wondered whether the banging during the night had just been a bad dream. Then I heard someone laughing from the top bunk on the left side of the room. "They left during the night," he said with a huge grin. Seeing the confused look on my face he added with a chuckle, "Your snoring drove them out."

"Yeah . . . sorry about that," I muttered. "My allergies have been bothering me and I snore when I get stuffed up."

He laughed again. "Actually, your snoring didn't wake me. It was the German guy pounding on the floor next to you that woke me up!" He swung his legs over the side of his bunk and slapped his knee with delight. "Man, was he furious! It was the funniest thing I ever saw! You'd be snoring away and he would start pounding the floor next to your little tent until you shut up. Then you'd start in all over again a few minutes later and he'd start pounding again. The guy was a real asshole." I nodded in agreement, remembering how angry he had been.

"But the best part . . . " He tried not to laugh, but couldn't help it. "The best part was when he started shaking your little house there.

The whole thing was rocking back and forth and everyone in the room woke up except you! I thought for sure that guy was gonna flatten your igloo, or whatever that thing is. Oh man, was it funny."

"Well I'm glad you had a good time," I laughed, "because I sure didn't. Hopefully it won't be as bad tonight," I said.

"Ahh . . . screw them," he said sympathetically. "It's not your fault you snore. It's their problem. What do they expect when they share a dorm room—that no one's going to snore? Let them pay for a private room if it's going to bother them so much."

When I returned to the room later that night, I dreaded a repeat of the previous evening. But to my pleasant surprise, my snoring must have driven my floormates out of *Uno House* altogether, because after the first evening I never saw either of them again.

The next few days in Kyoto were pleasant enough, but despite my best efforts to see what Kyoto had to offer, I couldn't understand why everyone was so in love with the place. To me, it looked like most other modern cities. Assuming that its magic would be found in its historic sights, I dutifully visited as many different temples, shrines, and palaces as I could. They were nice, but I didn't see what all the fuss was about.

In an attempt to explore the city further, I rented a bicycle and spent the next two days riding around the residential districts in a search of the "real" Japan. But it was hard to find—at least on the surface. From the outside looking in, Kyoto was a modern city that had been built up around its old temples and shrines. It was an attractive city, magnificently maintained and with a tradition and reverence for the past. But all the same, it was modern on the outside. To me, the real Kyoto was different from what I had imagined I would find.

It was only when I walked around the old-style homes in Kyoto's Gion District one night, and spotted two of the elusive, white-powdered Geisha women, clip-clopping along the streets on their elevated wooden sandals, that I felt I had glimpsed a part of the old Japan I had expected to see everywhere in Kyoto. Basically, I was looking for a Japan that didn't exist anymore—at least not on the outside, anyway.

Over the next few weeks, I came to realize that Japan was like a book. To the casual observer like myself, all that could be seen was its modern cover. The real Japan was hidden safely beneath this modern exterior and still permeated most aspects of Japanese life. But without an insider's view of the cultural nuances and traditions that still played a role in the lives of the Japanese people, it was hard for an outsider to read.

It was only after I had left Japan that I discovered how accurate my initial impressions of Kyoto had actually been. A travel book entitled, *Japan: Land of Myths and Legends* offered the following description of Kyoto:

> When in the West we speak of a 'beautiful city,' we often have in our minds a place which, viewed from some point of vantage, presents a pleasing overall prospect. Kyoto is not like that at all. If your first sight of Kyoto is from the platform where the bullet train deposits you, its superficial ugliness can move you to despair . . . Kyoto's beauty is elusive and has to be sought out with patience and forethought.
>
> . . . Part of the beauty of the great monuments of Nara lies in the impression of strength they convey. But the private, elusive beauty of Kyoto is far less vigorous a thing, and it is easily spoiled. Talk too loud, look too hard, think too much, and it is gone.

Most visitors to Japan love Kyoto because it's as close as you can get to the real Japan. But whatever the reason, I just didn't see it while I was there. For me, it was a pleasant place to visit but it didn't hold any special magic. Maybe I just looked too hard.

The nail that sticks up gets hammered down.
                                  —Japanese Proverb

Instead of taking the *Shinkansen*—the super-fast "bullet" train—from Kyoto to Tokyo, I took the less expensive and slower moving Japan Railway (JR). The *Shinkansen* would have cut the eight-hour trip in half but I didn't want to see the countryside at 168 miles per hour. The standard JR was good enough. It was clean, comfortable, and quiet. So quiet in fact, that I almost couldn't stand it. It was like sitting in a library. Almost no one talked. And when they did, it was in soft, hushed tones. Everyone seemed so controlled. The only time there was any sense of life on the train was when a group of high school girls piled on. But even their giggling and sporadic comments seemed restrained and reserved.

Without much to focus on inside the train, I turned my attention outside the window and watched the mountains and green, low-rising hills trickle slowly by in the distance. The countryside was clean and peaceful and dotted with homes and small towns that were built along the base of the hills and the valleys between. There wasn't much undeveloped land, and the closer we got to Tokyo the more congested the landscape, and the train, became. About twenty minutes outside of Tokyo, the train began to fill with passengers. At each successive stop, more and more people slipped silently inside. By the time we arrived at Tokyo's Central Station, the train was packed.

I stepped off the train onto a spotless platform crowded with blue-suited Japanese men and nicely dressed women. After everything I had heard about the overly crowded stations in Tokyo, I expected to find myself in a maze of confusion, lost in an unfamiliar and bewildering environment. Instead, I entered a well-organized, beautiful station that was easy to navigate and user-friendly to foreigners. Not only were there easy to follow and useful signs in English, there were helpful tourist information centers and telephone help-lines to make traveling in Tokyo, and throughout Japan, as hassle-free as possible. In addition, the station was lined with stores and shops filled with a variety of artfully displayed merchandise where passengers could make last minute purchases before boarding their train. The station was so clean and modern looking that it seemed more like an underground mall than a train station. And like most big metropolitan cities with a lot to offer, Tokyo was an easy city to keep occupied in after you arrived.

I spent my mornings wandering around temples and parks and the afternoons exploring the high-class department stores where kimono-wrapped hostesses greeted each new customer with a courteous smile and a bow—the perfect complement to the enormous selection of exquisitely wrapped packages and exotic food products inside.

In the evenings I strolled along Tokyo's neon-lit streets, stopping occasionally into one of the noisy video arcades and Pachinko Parlors that lined every sidewalk, to watch the Japanese gamble the night away in long, brightly-lit, smoke-filled rooms. Well-dressed, stoic-faced businessmen sat like automatons in front of vertical pinball machines for hours at a time, amassing huge buckets of small silver balls that they redeemed for prizes, which they then redeemed for cash—a clever set-up for circumventing the laws which forbid gambling directly for money.

Every now and then I splurged for a drink at one of the many nightclubs in Repongi or Shinjuku, two of Tokyo's most popular entertainment districts. The bars in Tokyo were like most clubs in any major city—dark, dimly-lit places with blaring music and the usual assortment of bar-flies who sit, smoke, and idly drink the night away until last call is announced and they have to head home.

Tokyo was an interesting place to spend some time, but after awhile, the crowded streets, glass-enclosed office buildings, neon-colored arcades, and ubiquitous, blue-suited businessmen started to get to me. I was anxious to find a city in Japan that wasn't so high-tech and super-modern. I wanted to find a place where there were no Pachinko Parlors and no vending machines that sold everything from beer and sex toys to vitamins and hamburgers—a place where the Japanese still lived the same way they had lived for generations.

A search of my guidebook revealed just what I was looking for—

Kurashiki and *Tsumago*—two secluded little towns a few hours north of Tokyo, off the main railway at the foot of the mountains. Both towns were described as places where visitors could step back a hundred years and experience the old Japan. They sounded perfect. Until I got there.

In *Tsumago*, I had hoped to find a secluded, out-of-the-way, mountain village where the Japanese still clung to their old culture, untouched by the modern world. What I found was a major tourist spot where even the Japanese went to see what life was like in the old days. Large groups of Japanese families wandered up and down the narrow lanes of the recreated village of *Tsumago*, gazing at the preserved wooden houses and old merchant shops along the streets, as if they were tourists in a foreign land. When they were done gaping at the renovated houses and shops, they strolled into the little souvenir stalls with the rest of the tourists to take a part of the old Japan back home with them. *Tsumago* was a pleasant side trip from Tokyo but, unfortunately, it wasn't the traditional Japanese city I had hoped to find.

It was no different in *Kurashiki*. Instead of finding a place where I could "step back a hundred years and experience the old Japan," I followed groups of camera-toting Japanese men and women through a secluded old section of *Kurashiki* that had been preserved as an historic area.

I was quickly discovering that the "old" Japan could only be seen in re-created villages or historic locations set up specifically for local and international tourists. Present day Japan was ultra-modern and immaculately clean. And aside from a few unique-looking temples or parks, like the one in *Nara* where deer ate out of the hands of visitors, every city in Japan was practically inter-changeable with every other.

When I arrived back in Tokyo, an American who had traveled all across Japan told me, "Once you've seen a few Japanese cities, you've seen them all." If Honshu, Japan's main island, was representative of other Japanese cities, then I had to agree.

I had read somewhere that most of the cities in Japan resembled one another because many of them had been built over the past forty years and used the same "cookie-cutter" approach to building design and city planning when the country was modernized after World War II. However, after speaking with a number of foreigners who had lived and worked in Japan, I began to suspect that there was also a cultural reason why their cities looked so similar.

A Canadian who had been teaching English in Japan for over a year told me that Japanese society didn't encourage individuality. "There's a group-think mentality in their culture," he explained. "The group means everything in Japan and affects every part of their lives, from family and friends, to relationships at work. Most Japanese feel the need to blend in with everyone else. Their goal in life is to look the same, behave the same, and live the same." If what he said was true, it was no wonder every city looked identical.

I mentioned what the Canadian had told me to two British girls I had met on a train. "It's true," they agreed. "I'll give you an example," one of them offered. "I don't know if you know this but the Japanese are a pretty racist people. To the Japanese, all non-Japanese are *Gaijin*—foreigners—and are considered inferior. And black people have always been viewed even less favorably than whites in Japan.

"Anyway," she continued, "I started to see more and more Japanese girls dating black men, which I thought was unusual, given their attitudes towards blacks. When I asked a Japanese girlfriend of mine why Japanese girls were suddenly so hot on black guys, she laughed and told me it was because Rap Music is now popular in Japan. That was her explanation. Rap Music is popular, most Rap Artists are black, so black people are now okay. Suddenly it's cool to have a black boyfriend, and all the Japanese girls want one."

Her friend added, "They all do what the others do. They think much differently than Westerners, so it's hard to understand their ways if you haven't lived here awhile. You've got to learn to read between the lines because most of the time they won't come right out and say what they mean. It's hard for us because we're used to people saying what they think. But what the Japanese don't say is sometimes more important than what they do say. It just takes a bit of getting used to. I've been here almost a year and a half and I'm still not used to it. After you've lived here awhile you'll see what we mean."

I laughed and said, "I think I'll take your word for it. Japan's a pretty expensive country to travel in, so I don't think I'll be here long enough to find out."

In two weeks time, I had raced through half a dozen Japanese cities and spent more money than I had originally intended. It would have been interesting to see some of the other islands in Japan, but I couldn't afford it this time around. Besides, I still wanted to see one more city before I left Honshu—the first city in the history of the world to feel the effects of a nuclear bomb. Hiroshima.

*The two best things about traveling are arriving in a new city
and leaving it.*

— Andrew B.

"Mind if I sit here?" I asked the two people seated at the table in front of me. It was my second night at the Hiroshima International Youth Hostel and I decided to splurge for a home-cooked meal in the hostel dining room instead of walking down the hill to find something to eat.

The person closest to me lifted his head from his plate. "No, not at all. Go right ahead," he said in a British accent. The second person was Japanese. I had caught him with his mouth full of rice, so he indicated his consent with a tilt of his chopsticks toward the unoccupied chair beside him.

Meals at the hostel were served cafeteria-style. Guests who had paid for meal coupons handed them to the cooks at the kitchen counter in exchange for their meal. The food that evening was shrimp tempura and was served with a bowl of soup and a side of vegetables. A huge metal pot of rice, as well as pitchers of water and green tea, were made available on long tables that had been set up in the middle of the large, square dining room.

Not long after I sat down, the Japanese man finished his meal and walked off. Left alone at the table, the British guy and I introduced ourselves and filled each other in on where we had traveled before arriving in Hiroshima.

His name was Andrew and he told me he was a twenty-eight year old entertainment lawyer who worked for a prestigious London law firm that represented famous rock stars. He was on a three-month sabbatical from work and had been traveling for less than a month. As he told me about himself, there was a hint of sadness about him that I couldn't put my finger on. It sounded like he had an interesting job back home and had been fortunate enough to get a sabbatical to travel, so I couldn't understand why he didn't seem happier. At first I thought he just wasn't thrilled with Japan. But slowly, he started to open up and give an explanation for his lack of enthusiasm.

Spearing one of his shrimp with a chopstick, he said, "Every time I tell someone I represent rock stars they think I've got this brilliant job. But it really isn't all that brilliant. I mean, these guys are all sitting around these massive conference tables in blue jeans and running shoes while I'm doing this incredibly boring job—all the while trying to be serious, and wishing I could be dressed like them instead of in my bloody suit."

He frowned and took a bite of his shrimp. "But instead, I have to pick over every word in their contracts and act as though it's all terribly important. And they don't really give a shit, do they? And when I thought about it, neither did I. That was when I realized I wasn't happy with my work. So I asked for a leave of absence for a few months. I told them I wanted to travel."

Without any prompting he added, "You see . . . I had traveled for about six months a few years ago and had a great time. I was really happy when I was traveling. So I thought that if I traveled I would be happy again. But the closer the date came for me to leave, the more I realized I didn't want to travel. I just needed something else to look forward to while I was at work and not wanting to be there."

When he paused to take another bite of his shrimp I asked, "So why didn't you just stay at home and look for something else to do that you liked better?"

He speared another shrimp with his chopstick. "Well, that's the thing, you see. After telling everyone I was going off to travel, I felt I had to go. So here I am." He leaned back in his seat with an embarrassed frown, looking about as lifeless as his speared Shrimp Tempura.

I was at a loss for what to say. It sounded like he wanted some advice to help him sort things out but I didn't want to say anything without giving it some thought. I sat there thinking of a reply while Andrew went off to buy us some beers from the vending machine in the lobby. When the kitchen staff began to clean up around us, we decided to continue our conversation on the front porch of the hostel.

We sat outside in the warm summer air, listening to the crickets and drinking our beers. As I gazed at the wooded hillside below the hostel, and breathed in the pine-scented evening air, I felt an incredible sense of satisfaction. Everyone I knew at home was busy working and going through their same old day-to-day routines while I was relaxing on a hillside drinking a beer in Hiroshima, Japan. I thought about how lucky I was to be traveling and seeing the world.

As I reflected on my good fortune, I realized what Andrew's problem was. He wasn't focused on his trip. He was going through the motions physically, but mentally he wasn't into it. He needed to change his attitude. I took a sip from my tall silver can of *Asahi* beer and offered him my perspective on his problem.

"Look, Andrew—no one can tell you what to do about your job. You're the only one who can decide whether or not you like your work. If you really hate it, you should try exploring other things. And even though you studied to be a lawyer, there are probably lots of other ways you can use your background and experience to do things you find more interesting. Or you can try something completely different. Sooner or later you're bound to find something to be passionate about. In any case, unless you've decided that you'd rather be back in London, you should focus on the fact that since you're already here, you should try to make the best of it. You may have gone off traveling for the wrong reasons, but I think you can get at least three good things out of your trip."

Andrew tapped his beer can nervously and leaned back on his elbows. "Such as?" he asked, uncertainly.

"Well, to begin with," I said, "you'll probably get a more objective perspective on things while traveling than if you had stayed in London. Maybe the time away will help you sort things out. A second benefit might be that opportunities could come up while you're traveling that might not be available at home. Who knows—you might meet people and see things while you're traveling that will change your life." I looked at him to see if any of my points were hitting home.

"You've only mentioned two reasons. You said there were three," he laughed.

"Well, the last thing—which I think is the best reason of all, is that you've got the chance to do something most people never get to do. You've got your whole life to work and somewhere along the way, you'll figure out what you want to do. But it may be really hard for you to get the time to travel for three months again. So why not enjoy it while you can?" I drank the rest of my beer and waited for his reaction.

Andrew leaned forward and sighed. "Well, that's the strange thing, you see. I do enjoy traveling. But only until I get to where I'm going. Then when I'm there, I can't wait to leave and go to the next place. The part I like best, I think, is just having something to look forward to. But once that's over, I'm not happy anymore and need something else to look forward to again."

"It's the same thing with girls," he added with a sad smile. "Whenever I meet a new girl, I'm crazy about her and think about her all the time. Then, after we've been going together awhile, I get bored and can't wait to meet someone else." He sat back and frowned.

I shrugged and said, "It sounds like you're afraid to make a commitment. Which is why you only go after short-term goals. Once you arrive in a new place or win over a new girl your goal is accomplished. You're then left without any goals until you pick a new place to go to or find another girl to go after." He nodded slowly, seeming to think I had made a good observation.

I wanted to end the conversation on a positive note so I added, "I think the only thing you really need to find is a worthwhile long-term goal. Something you really like and find meaningful. Plus a willingness to make a commitment—to a career and to a relationship. It may take some time to come up with something, but you'll figure it out eventually."

"Maybe you're right," he said slowly. He shrugged and gave a half-hearted smile.

I checked my watch and saw it was after midnight. Tired and talked out, we decided to put our conversation on hold for the night. Besides, I wanted to get to bed so I could get an early start to the *Hiroshima Peace Memorial Park* in the morning. When we said good night, Andrew said, "A couple of people from the hostel are going to Miyajima Island tomorrow afternoon to see the floating shrine. If you get back from the museum in time, you should come along."

"That'd be great, thanks," I said. "I should be back at the hostel around one o'clock. If you haven't had lunch by then, I'll stop by and get you."

I woke up early the next morning, and after a light breakfast of rice and eggs, hiked down the hill from the hostel and jumped on a local bus to the city. The bus sped down the highway past shiny, new, road signs, tree-lined exits, and fastidiously clean streets. I gazed at the peaceful, suburban roads outside the window as we rolled quietly towards the center of Hiroshima. It was hard to believe that less than fifty years before, the city had been virtually obliterated by an atomic bomb. Twenty minutes later, I stepped off the bus directly across the street from the *A-Bomb Dome*—the only building that had survived the atomic blast on Hiroshima.

Up until 8:14 A.M. on August 6, 1945, the *A-Bomb Dome* had served as Hiroshima's Industrial Promotion Hall. At 8:15 A.M., one of three American B-29 planes dropped a single nuclear bomb, code-named *Little Boy*, over Hiroshima. The Promotion Hall stood directly below the epicenter of the bomb and by some incredible fluke, miraculously endured the blast that exploded just 1,900 feet above its roof. Most of the building was blown to bits, its metal girders twisted and bent. But the metal dome and the shell of the building stood intact while virtually every other building radiating for miles from the epicenter of the bomb had been flattened.

Behind the *A-Bomb Dome*, narrow footpaths wound between closely cropped, bright green lawns toward the Peace Museum at the rear of the Park. Inside the museum, the atmosphere was subdued and respectful. In addition to detailed accounts of what the residents had been doing at the time the bomb fell, the museum's exhibits showed the destructive power of the bomb. There were remains of melted tiles, shreds of clothing, and imprints of human shadows permanently seared onto granite steps from the 7,000 degree Celsius (12,632 degrees Fahrenheit) surface heat from the blast. Over 200,000 people died in the explosion and thousands more suffered from radiation poisoning, the effects of which still show up today.

Solemn-faced visitors shuffled quietly past the exhibits, silently reading the explanatory signs near each display and casting nervous glances at one another, all of them numbed into silence by the graphic displays facing them. The Peace Park and Museum were built in tribute to the victims of the bomb and as a reminder to future generations of the destructive power of atomic weapons. After seeing the film clips and exhibits documenting the destructive force of nuclear weapons, I was a believer.

Before returning to the hostel, I stopped off at a travel agency a few blocks away from the Hiroshima train station to buy a ferry ticket to South Korea for later that week. I had telephoned the travel bureau the day before and been assured that tickets were still available for Thursday's ferry. Of course, when I arrived at the travel center to purchase the ticket, I was told that all the ferries to Pusan, South Korea were booked solid for the next week and a half.

"But that's impossible," I argued. "I called yesterday and the man on the phone assured me there would still be tickets left for one of this week's ferries if I came in today. This really screws me up," I said angrily to the young woman who was waiting on me.

The Japanese don't like confrontation, and when I raised my voice, it made the poor ticket girl very anxious. To appease the unpredictable foreigner, she dashed around the office checking schedules and book- ings, hoping to find some way to get me on a ferry later that week. Meanwhile, I counted my Traveler's Checks and tried to figure out how much it would cost me to stay in Japan for another week and a half. My *Yen* had been disappearing like crazy and I was cashing in new Traveler's Checks almost every other day.

The ticket girl checked all the available options then said nervously, "I am sorry, but all the ferries for the rest of the week are full." Sens- ing my apparent frustration, she quickly added, "there is still room avail- able on today's ferry however, if you would like to go on that one."

"Today?" I wasn't sure I wanted to leave so soon. "What time does it leave?"

"The ferry leaves from Shimoneseki at five o'clock," she replied.

We each checked our watches to see how much time I had. Shimo- neseki was on the northwest coast of the island, a few hour's train ride from Hiroshima. The only way I could possibly make it there on time would be to take the "bullet" train. Rather than watch my money dwin- dle away in Japan for another ten days, I decided to go for it. I booked the ticket then caught a bus back to the hostel to pack my things.

After quickly throwing my things in my backpack, I checked out of the hostel and went upstairs to say goodbye to Andrew. He was read- ing a book in his room and looked shocked when I came in with my backpack dragging behind me. "Well, it looks like I'll be taking off sooner than I thought," I said.

After filling him in on the problem with the ferry tickets, Andrew shook his head sadly and frowned. "That's a bloody shame," he remarked. "The best part of the trip would have been having a few days to look forward to leaving. And now they've taken that away from you."

I laughed and replied, "I hadn't thought of it that way Andrew." But from Andrew's way of thinking it made perfect sense. He savored the anticipation of arriving and leaving and felt I was being denied half the enjoyment of traveling.

"Andrew," I asked curiously, "haven't you ever heard the expression, *it's the journey, not the destination*?"

"Yes," he replied with a grin. "But I always thought they had it the wrong way around."

Typhoons, Snakes, and Gorges

The Little Engine That Could

No wind favors him who has no destined port.
— Michel De Montaigne

I gazed out at the South China Sea from the stern of the whitewashed ship and felt a merciful sense of relief as I watched the rolling waves fill the distance between Taiwan and me.

During the two weeks I had been on the tiny island, I had been through two typhoons, an earthquake, and so many torrential rains that I had lost count. And the funny thing was that I had gone to Taiwan to get away from the lousy weather I had hit when I arrived in South Korea after leaving Japan.

I had spent two pleasant and uneventful weeks traveling around South Korea, seeing an endless array of temples, palaces and burial mounds, before the wet weather finally drove me out of the country. The day after I arrived, it started to rain a little each afternoon. By the end of the second week, gray clouds had become a permanent part of the South Korean landscape and the rains had become heavier and more frequent with each passing day. While stuck in my room one rainy afternoon in Seoul, I read in my guidebook that the Portuguese had named Taiwan *"Isla Formosa"*—beautiful island. After almost two weeks of non-stop rain in South Korea, that was good enough for me. The following morning I bought an airline ticket to Taipei, the capital of Taiwan.

As luck would have it, the day after I arrived Taipei was hit by *Typhoon Polly.* Drenching rains and gusting winds battered the city for the next two days, imploding my cheap New York umbrella and soaking me to the skin whenever I ventured outside. The winds started to die down a bit by the end of the second day, and on the morning of the third day, the sun finally had the guts to show itself again without fear it would be blown out of the sky. I took advantage of the break in weather and wandered around the city as fast as I could, hoping to make up for lost time.

One of the more interesting places I visited was the *Chiang Kai Shek Memorial*, a huge, white structure crowned with a double-tiered roof of attractive, blue-glazed tiles. The exhibits in the Memorial chronicled Chiang Kai Shek's life from his early years in China and his association with Sun Yat Sen, who also happened to be Chiang's father-in-law and President of the Chinese Republic, through his unsuccessful struggle to maintain political control of mainland China. When Mao Tse Tung's Communist forces defeated Chiang Kai Shek's army in 1949, Chiang and his followers fled to Taiwan. And though the People's Republic of China has ruled Mainland China since 1949, the Taiwanese government continues to claim absentee sovereignty over China, with plans to return to the mainland one day to replace the current Communist government.

From the Memorial, I walked through the narrow, congested streets of Taipei to a place called *Snake Alley*, a narrow market street lined with food vendors and shops, whose specialties included snake soups, drinks and various medicinal concoctions such as snake penis pills—which was fortunate for me, since I was running low on them at the time.

Hoping to witness a snake transaction, I hung around the snake stalls waiting for customers to arrive. I didn't have long to wait. At a stall to my left, a nicely dressed, middle-aged Chinese man examined a black wire cage filled with dozens of snakes. The vendor watched closely as the man pointed carefully to the snake of his choice.

With a quick nod of his head, the vendor scooped the snake from the tangled web of black knots and held it up for the man's approval. When the man grunted his satisfaction, the vendor attached the head of the snake to a clip affixed to the wall of his stall. With a single cut from a long, thin knife, he deftly sliced the snake open from head to tail. With a second cut he removed the snake's gallbladder, then carefully collected the snake's blood in a small metal cup.

When the last of the blood had been drained from the snake, he placed the gallbladder in the cup and handed it to his customer. The man paid for his drink then walked over to one of the nearby food stalls that lined the length of *Snake Alley*. Setting the cup down carefully so as not to spill its contents, he ordered some food to accompany his snake cocktail. While eating his meal, the man drank the contents of his cup slowly, savoring each sip of his precious drink until it was finished. I was curious to know what a snake cocktail tasted like, but didn't feel like having a snake killed to find out. Instead, I settled for some old-fashioned Chinese noodles and rice soup at a small food stall further up the alley before walking back to my hostel through the noisy, crowded streets of Tapei.

The clear sky over Taipei didn't last long. A few days later, a second typhoon—*Typhoon Omar*—belted the city with another bout of high-velocity winds and torrential rains that blotted the sky with a perpetual twilight that seemed to last forever. A day and a half later, the black ceiling of clouds that had settled over Taipei finally blew off to sea. Later that week, it was rumored that a third typhoon was on its way. I packed my bags and bought a train ticket south.

The western side of Taiwan is flat and makes up the bulk of the country's agricultural land. The eastern side of the island is much more varied—steep and craggy, with a long mountain range that divides Taiwan in half from north to south. Compared to Taipei, the rest of Taiwan was quiet, peaceful and unpolluted. It was also much more scenic. The train ride along the east coast offered stunning panoramas of the Pacific Ocean. Running dangerously close to the edge of the rocky cliffs below the train, the harbor roads that hugged the coast were almost within spitting distance of the dark, blue water and offered even more spectacular views than from the train. But the most impressive part of the journey was a place called *Taroko Gorge*, a nineteen-kilometer road that had been blasted through Taiwan's Central Mountain Range to allow access between the east and west coasts of the island.

From the eastern side of the island, buses and cars entered the gorge from a narrow two-lane road that ran through a small, one-street town on the outskirts of *Hualien*—a medium-sized city, only a few hours by train from Taipei. I arrived in *Hualien* with an American named Bryan who was also on his way to the gorge. From the station, we took a local bus to the little town that sat at the mouth of the canyon. A short walk down the town's only street brought us to a bus stand where we were told to wait for the next bus going through Taroko Gorge. Forty-minutes later, we were still waiting. Leaving Bryan to watch our packs, I walked into a local shop down the street to ask when the next bus was scheduled to leave. An old Chinese man who spoke a bit of English told me that a bus had left an hour earlier and was probably the last bus that would leave that day. Rather than wait around to see if he was right, we decided to try our luck and hitchhike through the gorge.

As we soon learned, however, Chinese drivers aren't anxious to give lifts to foreigners. We tried to flag them down but they usually sped by without a passing glance. After almost an hour with no luck, an old, dirt-encrusted cement truck slowed to a rumbling halt in front of us. We peered inside the truck and saw a young Chinese man in a dusty, plaid shirt. Bouncing up and down with the vibrations from the engine, the man grinned and waved us in.

Bryan and I grabbed our packs and climbed in. The driver slid the stick-shift into gear and hit the gas. After a moment's hesitation, the cement truck kicked forward with a rumble then went bouncing along the road towards the black hole at the entrance to the gorge.

I was dumbstruck by the sight in front of us as we entered the narrow winding road leading into the gorge. To the left of the cement truck, heading in the opposite direction, cars and buses threaded their way between us and the solid rock face of the mountain. On our right, directly below the window where I sat, spectacular, sheer cliffs dropped straight down to a rushing, white-water river 1000 meters below us. As we drove further into the gorge, the road twisted and turned through the black interior of the mountain, throwing us into frightening stretches of semi-darkness before it snaked its way back along the sunny cliff to follow the narrow rapids in the canyon.

The views from the gorge shifted and changed with each bend of the road. One minute, the river was rushing madly over the rock bed in the canyon. The next, it was hidden from view by the massive rock face ahead of us. When we swung back towards the edge of the mountain, it reappeared as a peaceful, flowing stream, gently lapping the rocks in its path until it picked up speed around the next turn. I couldn't take in the sights fast enough. The trip through the gorge was better than a ride at Disneyland. Especially in the cement truck, which bounced and rocked like a stagecoach around every turn. I wanted the ride to go on forever, but before we knew it, we were through the gorge and slowing to a halt.

We had asked the driver to let us out at a place called *Tienhsiang*, a village at the top of the gorge between the towering cliffs of the Central Mountain Range. We planned to spend the night on the mountain before going through the rest of the gorge the next day. When we reached our destination, the driver down-shifted the noisy cement truck and pulled over to the side of the road to let us out. We thanked him for the lift, then hiked up the steep hill ahead of us.

My guidebook recommended a place called *The Catholic Hostel*, a Swiss-like chalet on a hill in the mountains. Nestled among trees and cliffs, the hostel was in a beautiful location. It was a steep hike up the hill though, and when we reached the top, we dropped our backpacks to catch our breath, praying there would be beds available.

At the crest of the hill was a large, two-story wooden house. As we approached the main building, I noticed someone seated on the rail of the balcony, with his back propped up against the vertical beam of the rail and a writing pad on his knee. When he noticed our approach up the path, he put his pen down and waved.

"Any beds available?" I called out as we got closer to the house. "You can prob'ly rent out the whole place if you like," he laughed. "I think we're the only ones here—though I wouldn't swear to it, 'cuz I only just arrived about an hour ago myself." Balancing himself precariously on the railing, he reached out to shake our hands. "Name's Dan," he said. When the introductions were over he told us, "There should prob'ly be someone inside the house you can see about renting a bed for the night."

We checked in and were assigned beds in the same cabin as Dan. The room was clean and fairly large, with enough beds for about twenty-five people. I surveyed the empty bunkbeds and picked one that looked like it had a firm mattress. All sorts of things were spread out on the beds on Dan's side of the room so I assumed some other people had checked in before we'd arrived. I pointed to the gear on the beds and remarked to Dan, "Looks like some other people showed up while you were out."

He looked where I was pointing and laughed. "That's my gear!" he said happily.

"All that stuff is yours?" I was amazed that one person could lug all that stuff around.

"Yeah," he replied sheepishly. "I think I might've over-packed a bit before I left Oz."

"What's 'Oz'?" Bryan asked.

"Short for Australia," Dan replied.

"Where have you been putting all that stuff?" I asked.

Reaching behind his bed he pulled out one of the biggest backpacks I had ever seen. "Got a nice big pack!" he beamed.

Dan was a twenty-four year old Australian from Canberra. He had bought a round-the-world ticket in Australia and intended to see as much of the globe as possible before his money or his Visa credit ran out. By the time we met up, he had been traveling for about a month and had spent most of that time in Japan before arriving in Taiwan. Though he'd never been too far from home before, he didn't appear to be nervous or cautious about traveling around the world on his own. On the contrary, he brought a great sense of curiosity and wonder to everything he came across—no matter how mundane or trivial it seemed to others. Which was a good thing, since he was kind of hapless in a way. During his first month of travel, he had lost plane tickets, left personal items behind, missed travel connections, and overpaid for things he was expected to bargain for. But none of it dampened his enthusiasm. He just laughed it all off and moved happily on to his next misadventure.

A good case in point was his trip through Taroko Gorge. Like Bryan and me, Dan had also missed the bus from the little town outside of *Hualien*. But instead of trying to hitch a ride or wait for the next bus, he decided to walk the nineteen kilometers through the gorge.

"You walked here?" I asked in amazement.

"Yeah, I didn't figure it would be as far as it was. Turned out to be a lot harder than I thought, though—especially with the pack on."

"How long did it take you?" Bryan asked.

"Dunno. I had to stop a coupla times in the tunnel when it started to rain. I also stopped a lot of times to have a look at the gorge. The sights along the ridge were unbelievable, weren't they? So, to answer your question—I dunno," he laughed.

"It took me all day though," he continued. "I started this morning and didn't get here till late afternoon. The worst part was when I got out of the gorge and made my way up here to the hostel. It started to rain like crazy on the way up, which is why my gear is spread out all over the beds. My whole pack got soaked. I just hope it all dries out by morning." He got up and felt a couple of his shirts to see how wet they were. Draping some of the shirts over the frames of the beds he sighed and said, "It's going to take awhile to dry in this mountain air, I think."

When I left the cabin to get washed up for bed, the air was cold and the sky was jet black. I looked up and saw thousands of tiny, bright-white stars shining like little diamonds against the black backdrop. It was peaceful, quiet and beautiful on top of the mountain. And it wasn't raining for a change. Maybe Taiwan wasn't such a bad place, after all.

The following morning, the three of us took a bus from *Tienhsiang* toward the west coast of Taiwan. An hour after we set off, the bus driver pulled over at a small rest area in the middle of nowhere so the passengers could buy some refreshments. After the last of the passengers had filed out, Dan grabbed his pack and hopped off the bus.

"You're getting out here?" I asked with surprise.

"Yeah. When I was in Japan I met the guy who wrote the *Lonely Planet Guide to Taiwan*. When I told him I was going there after Japan, he told me about a great place to go white-water rafting. It's supposed to be right around here somewhere."

I looked at the little refreshment shack and shook my head doubtfully. "Around here? Do you know *where* exactly?"

"Well, not exactly," he laughed. "But I'll find it. He told me this is where I'm supposed to get off the bus. You're both welcome to come along if you'd like."

Bryan thanked Dan for the invitation, but declined the offer since he had to be back in Taipei the following afternoon. I had no intention of searching for a river in the middle of nowhere, and decided to stick to my original plan and go through the rest of the gorge until I reached *Taichung* on the West Coast. Besides, the sky had started to cloud up again and I didn't want to get stuck on the mountain in the middle of another storm. I bought a soda and some Chinese cookies from the little food stall and ate my breakfast beside a tree as I watched a pack of ominous-looking clouds settle over the treetops across the valley. I had no clue where we were but I was glad we wouldn't be staying there too long.

Before we got back on the bus, I walked to the edge of the cliff near the side of the rest stop to take a look around. In the valley below, a narrow stream flowed gently between steep, rocky cliffs. Dense trees covered the sides of the mountain as far as I could see.

From where I stood, the only sign of civilization was the rest stop—which wasn't very encouraging. Other than the old Chinese couple who ran the little food shop, it didn't look like there were any other people for miles around.

Soon after I finished my breakfast, the driver started the engine and the passengers began to climb back on the bus. "Are you sure you want to get off here?" I asked Dan with concern. "It looks like it's going to start raining any minute now."

Dan looked at the clouds overhead and shrugged. "Hmm, does look like rain again, doesn't it? Should make the river good and full for rafting though, I reckon."

Dan's optimism was commendable. I wished him luck and boarded the bus.

The driver reversed the bus out of the narrow rest area and turned slowly back onto the dirt road which led down the mountain. Soon after we set off, I heard raindrops begin to tap lightly against the windows of the bus. Not long afterwards, the rain came pouring down around us, beating against the roof of the bus like thousands of little drums gone out of control.

I turned in my seat and looked out the back window. The mountain was barely visible through the dark clouds and thick rain that had settled over it. As I thought of poor Dan stuck on top of the mountain in the middle of nowhere, I couldn't suppress a laugh as I imagined him getting drenched all over again.

She tugged and pulled and pulled and tugged and slowly, slowly, slowly
they started off. . . . Puff, puff, chug, chug, went the Little Blue Engine.
"I think I can, I think I can . . . "
— From The Little Engine That Could, by Watty Piper

Four days later, I was holed up in a town called *Chiayi*, a small, rural city halfway down the western coast of Taiwan.

I arrived at night in the middle of a torrential downpour. And despite my umbrella, I got soaked walking from the train station while searching for a place to spend the night. Most of the hotels listed in my guidebook turned out to be dead-ends. Either the guesthouses had closed down or the house numbers were wrong. Either way, I wasn't having much luck finding a place to stay.

It was dark and wet, and hard to find my way along the unlit streets. After an hour of wandering aimlessly, I walked into a bakery to ask directions to one of the hotels listed in my guide. As soon as I entered, a young Chinese couple inside the shop asked me if I was American. They had just returned from California after a year of studying abroad and were thrilled to see an American in *Chiayi*. When they had paid for their purchases, they offered to help me find the hotels I was looking for. We left the bakery and walked over to their little motorbike which was parked beneath the awning of the bakery. Despite my protests they insisted that I ride with the husband since I had a big pack to carry. Driving slowly enough for his wife to keep pace alongside the motorbike, we puttered off down the muddy, puddled streets of *Chiayi*.

The first few places we tried were duds—nothing but old, abandoned houses. The next place matched the address in my guidebook and looked open. Leaving his wife outside to watch the scooter, the husband and I went inside to check out the rooms. The woman inside the shabby, wooden entranceway didn't speak English, so my Chinese friend told her in Mandarin that I needed a bed for the night. The woman took a set of keys from a wooden cupboard behind her, then led us slowly up an old, creaky staircase and down a long narrow hall lined with rooms on the left side of the floor. Selecting a key from the assortment in her hand, she unlocked a door in the middle of the hall and nudged it open to show me the room.

I edged my way inside the room and took a look around. Directly behind the door, and filling almost the entire floor of the dimly-lit room, was a worn, striped mattress, partially covered with old bedding. Next to the door, a small, rotating, metal fan sat lifeless, its plug twisted around its curved, plastic base. A tiny table lamp with a weak, yellow bulb glowed on the floor near the fan and sputtered like a candle when I stepped near it. Why the old woman thought I would want to rent the room was beyond me. What was even more surprising, was that she wanted five dollars a night for it. With a sigh and a shrug to my Chinese companion, I turned to the woman and said, "I'll take it." I didn't have much choice. It was still pouring outside and I was tired. Besides, I felt guilty dragging my kind Chinese friend and his wife around in the rain.

The woman closed the door and led us back down the creaky stairs so I could register. My Chinese companions wished me a pleasant stay in *Chiayi*, then rode off down the street in the rain. I grabbed my pack and went upstairs to my dungeon to go to bed.

When I woke the next morning, the sun was blazing. And by early afternoon, all the puddles in the streets had disappeared, leaving no trace of the previous night's storm. When I ventured outside, I found that *Chiayi* was a likeable little town—small enough to feel familiar, yet big enough to wander around without getting bored. It was even commercial enough to warrant a McDonald's. After almost two months of eating nothing but noodles, vegetables, rice, and Chinese soft drinks, McDonald's quickly became my restaurant of choice in *Chiayi*. By coincidence, it was also the favorite spot of someone I hadn't expected to see again.

My second day in *Chiayi*, I went back to McDonald's for lunch and while standing on line at the counter, I saw a pair of familiar-looking hiking boots coming down the stairs to my left. The person's body was hidden from view by a wall but there was something oddly familiar about those boots. When the legs descended the stairs, a huge backpack suddenly came into view. The face was hidden beneath a floppy, straw hat but there was no mistaking that backpack.

"Sorry, but Australians aren't allowed in here!" I called out from below the stairway.

Seeing me at the foot of the stairs, Dan almost dropped his tray. "If I'd have known they let Americans in here, I never would've come in!" he laughed.

When the shock of seeing each other was over, we grabbed a vacant table and filled each other in on where we'd been the past few days. Dan shook his head and laughed when I asked him where he had gone after we left the rest stop. "I never saw so much rain! I shoulda stayed on the bus with you. I walked for about an hour in the blasted storm after the bus pulled away. Got soaked—and had to lay all my stuff out again to get 'em dry. I think my clothes have been wet more than they've been dry, come to think of it."

"How was the white-water rafting?"

"I never got to go. Turns out it's not the right season for it, or something like that. I couldn't get the full explanation since the guy I spoke to didn't speak much English. When I found out there was no white-water rafting, I tried to leave the mountain but couldn't, 'cuz the roads were rained out and the bus couldn't get to us. A bus finally made it through this morning and dropped me at a place called Tai-chung. When I heard there was a McDonald's in Chiayi I bought a ticket on the next train out. I arrived about an hour ago and came straight here from the station."

Since Dan hadn't arranged a place to stay we went back to my hotel to see if there were any rooms available. The old Chinese woman showed him a small room on the third floor that looked even worse than mine. After a quick look at the room, he shrugged his shoulders and with his usual positive outlook, tossed his big pack on the bed and said, "Looks aw'right. I've stayed in worse."

In addition to boasting a McDonald's, Chiayi's other claim to fame is being the gateway to a mountain called Alishan, one of the most scenic places in Taiwan. An old, narrow-gauge railway, built by the Japanese during their occupation of Taiwan in the 1930's, still oper-ated from Chiayi to Alishan and was supposed to be a great trip up to the summit. And though I wasn't anxious to spend another night on a mountain after the rainy night I had spent on Tai Shan in China, I didn't want to leave Chiayi without seeing Alishan.

The following morning, Dan and I set off for the railway station across town with a British guy named Stephen who was also staying at our hotel. We purchased tickets for the morning train then bought some bananas and bread to take with us before boarding the small, four-carriage, red and white train. At 10:00 A.M., right on time, the little train inched slowly from the station and started its ascent up the mountain. The train was so small, and moved so slowly, that I felt like I was riding a toy. The total distance from Chiayi to Alishan was only 71.4 kilometers, but because of the steep elevation—2,216 meters to the top—the train practically crawled up the mountain, wheezing past fifty tunnels and eighty bridges on the way up, like a pack horse struggling under a heavy load.

The scenery along the way was incredible. Lush palm trees, bamboo forests, and dense jungle growth were slowly replaced by old cedar and pine trees as we moved from a tropical and sub-tropical environment to a temperate forest during our ascent. About halfway up the mountain, heavy rain and fog cut our visibility to a few feet outside the steamy windows. Without much to look at, the slow climb up the mountain seemed even slower. To make things worse, the engine broke down and we had to wait in the hot, humid train car while the conductor and engineer tried to figure out the problem. An hour and a half later, the engine was fixed, and as the toy train continued its uneasy struggle up the mountain, we went from sweating to death in the tropical zone to freezing to death in the temperate zone.

I felt sorry for the little train as it choked along, grunting and wheezing like an old athlete whose body no longer has the energy to go the distance. I kept expecting it to give a final cough and die, exhausted from the effort, but it never did. It just kept plugging slowly up the hill, until eventually, it reached the top. A trip that was supposed to take three hours took seven, but at least we made it.

By the time we arrived at Alishan, night had already settled over the mountain. With no clue where to go, we followed the locals down a long path from the station to some hotels located a short distance away. After checking a few out, we selected an empty bungalow with big, clean, comfortable rooms that reminded me of ski houses in New England.

The night air was cool and invigorating, and after spending the past few nights in that hell hole in Chiayi, I was looking forward to getting a good night's sleep. Dan however, with all his youthful enthusiasm and zeal for mountains, was planning to climb to the summit the following morning to see the sunrise. Stephen was more in line with my way of thinking, and planned to sleep in, as well.

Before we went to bed, Stephen and I told Dan not to wake us in the morning. Dan shook his head and laughed. "I can't believe you guys. Don't you want to see the sunrise from the top of the mountain?"

"It'll rise without us," I replied, as I got ready for bed. "If it doesn't, then you can wake us."

After a great night's sleep, I woke to a perfect, mountain morning. The air was crisp and refreshing and the sky above Alishan was a deep and cloudless blue. I made a pot of Chinese tea on the electric burner in the kitchen and sat in the small sitting area in front of the window, listening to the birds chirping outside. Stephen wandered out of his room shortly after me, and poured himself a cup of tea. Half an hour later, Dan came bounding through the screen door, full of energy. "Nice mountain!" he belted cheerfully. "Lotsa trails and good views from the top. The sunrise was a little disappointing though. Too much fog. But it was worth it, all the same. You shoulda come along, ya' lazy bastards!" He poured himself some tea then went back in his room to take a nap while Stephen and I went out to find breakfast.

We spent the rest of the day hiking around different mountain trails that wound in and around the leafy forests of Alishan until it was time to catch the afternoon train back down the mountain. The little train moved a lot faster going down than it did coming up, and we arrived back in Chiayi just a few hours after we set out.

Before we left the station, Stephen bought a ticket for the afternoon train to Tapei. His two week holiday was at an end and he needed to get moving to catch his flight back to England the following morning. By some strange coincidence, Dan and I had each bought ferry tickets to Macau the week before we met at Taroko Gorge. The ferry was scheduled to leave the following week from Kaohsiung, a port city in the south of Taiwan. From Macau, we each intended to hop on the forty-five minute JetFoil to Hong Kong. Since coincidence had thrown us on the same boat, we decided to travel together to Hong Kong.

After two more days of doing nothing more taxing than eating and relaxing in the friendly town of Chiayi, Dan and I found ourselves happily situated on the white, sun-washed deck of the MACMOSA— short for "*Mac*au and For*mosa*." With our backs to the sun, we leaned contentedly against the railing at the stern of the ship. With the care-free attitude of travelers on the move, we watched Taiwan shrink across the deep blue waves of the South China Sea, while high above our heads, dark rain clouds moved towards the little island of Taiwan like moths to a flame.

As Dan and I watched the approaching storm head steadily towards Taiwan, we sighed, relieved that for once, we had escaped in time.

A Hell Hole in Hong Kong

Seems Like Old Times

Temptation in Thailand

Are you sure that wasn't a rat? 'Cuz if it wasn't, it was the strangest looking cat I've ever seen. And if it was, I think we oughtta get out of here.
—Dan, after checking in to ChungKing Mansions in Hong Kong

"Dat elebator is stuck on dee six floor. You need du use dis one." A short, dark-skinned man from India stepped out of the elevator car to our right and held the doors open for everyone who had been waiting for the stuck elevator in front of us. The crowd of people around Dan and me shoved their way en masse to the one working elevator. Stuck in the middle of the crowd, we were swept helplessly inside. When the mad rush was over we had secured a spot in the middle of the car, squashed against a group of turbaned Sikhs just inches in front of us.

The elevators in Hong Kong's ChungKing Mansions were in use twenty-four hours a day and it was nothing short of a miracle that they didn't break down more often. Even when they were running smoothly, I never felt safe in them. The complex was made up of five blocks of buildings, with each block having sixteen floors and two elevators per block. When one of the block's elevators was stuck or out of service, the second one became a deathtrap, as swarms of Indians, Africans and other temporary residents scrambled to get inside.

"*BRRRRRNNNNNNGGGGGGGGGGGG!!!*" The alarm in the elevator signaled an overload condition as soon as one too many people squeezed on. "Sumbuddy 'ave du git owt," one of the Indians called out from the back of the car. No one in the packed elevator car moved. "*BRRNNNGGGG!!! "BRRNNNGGGGGGG!!!*" To be heard above the alarm, another Indian man shouted more loudly, "We going nowhere less sumbuddy git owt."

A large African man behind me let out a sigh. He glared at the people who had stepped on last and yelled, "Mon, dee elevator won' move unliss someone git off!"

When no one stepped off, a couple of young African men in front of me jumped in the air. By easing the weight on the floor for a few seconds they tricked the elevator into thinking someone had stepped off. The alarm stopped and the doors closed. As the car began its ascent, I held my breath and prayed I wouldn't plummet to an untimely end in Hong Kong's most notorious backpacker tenement.

Despite its hazards, ChungKing Mansions had the unbeatable benefits of price and location. Situated on *Nathan Road*, a few short blocks from the Harbor, the building complex was in a great spot. With guesthouses scattered on almost every floor, it was easy to find a bed to meet anyone's budget—from single and double air-conditioned rooms for ten dollars and up a night, to crowded, un-airconditioned dorms with four to twelve people laid out on bunkbeds for five dollars a night.

Some of the places were maintained pretty well. More often than not, though, they were dirty, cockroach or rat-infested rooms where you got what you paid for. The place Dan and I checked into was somewhere in-between—somewhere in the "hold the rats but give me the roaches," budget range. For five dollars a night we checked into the dorm rooms at *The Friendship Traveler's Hostel*, a moderately clean hostel on the sixth floor of Block B.

There were four bunkbeds in my room. I took the top bed near the window, on the left side of the dorm—a choice spot, since it was farthest from the door and closest to the overhead ceiling fans. Most nights, the two rotating fans kept the room from getting too hot. On some nights though, it got so sticky and humid in the crowded room that I thought I would sweat to death before morning. Dripping with sweat, I would pull off my sheet and lay on my bed in my underwear while I waited for the ceiling fan to rotate back to my end of the room. While the other seven people in the dorm slept soundly around me, I listened anxiously in the dark to the hum of the fan's motor, grateful for the two or three-second breeze that bathed my body before it spun away from me again. On a few of the hotter nights, when the heat became too unbearable, I would climb down from my bunk in the middle of the night and take a cold shower to cool off before going back to bed.

To get away from the hot, crowded streets during the day, Dan and I took ferries to the islands off the coast of Hong Kong. *Lantau*, *Peng Chau* and *Cheng Chau* were short commutes by ferry and great escapes from the hectic pace of Hong Kong, except on the weekends, when local residents flocked to the islands in search of relief from the crowds and the heat. At other times, we rode the Star Ferry back and forth between Hong Kong and Kowloon to cool off when the heat became too intense. The ten-minute boat ride across the huge harbor, with its cool breezes and choppy waves, was usually enough to cool us down before finding relief in the air-conditioned shops and restaurants in the city.

Hong Kong had a charged energy I liked—similar to New York, but a lot more scenic. An impressive skyline of modern skyscrapers formed an imposing backdrop for the amazing array of cruise ships, tugboats and small sampans that swayed gently in the rough waters of Hong Kong's immense harbor. At night, the city looked even more dazzling, especially from the top of Victoria Peak, where you could see over the tops of the skyscrapers and gaze across the harbor to Kowloon and the New Territories, all the way to the border of mainland China.

Aside from its sights, Hong Kong was also a great place to eat. Most of the backpackers at ChungKing Mansions loved Hong Kong because there were so many McDonald's and Pizza Huts scattered throughout the city. But for just a few dollars more, there was an unbelievable selection of Chinese restaurants, Vietnamese food, American food, and practically anything else you could desire. Unfortunately, Dan's idea of a gourmet restaurant was a McDonald's with place settings. One afternoon, as I watched him sip his fourth McDonald's milkshake of the day, I shook my head and laughed. "Congratulations! You've just set a new world record for the most chocolate milkshakes consumed by an Australian in Hong Kong."

Dan held his cup out proudly and grinned. "You mean I can stop drinking the blasted things now? *Thank God!*" He took another sip from his straw and said with a straight face, "You know, I really don't know what I would do if there were no McDonald's here."

"Yeah, you might have to eat something healthy—probably throw your whole system off," I replied.

He finished his drink with a loud smack of his lips and leaned back in his red plastic chair, looking very content. A few seconds later, he leaned forward and said, "Actually, I've just about had my fill of Hong Kong. It's a terrific place to shop, but I've already bought a Walkman and a camera and don't need anything else. Any idea where you'll be heading after you leave Hong Kong?"

"No, not really. How about you?"

"Dunno. Got any ideas?"

"I've heard Vietnam is supposed to be a pretty good place to travel," I said. "I met some people when I was in China who had just come back from there. They had a great time and told me to get there before it turns into a major tourist spot like Thailand."

"Vietnam, huh?" Dan mused, while shoving his straw to the bottom of his cup and slurping the last few drops of his milkshake.

"What do you think?" I asked.

"Can we fly from here or do we have to go to Bangkok or some place first?"

"I'm not sure. Let's find out."

We spent the rest of the day getting information from the different travel bureaus along Nathan Road and quickly learned that the best way to get to Vietnam was to fly from Bangkok. Visas were easier to get from there and flights were less expensive than from Hong Kong—even when we figured in the airfare from Hong Kong to Bangkok. We decided to go for it and booked two tickets to Bangkok on *Air Lanka* for Saturday night.

We checked out of the hostel early Saturday afternoon and walked to the bus stop half a block down from ChungKing Mansions to wait for an airport bus to Hong Kong's *Kai Tak International Airport*. While waiting for the bus, we struck up a conversation with a Welsh traveler named Colin who was booked on the same flight as us. He had come to Hong Kong three days before with the intention of finding work. After the third day, he couldn't stand the thought of living in Hong Kong and booked himself a one-way ticket to Thailand.

"I don't know wha' it is about this place, but after I got here the thought of workin' an livin' here gave me the willies, so I decided to get out," he said in a strong, working-class British accent.

"Where are you planning to go after Thailand?" Dan asked curiously.

Colin shrugged. "Dunno. I like Thailand. Maybe I'll hang aroun' there for awhile till I decide wha' I want to do next. I defini'ly don't want to go back to London yet, that's for sure."

The three of us sat together on the bus to the airport and asked to be seated next to one another on the plane. During the flight, Dan and I told Colin we were heading to Vietnam from Bangkok and asked if he wanted to join us. By the time our Air Lanka flight touched down in Bangkok, we were joking around like old friends and Colin told us to count him in for the trip to Vietnam.

The customs check at Bangkok's Don Muang International Airport was fast and efficient, and less than twenty minutes after our plane landed, we left the air-conditioned comfort of the International Arrivals Hall and stepped out of the terminal into the humid, polluted air of Bangkok.

Tired and hot, we decided to splurge for a taxi to the city instead of sweating it out on a crowded, local bus. We tossed our packs in the trunk of the first air-conditioned cab we could find, and sat back and relaxed inside its nice, cool interior. After securing the trunk, the small Thai driver climbed behind the wheel and glanced at us in his rear-view mirror. "Where you want to go?" he asked, in his pleasantly accented broken English. Colin and I had each been to Bangkok before and said, "Kao San Road" at the same time. The driver hit the gas and our taxi was soon swallowed up in a sea of exhaust fumes from a herd of cars, motorscooters, and three-wheeled Samlors—better known as *Tuk-Tuks*, due to the throttling noise of their engines.

As we sped along the noisy, congested highways of Bangkok, our Thai driver weaved in and out of the jungle of vehicles around us with road-handling skills that would have made any New York City taxi driver proud. As we sped along, I kept my eyes open for familiar sights, and when I spotted the *Democracy Monument* at the traffic circle a mile ahead of us, I knew we were almost at *Kao San Road*. I hadn't been to Bangkok for four years, but suddenly it felt like I had been there yesterday. The driver veered around the right side of the monument then made a right-hand turn down a narrow unlit street. A few blocks down the road, he made a quick left.

Colin glanced over at me and smiled. "Is it startin' to look familiar?"

"It sure does," I replied. "Wow, it feels so strange to be back here again."

Dan gazed out the window at the various handicraft shops and curbside cafes that lined the long street. "Where are we?" he asked curiously.

The driver swung the taxi to the side of the curb to let us out. Colin hopped out of the car and flashed a wide grin at Dan. "You're in the place every backpacker in the world comes to sooner or later, lad. Welcome to Kao San Road."

The less things change, the more they remain the same.

— Sicilian Proverb

"This place hasn't changed at all," I said to Colin when I stepped out of the cab.

"Kao San Road never changes. That's wha' I love about the place," he replied, as he popped open the trunk of the taxi. "You'll prob'ly run into the same people you saw four years ago."

After paying the driver for the ride, we grabbed our packs and walked up the street in search of a guesthouse to spend the night.

"There used to be a pretty decent place over there on the corner," I said, pointing to the end of the street. "There it is—the *Ploy Guest House*. Let's check it out."

The guesthouse was on the corner of Kao San and Chakraphong roads, across the street from a Buddhist Temple named *Wat Chana Song Khram*. The place wasn't as clean as I had remembered it, but the rooms weren't bad. After a quick look around, we checked in and dropped our packs off in a large, bright room with three single beds. There were so many guesthouses on Kao San Road that it really didn't make much difference where we stayed. At three dollars a room, we could change places every night if we wanted to.

Dan and Colin were tired and decided to wash up and call it a night, but I was hungry and wanted to have a look around before going to bed. Though it was close to midnight, there were still people in some of the cafes along the street. And though most of the restaurants and street vendors were starting to close up, some were still hoping for a few last sales.

Forty or fifty guesthouses lined both sides of Kao San Road, most of them with open-fronted restaurants facing the sidewalks. Some of the more popular places showed videos in the evenings in order to attract customers. Though most of the movies had already ended, there were still some people lounging around the various restaurants, sipping fruit shakes or eating ice-cream while the Thai staff cleaned up around them.

I walked into the restaurant of the *Hello Guesthouse* and ordered a watermelon shake and a noodle dish called *Pad Thai*. Not long after I placed my order, a young Thai waitress carried my food to the table. Leaning lazily against an empty chair next to me, she gazed sleepily out at the street while I ate my meal. The girls in the restaurants worked long shifts. Shuffling around in their sandals for hours at a time, they served an endless number of Westerners from morning till night. Whenever they could, they took small breaks between customers—sitting in empty chairs while they took orders, or leaning against chairs and empty tables when they weren't busy.

It didn't take long for the familiar sights and sounds of Kao San Road to drift back to me: Tuk-Tuks sputtering by, their engines throttling unevenly as they wandered up and down the street looking for late-night passengers; Thai waitresses speaking to one another in the sing-song, high-pitched tones of the Thai language; And suntanned, Western travelers drifting slowly along the street outside, each of them dressed in the unofficial travel uniform of long-term backpackers—baggy shorts, T-shirts and flip-flops.

When I finished my meal, I took a slow walk up the street to further rekindle my memories. As I strolled up and down the long, narrow road, I looked with familiarity at all the shops, restaurants, guesthouses and sidewalk vendors that lined the street. Surprisingly, other than the addition of a pizza restaurant and a few upscale shops selling leather coats and cowboy boots, nothing had really changed. Kao San Road was still the dynamic market of Thai handicrafts, jewelry, music cassettes, T-shirts and clothing that I remembered. Above all, it was still a lively, energetic refuge for international backpackers, and the preferred crossroad for travelers heading east toward Indonesia and Australia or west toward Europe. Sooner or later, everyone stopped at Kao San Road. And though I hadn't been there for four years, nothing had changed too much during my absence. The faces on the travelers were different, but other than that, it was the same place. It felt good to be back.

After breakfast the next morning, Dan, Colin and I split up to gather information and prices to Vietnam from the various travel offices scattered along Kao San Road. An hour later, on my way to the next travel shop along the street, I spotted Dan a few shops down from me, happily browsing through stacks of music cassettes. Feeling like a truant officer who had just caught a student playing hooky, I approached him with a disapproving look. "How many travel places have you checked out?" I asked.

Embarrassed that he had been caught dodging his assignment, he stammered, "Well, um, . . . uh . . . *one* so far." Then added with a sheepish grin, "But it was a *really* good one." With a sigh of resignation, he reluctantly placed the cassette he was holding back on the table. "Aw'right, aw'right, I'll keep checking," he laughed. Not taking any chances, I stood guard by the table until he entered a travel agency up the street.

Two hours later, I found Colin and Dan sipping banana fruit shakes at a restaurant halfway up Kao San Road. They were ogling a couple of German girls in shorts and tank tops who were standing by the curb in front of them. I couldn't help laughing at how obvious their stares were. "You guys look like you just got out of prison," I laughed. "Put your eyes back in your heads."

I pulled a chair up to their table so we could review the information we had gathered. As it turned out, the travel shop near our hotel had the best prices, so after lunch, we decided to go straight over and buy three tickets to Vietnam. The friendly Thai woman in the travel office sat us down, and after offering us some tea, said, "I need four or five days to get the visas. Today is Sunday. If I send the paperwork in tomorrow, I can maybe get your visas by Thursday or Friday. When do you want to go?"

We discussed our options. Colin and I had each been to Thailand before and didn't particularly care to spend a week in Bangkok waiting for the visas. Dan didn't care where he went since it was all new to him anyway. We agreed that our best bet was to spend some time relaxing on a beach outside of Bangkok while our visas were processed.

"Is there a flight next Sunday?" we asked.

"Yes. There is an evening flight to Ho Chi Minh City."

"Perfect—we'll leave Sunday," we replied.

We completed the necessary paperwork and handed over our passport photos for the visas. When we were all paid up, the woman reserved three seats to Ho Chi Minh City—better known as Saigon—for a week from Sunday.

We returned to the hotel and talked about where we wanted to spend the next week. Dan read descriptions of the different islands from his guidebook while Colin and I spread out a map of Thailand. "Well, where to lads?" Colin asked, as he perused the map.

"How about Koh Samui—or Kao Phanghan?" Dan asked.

"Great places, but too far south," I said. "We'll lose two days getting down there and back."

"Yeah, that's true," Colin agreed. Then said, "I've got it—let's go to Koh Samet. It's only a few hours south of Bangkok. I was there a few years ago. It's a nice place—small, and much less crowded than the places further south."

"Sounds good to me," I said. "Dan?"

"Okay by me."

Colin folded the map and nodded his agreement. "Then Koh Samet it is."

Lead me not into temptation; I can find the way myself.
                                                          — Rita Mae Brown

The following morning, we took a "Tuk-Tuk" to the Eastern Bus Terminal on Sukumhvit Road. The cross-town traffic wasn't bad and we made it in about twenty minutes, which was pretty good for a "Tuk-Tuk" at that time of day.

After purchasing tickets to a town called Rayong, we boarded an un-airconditioned, local bus from the loading bay behind the terminal. Soon after we were seated, the bus backed out of the bay and inched its way through the congested city streets, bouncing in and out of potholes, and blasting its horn at every little motor scooter that weaved through the lanes of traffic in front of us.

After clearing the downtown congestion, the driver accelerated onto an access ramp that led onto a four-lane highway. Free from the constraints of city stoplights, we cruised down the highway at record-breaking speeds. For some reason, our driver wasn't merely content to drive as fast as he could—he also felt he had to pass every vehicle ahead of him. Expecting nothing short of disaster before we reached our destination, I sat helplessly glued to my seat while our crazy driver maneuvered the bus like a stagecoach out of control until we screeched to a halt in Rayong two hours later.

We hopped gratefully off the bus and piled into a *Songthaew*—a small pick-up truck with two benches in the truck-bed for passengers. *Songthaews* served as taxis along fixed routes, and since they usually didn't take off until they were filled with passengers, we squeezed onto the most crowded one we could find. When there was no more room for anyone to stand, sit, or hang on, the driver started the engine and drove to Ban Phe, a small seaside town thirty-minutes outside of Rayong. The island of Koh Samet was six and a half kilometers off the coast. After an hour wait, we boarded the next ferry and took off on the last leg of the trip.

As the ferry plowed through the clean, green-blue water towards the island, I felt the dirt and soot of Bangkok melt off me. The warm, ocean breeze carried the scent of the beaches out to us, while the cool, wet spray of the waves that crashed against the sides of the ferry cooled us down from the hot afternoon sun. I closed my eyes and relaxed.

Forty minutes later, the slowing of the engines roused me from my peaceful reverie as we made our final approach to the island. As we drifted into the harbor, the crew on the ferry tossed long, thick ropes to the shirtless Thai workers who stood waiting by the dock. When the ferry was firmly secured to the wide wood pilings by the pier, we grabbed our packs and stepped off the dock into the soft, white sand of Koh Samet, our island home for the next week.

Koh Samet is maintained and protected from overdevelopment by the Thai government as a National Park, so it isn't a big tourist spot for foreigners on the scale of say, Koh Samui, Pattaya, Pukhet or some of the other more popular spots further south. Due to its proximity to Bangkok, though, it receives a lot of local tourists during the high season and on Thai holidays when people flee out of Bangkok for the beaches.

We arrived during the low season so it was fairly deserted the whole time we were there. And because there weren't that many guesthouses along the southeastern part of the island where we stayed, it was almost like having the place to ourselves, which was fine during the day, when all we wanted to do was swim and lay out in the sun. But it got a little boring at night, since there wasn't much to do after dinner other than watch video movies at some of the guesthouses up the beach.

In the mornings, we walked along the beach and had breakfast at the different guesthouses to sample their menus. We stuffed ourselves with fresh fruit shakes, baked breads, and huge fruit plates of papaya, watermelon, jackfruit, and various other island fruits I wasn't familiar with. After breakfast, we rented lounge chairs for a few Baht, and laid out on the clean, white sand beach, soaking up the morning sun until the rays got too intense. After breaking for lunch, we took afternoon swims and sat in the shade of palm trees until the sun went down. It was a nice, easy-going pace, and not too hard a life to get used to.

After five days of lounging around the beach, however, I started to get restless for a new environment. I checked my map and saw that *Pattaya*, a resort town where foreigners from Europe and Asia went to party with Thai girls, was on the way back to Bangkok from Rayong. I had no intention of fooling around with any Thai call girls, but had heard so much about the place that I thought it might be worth a stopover for a day or two.

Colin hadn't quite had his fill of sand and sun so he preferred to hang out on Koh Samet for another few days rather than go to Pattaya. "I went there a coupla years ago," he told us. "It's too temptin' a place—all them young Thai girls throwin' themselves at ya'. If I go again I know I'll do somethin' I'll regret." He tapped his fingers nervously against his beach chair and contemplated the thought of going to Pattaya like an alcoholic tempted by a shot of whiskey. After a bit of an internal struggle, he grimaced uncertainly and said with some reluctance, "Nah, I'd better stay put. If you guys wanna go though, don't worry abou' me. I'll 'ang out 'ere for a coupla days, then meet you back at Kao San Road on Saturday or Sunday."

I turned to Dan. "So, how about it Danny-boy—feel like seeing what Pattaya's all about?"

Dan sat slumped in his beach chair, reading a guidebook on Vietnam, while the hot, morning sun slowly cooked his white skin to the color of a lobster. He looked up attentively at Colin and me. "Massage bars? Thai hostesses? Cold beers? Sounds aw'right," he mused aloud. Reaching for the sunscreen by his chair, he spread a puddle of white cream on his already burnt skin and nodded his approval. "Count me in."

When Dan and I boarded the ferry at Koh Samet the following morning, the sun was like a shimmering, yellow fireball in a clear, blue sky, bright and hot, with no escape from its rays. But despite the heat, it felt good being back on the water again, feeling the spray of the waves as the old, wooden ferry thumped its way across the Gulf of Thailand towards the fishing village of Ban Phe on the mainland.

After we docked at Ban Phe, we stepped off the ferry and waited on the dusty, dirt road in front of the pier for a Songthaew to take us to Rayong. After a hot, forty-five minute wait, a crowded Songthaew sped by without stopping. Seeing us waving energetically on the road, the driver hit the brakes, kicking up a cloud of dust in front of us. Dan and I jogged down the road and hopped inside the pick-up truck next to the other passengers already seated inside. When we were safely on board, the driver hit the gas and raced back down the dusty road toward Rayong, where we caught a long distance bus for the two and a half hour trip to Pattaya.

As we neared Pattaya, the skyline from the highway reminded me more of Florida than of Thailand. Tall, white, luxury hotels with rolling golf courses and long, clear-blue swimming pools had been built along the waterfront side of the city. If the traffic along the Sukhumvit highway was any indication, Pattaya was going to be as crowded as any beach strip in Fort Lauderdale during Spring Break.

The bus turned off the highway and drove down South Pattaya Road toward the center of the city, a four-kilometer area that stretched between Pattaya Beach Road along the gulf, and Pattaya 2 Road along the beach. Almost all the streets within this strip were packed with shops, bars, restaurants and tourists, but Pattaya Beach Road was where the action was heaviest.

Before we even got off the bus, I could feel the energy on the streets. Motorcycles and mopeds sputtered all around us, leaving long trails of black exhaust in their wake, their seats loaded down with three or more Thais on them. Foreign tourists crowded the strip and the side streets up and down the beach and everywhere I looked, I saw outdoor bars and night clubs with scantily-clad Thai women beckoning tourists to step inside.

I stepped off the bus behind Dan and noticed him gawking at a pretty Thai girl walking arm-in-arm with a stocky, middle-aged European at least twice her age. Dan gaped at them until they walked past. "That guy's old enough to be her father! What could she possibly see in him?" he remarked, curiously.

"Money," I replied.

He frowned and lifted his backpack. "This town looks pretty crowded. Think we'll have trouble finding a room?"

"I hope not. But we'd better hurry and start looking before it gets too late," I answered, as I flipped open my guidebook and checked out the hotel listings for Pattaya.

As it turned out, we had nothing to worry about. There were hundreds of hotels and guesthouses all around Pattaya—more than enough to accommodate the huge number of tourists who went there all year long to enjoy the water sports, beaches, and sex. Not necessarily in that order.

Dan and I found a clean, little hotel on a quiet side street in South Pattaya, close to Pattaya Beach road. After dropping our things off in our room, we went out to get a feel for the city before going for dinner. It didn't take long before we spotted Pattaya's main attractions, or rather, before Pattaya's main attractions spotted us.

"Hello! You very handsome! Come inside! You want meet pretty girl?" Dan and I shot quick glances down the street to our right and saw three girls outside a nightclub smiling and waving at us. Dan turned around to see if they were calling to someone behind us.

"I think they're talking to us," he said with surprise.

"Well actually, I think they're talking to me."

"Why's that?"

With a playful grin I said, "They said 'handsome,' didn't they?" We waved to the girls and continued walking. Each street we passed was the same. Small groups of dark-haired, attractive Thai girls lingering outside the bars and clubs along the sidewalks, flirting with tourists and trying to entice them to come inside. To our surprise, plenty of tourists answered the call. It was only late afternoon, and still light outside, but already the bars and massage parlors along the streets were busy with customers—most of whom weren't Asian.

As we walked along the strip, I was amazed to see how many Western men were coupled up with young, Thai women. Everywhere we looked, Westerners zipped along on little, Honda motor-scooters with Thai girls clinging happily to their waists, their long, silky black hair whipping behind them in the breeze. The more well-healed tourists cruised by in jeeps, their Thai escorts flashing great, white smiles from the front and back seats. It was like one big party, and everyone with money was invited.

For a change of pace from the Pad Thai and other noodle dishes we had been eating day in and day out since we had arrived in Thailand, we decided to have dinner at a Pizza Hut along Pattaya Beach road. It wasn't cheap compared to Thai food, but it was worth it, until we stuffed ourselves so full of pizza we couldn't move. The pizzas were good, but the toppings were so filling, and the crusts so buttery, that I actually felt queasy when we got up to leave. Dan had eaten even more than I did. Rather than walk around in our bloated states, we went back to the hotel to relax for a while before going out to see the nightclubs.

Fluorescent lights from all of the street stalls and bars lit the black, night sky like an outdoor carnival. Pattaya Beach Road was packed.

Groups of pleasure-seeking tourists huddled along the strip, checking out the girls in the outdoor bars and clubs, while their souvenir-minded counterparts browsed at little stalls along the sidewalk, searching for cheap sunglasses, T-shirts, and other inexpensive souvenirs with 'Pattaya' emblazoned all over them.

Dan and I found it easier to walk in the street near the curb than along the crowded sidewalks. Avoiding the sidewalks also made it easier to fend off the advances of the Thai girls who pulled at our shirts to get us to stop inside their clubs. Every now and then, though, oncoming cars would force us back on the sidewalk and the girls would make us promise to come back later in the night before they would let us get away.

"This is unbelievable," Dan said, after slipping gently away from a very cute, and very young-looking, Thai girl. Deftly fending off the advances of another young girl ahead of him, Dan laughed and called back over his shoulder, "If the girls in Australia were this willing, I would never have left!" I was too busy skirting around two women lunging for my shirt to answer him.

Further down the strip, an outdoor bar had set up a full-sized boxing ring in the hopes of drawing customers through the lure of Thai Boxing Exhibitions. While Dan and I scanned the list of fight schedules, a group of Thai hostesses laughed and ran toward us. We jumped quickly back in the street and kept walking.

A few blocks further on, we turned off of Pattaya Beach Road and made our way down a busy side street. Halfway up the street and off to our right was a short, wide square with three large outdoor bars in its center, and topless clubs lining its sides. We walked past the outdoor bars and sauntered slowly past the different clubs, catching glimpses of the action inside as customers entered and exited. As we wandered near each club, Thai hostesses swung the doors of their bars open to reveal naked girls dancing to loud, pulsing music on stages lit up with multi-colored lights. While we peeked inside, they enticed us with, *"No cover charge"*; *"Come inside"*; *"Just have look."*

Dan and I evaluated our options as we walked around the square. On our second run around, we stopped in front of a club called "*Caligula*" that had two beautiful hostesses standing out front. With a seductive smile, one of the women opened the door and said, "Very pretty girls inside. Come look."

Dan and I stepped cautiously inside the dark entrance of the club as the door closed quietly behind us. Twenty feet inside the club was a large, elevated, rectangular stage ringed by a wide counter and tall bar chairs. Men, mostly Europeans and Japanese, sat around the counter, their faces illuminated by flashing, colored lights that were set beneath the plexiglass floor of the stage. They sat with frozen smiles on their faces, motionless except for an occasional sip from their glasses of beer, their eyes fixed on the girls gyrating to the booming music on the stage above them.

On top of the stage, eight raven-haired beauties were strutting their stuff to loud, pop music. Clad in little bikini swimsuits, they oozed sex as they swayed from one end of the stage to the other. Sliding their bodies seductively up and down shiny metal poles which led from the stage to the ceiling, they flashed slow, deliberate crotch shots to the men around the bar, who sat mesmerized, following every move the girls made.

Further away from the stage, other customers sat around small cocktail tables placed along the sides of the club, happily fondling the girls who were "on break." To keep the girls from drifting off to other tables, the men knew they had to keep buying rounds of drinks. I stood near the doorway taking it all in and couldn't help laughing. It all looked so pathetic. Dan and I were surrounded by a bunch of horny foreigners who sat staring and pawing at dancing girls like high-school kids who had never seen naked women before. I wondered if they realized how pitiful they looked. Especially the older men. Most of the men in the club were in their mid-twenties to late-forties, but some of them looked like they could have been grandfathers to the girls sitting on their laps. It was surprising what some guys would do for a couple of cheap thrills.

A few seconds later, a hostess came by to seat us. Taking the lead, she led us past tables hidden in shadows on our left, and escorted us to two recessed seats against the back wall. Two round cocktail tables stood in front of us, stacked with empty brown *Singha* beer bottles from the customers who had sat there before us. As soon as we were seated, an attractive, young waitress approached from the shadows to clear our tables and take our drink orders. Within minutes, Dan and I were sipping cold beers and gaping at the girls dancing on stage in front of us.

"God, that one on the left has got an unbelievable body," I blurted out loud, as I stared at a beautiful dancer with long, silky black hair on the left side of the stage.

Dan looked at the girl I was admiring. "Not bad," he agreed, taking another sip of his beer. "But I like the one with the short hair in the middle." The girl he was referring to was also great looking. They were all great looking.

The girl I was admiring stretched her legs around the pole in the center of the stage. I took a deep breath and tried not to stare but couldn't help myself. When the song was over, the girls put their string bikinis back on and left the stage to mingle with the customers. Without missing a beat, the girls who had been walking around or having drinks at the tables then went up to take their place back on stage. Dan and I were in the process of ordering another round of beers when two girls stepped out of the shadows and sat at our table. The one next to me placed her hand on my arm and asked quietly, "You buy me drink?"

I turned and almost fell off my seat—it was the girl from the stage that I had been gawking at. She was even more beautiful up close. She had gorgeous, almond-shaped eyes and long, thick, black hair which flowed over her tanned, perfectly shaped shoulders to the middle of her back. She also had the most perfect smile I had ever seen. Her teeth were so white they almost glowed in the dim light of the club. And her body was flawless—most of it visible, since all she had on was a string bikini. I stared at her with my mouth wide open, speechless, awed by her half-naked body just inches away from me.

"You buy me drink?" she repeated. The waitress waited for my answer. When I hesitated, the dancer placed her hand on my leg and inched her fingers slowly up my thigh. "Buy me drink," she said softly, while gently stroking my crotch. I looked at the waitress and let out a gasp. "Uh . . . Okay, yeah, sure—whatever she wants."

The rest of the night sped by like a blur. To keep my girl from leaving I kept ordering drinks, knowing I would be rewarded with continued kisses, stroking and mutual fondling. She had the softest skin I had ever felt and I couldn't keep my hands off her. It was pathetic. I was pathetic. But I didn't care. My libido had taken over and I was happy to relinquish control. After awhile, she breathed lightly in my ear, "You want sleep with me?" I breathed in the fragrance of her thick mane of hair while she continued to gently explore my body. "How much?" I immediately asked.

Hearing my words slip from my mouth, I jolted up. *Did I just ask how much?* I thought, suddenly starting to panic. I couldn't believe it. I was losing it and needed someone to yank me out of there—fast.

Where was Dan? I suddenly wondered. Why wasn't he trying to talk some sense into me before I did something I would regret in the morning?

When I turned to find him, my hopes for a speedy rescue were crushed. Dan was further gone than I was. Sprawled out on the seat to the right of me, I could barely see him beneath the long black hair and the tight embrace of the girl on his lap.

Meanwhile, my girl was signaling to a man behind the bar that I was interested in a price to sleep with her. The barman signaled back to her and she whispered in my ear, "Five-hundred Baht." With a sexy smile, she slipped her gentle, experienced fingers under my shirt and said, "Okay?" I felt myself starting to weaken. All of a sudden the song ended, indicating a change of dancers. It was my girl's turn to go back on stage. *No, not yet! Oh God, don't let her go. Talk about lousy timing!*

I watched as she took her place on stage with the other dancers and realized it was now or never. When her set was over she would come back, fondle my body again, and I'd go off anywhere with her. It was a done deal and she knew it. This was my last chance for a getaway "*Dan . . . Dan!*" I whispered urgently. I shook his shoulder—though it might have been his girl's shoulder. They were so tied up together I couldn't be sure.

With a sleepy look, he replied innocently, "What's up?"

I glanced back at the stage to make sure my girl was still up there and safely out of reach. "Listen, I've got to get out of here or I'm going to wind up in bed with her in about ten minutes," I said desperately. "What are you planning to do—take off or stick around?"

Dan tried to sit up but was having trouble disentangling himself from the girl on his lap. When she shifted her legs a little to let him up, I noticed that he looked like a mess. His shirt was pulled out from his pants and his hair was twisted in every possible direction. In his usual obliging way, he yawned and said, "I guess I'm ready," as he stood up to go. When his girl saw that he was planning to leave, she also stood up. Without a word, she smiled at him then disappeared in the shadows across the room.

I didn't want to leave the club without saying goodbye to my girl so I stood in the aisle near the stage and waited for her to dance in my direction. As she whirled around, she lifted her head and saw me. When her eyes met mine, I smiled and waved goodbye. She tilted her head and pouted her lips a little to let me know she was disappointed I was leaving. Then, without missing a beat to the song she was dancing to, she slid her left leg around the pole next to her and slowly caressed her thighs before flashing me a sexy smile and a wave goodbye.

It wasn't until I was out of the club and back on the street that I felt safe from my desire to turn around and toss the barman 500 Baht to take her with me for the night. I was thankful I hadn't, but knew that as long as I stayed in Pattaya I'd be tempted to go back.

When Dan and I boarded the bus the following morning for the two-hour ride to Bangkok I was relieved to put some miles between Pattaya and me. Colin was right—the temptations were just too great.

Fear of Flying

Good Morning Vietnam

Scarface

I'm not afraid to die. I just don't want to be there when it happens.
—Woody Allen

We pulled up to the airport with plenty of time to spare before our 5:00 P.M. flight to Saigon. It was a good thing too, since we needed the extra time to walk the cramps out of our legs from the hour and a half Tuk-Tuk ride from Kao San Road.

Why the three of us squeezed into one Tuk-Tuk with all our backpacks and daypacks was beyond me. At the time, it seemed like a good idea. Ten feet away from Kao San Road, it was a bad idea. But by then, it was too late to do anything about it. With our packs wedged uncomfortably between our knees and our chins, we were jammed inside the little, three-wheeled vehicle like sardines. The only way to pry us out would have been with a crowbar.

With the weight of my backpack on my knees, every bump in the road made me curse the thin padded seat beneath me. Our driver, on the other hand, was having a terrific time. Dodging his way in and out of the traffic mess around us, he chattered happily away in Thai, pointing to things on the streets as he spoke—totally oblivious to our heads smashing against the roof of the Tuk-Tuk whenever we hit a particularly nasty bump. Not that he could have heard us over the high-pitched throttle of the engine, but even if he had, all he would have heard was, "Oomphff!"; "Aarghh!"; "Aackk!" as Dan, Colin, and I got tossed around with every bump in the road.

Ninety-minutes later, we swerved into the drop-off lane at *Don Muang Airport*. We crawled out of the Tuk-Tuk like three old men with severe cases of arthritis. When the circulation returned to our legs, we swung our packs on our shoulders and left the heat of the late afternoon sun for the cool, airconditioned comfort of Bangkok's modern, international airport.

The Vietnam Airlines check-in counter wasn't hard to find. It was the only one with no passengers in front of it. "Not a very good sign is it?" Dan remarked.

I was a little nervous about the flight to begin with, so the lack of other passengers didn't make me feel better. And since Vietnam Airlines wasn't exactly a world-class carrier, I found myself wondering what their safety record was—assuming they had one. The description in my guidebook certainly wasn't very encouraging:

> " . . . Vietnam Airlines has suffered a bad reputation in the past. Basically, the problem has been old equipment, a lack of spare parts and lack of funds to set things right . . . "

That they used Russian Tupolev 134 planes didn't give me much confidence either. Not that I knew anything about Tupolev 134 planes, but anything built in Russia was cause for suspicion as far as I was concerned. When I saw we were the only passengers checking in at the counter, I wondered whether we had been the only ones dumb enough to buy tickets on Vietnam Airlines.

With nervous smiles on our faces, we walked up to the check-in desk. Two women dressed in simple, but professional looking uniforms, greeted us with pleasant smiles as we approached. Colin spoke up first. "We're 'ere to check-in for the five o'clock flight to Ho Chi Minh City," he said. Dan added hopefully, "Are there many other people going on tonight's flight?"

"Not so many," one of the women replied. Dan and I shot panicked looks at each other.

"Do you know if we'll be flying on one of those Russian Tupolevs?" Dan asked.

"No Russian airplane. We have new airplane we are using now."

"Do you know what kind of plane?" Dan probed.

She bit her lower lip, trying to remember, then said, "No . . . but it is a *good* one!"

"Is it safe?" I asked nervously.

She smiled and said diplomatically, "It is more safe than the one we used before." Her reply didn't comfort us much and when we walked towards gate number 33 for our 4:20 P.M. departure, we expected the worst.

As we approached the loading ramp, we were shocked to see a Boeing 737 parked outside the gate. We were even more stunned to see a blonde, Swedish woman as the Head-Stewardess. She was an attractive woman in her late forties, and smiled politely to each of us as we boarded the plane. When we remarked how happy we were to find ourselves on a 737 with a Swedish stewardess, she laughed and told us that the plane and flight crew—all Irish pilots—had been chartered by Vietnam Airlines to supplement their fleet of Tupolev planes. In addition to the Swedish stewardess, there were three other stewardesses and one male steward, all Vietnamese. The stewardesses, including the Swede, wore the traditional Vietnamese "*Ao dai,*" a blouse with long panels in the front and back, and slits on either side, that is worn over loose-fitting trousers.

Of the fifty or so passengers on the flight, there were only four other Westerners in addition to Dan, Colin and myself. Most of the passengers were Hong Kong Chinese traveling to Vietnam on business.

"Hey, this isn't too bad, is it?" Dan said, as we relaxed in our seats before take-off.

"It's a lot nicer than I expected," I replied. Then added, "I feel a lot better knowing we're on a 737 with Western-trained pilots and a professional-looking flight crew, I'll tell you that."

With a shake of his head, Colin laughed. "Bloody Americans—always worryin' and frettin' about somethin' goin' wrong. It's a wonder the lot o' you ever leave the country!"

"Who's worried?" I said, knowing full well I still had my doubts we would ever get off the ground in one piece. But as usual, my fears were unfounded. Shortly after all the passengers were seated the aircraft accelerated down the long runway and lifted effortlessly into the air.

An hour and twenty minutes after we left Bangkok, the flight crew announced that we were beginning our descent into Saigon. Dan peered out the window and commented curiously, "Doesn't look like there's anything down there." I cupped my hands against the window to my left but all I could see was blackness below the wing of the plane.

As we continued our descent I saw faint lights across a wide area far below us. I had expected to fly over a large city with bright lights emanating from highways and buildings, but instead, it looked like we were flying over a remote area in the country. Far below the left wing of the aircraft, the dim glow of small, yellow lights flickered feebly against the massive gaps of darkness around them.

The wheels of the plane rumbled noisily from the belly of the 737 as they were lowered for landing. With barely a bump, the aircraft touched down lightly on the ground and we sped across the dark tarmac like a bullet. As the wheels gripped the hard surface of the runway, the whine of the engines decreased in pitch from a deafening roar to a steady, even hum as we decelerated and taxied toward the arrival building. A few minutes later, the aircraft came to a full stop and the overhead lights were turned on to signal our arrival.

As the passengers unbuckled their seatbelts and popped open the overhead compartments to gather their things, the flight attendants walked through the aisles to pick up whatever stray cups and headphones hadn't been turned in prior to our landing. On her way to the front of the aircraft, the Swedish stewardess stopped by my row to pick up an empty water cup from the seat beside me. As she stooped by my seat, she glanced over and smiled. "Have you ever been to Saigon before?" she asked.

"No, this is my first trip to Vietnam."

With the cup in her hand, she stood up and leaned towards me. Speaking in a low voice so the other passengers wouldn't hear her, she cautioned, "Be careful on the streets—there are many pickpockets in Saigon."

Many of us have some of the war still inside us.
This creates difficulties in lives.
—Le Luu, Vietnamese Veteran and Novelist

We stepped off the plane at Saigon's *Tan Son Nhut International Airport* and crossed the dark tarmac to the customs hall across from the arrival gate. After collecting our backpacks, we entered a large, bleak room lined with rows of long, metal tables. One by one, we propped our packs on the tables so the customs officers could check their contents. After a brief inspection of our cameras, Walkmans, and cassettes, we were officially stamped into Vietnam.

On our way through customs, we struck up a conversation with a tall, friendly Swiss guy named Bart who was returning to Vietnam for the second time in six months. He had been so enamored with Vietnam during his first trip that he had decided to come back and explore those parts of the country he had missed the first time around. "I know a good place to stay if you'd like to take a taxi into the city together," he offered, as we walked out of the customs hall together. Happy to accompany anyone who knew where he was going, we grabbed our packs and followed him outside.

It was dark outside the terminal, and other than a few taxis parked out front, the grounds of the airport were fairly deserted. Bart walked over to one of the waiting taxis and negotiated a fare to a street called *Pham Ngu Lao* in Central Saigon. "Pham Ngu Lao is in District One," he informed us. "It's only about thirty minutes from the airport. There are a couple of cheap hotels there that are pretty good." After tossing his pack in the trunk, he sat in the passenger seat next to the driver while Dan, Colin and I piled into the back seat behind them.

During our drive to the city, I realized why Saigon looked so dark from the air. There were no streetlights. Though the streets were packed with people, the only illumination came from pale, yellow light bulbs that hung on the food stalls, shops and carts of street vendors that lined the sidewalks. It was like coming into a city during a black-out. From the air it looked deserted, but on the ground, it was a hive of activity, hidden by the cover of night.

After half an hour on a dimly lit road from the airport, the driver made a right-hand turn onto Le Loi Boulevard, one of central Saigon's main avenues. We drove past the Ben Thanh Market, one of the busiest markets in Saigon, then swung around a traffic circle in the middle of the street towards an unlit, dirt road that became Pham Ngu Lao Street. Halfway up the street, the driver stopped the taxi in front of a hotel. Pointing to the building in front of us, Bart said, "This is where I stayed the last time I was here—the *Vien Dong Hotel*."

The Vien Dong was an old, solid-looking, French style hotel with balconied floors that overlooked a central courtyard. The rooms were large and clean, with high ceilings and shuttered windows—a decent place for five dollars a night, per person. We paid for two double rooms, Dan and I in one, and Colin and Bart in the other.

After dropping our bags off in our rooms, Bart led us to a small, outdoor café a few blocks from the hotel. The owners of the little café remembered Bart and were happy to see him again. With big smiles, they cleaned the seats of four plastic chairs on the sidewalk and invited us to sit down. Right after we were seated, a young girl walked over with a small serving tray. With a shy smile, she handed each of us a small cup of freshly brewed coffee.

Bart stretched his long legs on the sidewalk in front of him and sipped his coffee with pleasure. He gave a friendly nod to some elderly men who walked by, and said happily, "I love this country—the people are all very nice and always smiling."

Dan tasted his coffee and nodded contentedly. "They also make a pretty good cup of coffee," he remarked with a smile.

We sat on the sidewalk drinking our coffees and relaxing in the warm, night air while the busy street life played around us. Vietnamese men and women zipped up and down the dark streets on motorcycles, scooters, and bicycles, their headlights barely illuminating the dimly-lit roads in front of them. Families strolled casually along the sidewalks, stopping at small roadside shops and food stalls on their way home, while their children ran behind them, pointing and giggling at the four strange looking foreigners sprawled out in little, plastic chairs in front of the café.

Actually, I felt conspicuous even when the kids weren't giggling at us. For the first time since I left home, I was suddenly very self-conscious of my nationality. It was foolish for me to feel that way since none of the Vietnamese acted any differently to me than to Bart, Colin or Dan, but all the same, I still felt a little uneasy.

For a lot of Americans back home, the Vietnam War was still a touchy subject. The fact that many Americans still harbored ill feelings toward the Vietnamese more than twenty years after the war was proof enough. And if some Americans were still sensitive about Vietnam, I hated to imagine what the Vietnamese thought. Aside from having their country bombed to pieces by American forces, almost ten percent of the total Vietnamese population had been killed or injured during the war. Though most Vietnamese in their twenties wouldn't remember much about the war, the people in their late thirties and forties or older, had either lived through it or fought in it.

I glanced over at two elderly Vietnamese men sitting next to us and tried to imagine what life must have been like for them during the years of fighting in Vietnam. Seeing me looking at them, they nodded their heads and smiled. I wondered whether they could tell I was American just by looking at me. And if they could, whether it bothered them knowing Americans were coming back to their country again. Even if it didn't, I still felt strange being in the place that had been the focus of the whole sixties generation, and even today, the subject of books, movies and TV shows about the war.

Looking at the young families on the street and the old men sitting peacefully beside us, it was hard to imagine the devastation and loss their countrymen must have lived through during their long conflicts with France and the United States. I smiled back at them and felt grateful for their warm welcome. And though it was an amazing experience to sit at an outdoor cafe in Saigon in the middle of the night and watch its incessant street life unfold around us, the flight from Bangkok and the excitement of being in Vietnam finally caught up to us. So after finishing our last round of coffee and settling our bill, we said goodnight to the two, smiling old men and returned to our hotel to get a good night's rest.

"Sszzzz! Thump! Crack! Whrrr!" The sounds from the courtyard outside our room jolted me awake from a sound sleep. I reached in the dark for my watch on the night table. The luminous hands on my watch showed 6:00 A.M. "What in the world is all that racket out there?" I mumbled aloud in the dark as I hopped out of bed and walked outside the room. From the balcony in the hallway, I could see a group of Vietnamese workers hauling bales of wood and aluminum poles through the courtyard below. On the opposite end of the courtyard, other workers were busy sawing stacks of lumber and hammering nails into thick posts of wood.

"What's going on?" Dan asked wearily, from inside the room.

"I don't know. They're doing some kind of construction work in the lobby," I replied, before closing the door and crawling wearily back into bed.

Dan moaned and pulled his blanket over his head to block out the noise. I covered my head with my pillow but it didn't help. The hammering and sawing from the construction crew echoed through the courtyard and reverberated throughout the room.

When we left the hotel a few hours later to find a place for breakfast, we inquired about the noise and were told that extensive renovations were being done in the hotel to accommodate the growing influx of tourists. When we learned that the construction crew began work at six o'clock every morning, Dan, Bart, and I opted to switch hotels. Not surprisingly, Colin wanted to stay right where we were. His main priority on arriving in a new city was to book a room as painlessly and as quickly as possible. Once he got settled into a place, he hated to move. But the rest of us had no desire to get woken up every morning at daybreak. We packed our things and told Colin, "You can stay here if you want, but we're moving to another hotel. There's no reason why we've got to live on a construction site when there are plenty of other decent hotels half a block up the street." Not wanting to foot the cost of a room by himself, Colin reluctantly agreed to switch hotels with us. Ten minutes later, we checked into the equally nice, and infinitely quieter, *Prince Hotel*, a short distance up the road.

We dropped our packs off in our new rooms, then went for breakfast at *Kim's Café*, a small, outdoor restaurant at the corner of the street. Kim was a young woman in her early twenties who ran the café with the help of her family. Westernized Vietnamese dishes and great fruit shakes made her café a popular hangout for backpackers staying at the hotels along *Pham Ngu Lao*. Unfortunately, it had also become a popular hangout for a growing number of Vietnamese kids in the neighborhood who hoped to make money from the travelers who ate there.

As we were soon to learn, it wasn't easy going anywhere in Saigon without attracting hordes of kids trying to sell us something. And at Kim's, we were sitting ducks. But worst of all, we were easy prey for the tough, little, ten-year old that we came to know as "Scarface."

*If a child shows himself incorrigible, he should be decently
and quietly beheaded at the age of twelve.*
— Don Marquis

We were new in town, and, like fresh meat, the kids at Kim's Café hovered over us like vultures. Five kids, ranging in age from nine to fourteen, came racing to our table as soon as we sat down. Shoving their bubble gum, postcards, cans of soda, and T-shirts in our faces, they shouted at once, "You buy, okay?"

Tired from having been woken up so early in the morning, we weren't in the mood to deal with a bunch of screaming children. But not wanting to be rude, we thumbed through their stuff to keep them happy. As nicely as we could, we told them that if they left us alone for awhile we might consider buying something after we finished eating. To our surprise, they understood everything we said and ran off to pester some of the regulars seated at the tables outside the café.

Colin laughed as he watched the kids run to the other tables. "Li'l buggers understan' English pretty well, don't they?" With a tired sigh, he leaned across the table for one of the hand-written menus next to Dan and said confidently, "Well, at least we'll get to eat in peace now."

"Don't count on it," I replied, warily. When Colin looked up, I nodded towards a small, barefoot boy outside the café who was staring at us. Dressed in dirty shorts and a ragged white T-shirt, he watched us with piercing, dark-brown eyes. For some reason, he hadn't been with the group of kids that had surrounded us when we first walked in. Free of competition, he saw his chance and decided to take it. With calm determination, he edged past the tables on the sidewalk and walked slowly and deliberately towards us. "Here he comes," I warned.

The boy walked with a little swagger, swaying his hips a bit, while leaning his shoulders back like a tough-guy who meant business and wanted to telegraph with his stride that he wasn't someone to be messed with.

Sauntering up to the end of the table, he placed his stack of postcards in front of Colin and me. Without so much as a hello, he demanded, in a voice that reminded me of Peter Lorre, "You buy postcards!" He was small and looked to be about ten years old. But somehow, standing eye-to-eye with us as we sat in our seats, his confident, menacing manner made him seem taller and older.

Colin sighed and flipped through the postcards, hoping that after he looked at them, the kid would walk off and leave us alone. I looked at this cocky, little boy, with his dirty, little arms leaning casually against our table, and was surprised to see that he was studying us in return, glancing at the four of us with an amused expression.

Seeing him up close, I noticed that he had two long scars across his face. One of the scars, the more noticeable of the two, ran straight across his face from cheek to cheek. The second ran vertically down his forehead, about an inch and a half in length. He actually wasn't a bad-looking kid, but the scars gave him a hardened, street-tough scowl.

When Colin finished looking through the cards, he tossed them back on the table. "Sorry lad, not interested," he remarked flatly. The boy shot a nasty glare at Colin and then turned his attention to me. With a quick movement, he slid the packets of cards next to my plate and quietly demanded, "You look."

I skimmed through the cards and said, "Maybe I'll buy something later. Right now I want to have breakfast, okay?" He took a deep breath and stared at me without a sound. Taking my comment as a promise to buy, he scooped up his cards and swaggered back outside of the restaurant.

When he walked away, Dan said, "Those are some nasty looking scars he has there. Wonder how he got them?"

"Well, he's a cocky l'il bastard, isn't he?" Colin replied. "Probably shoved his cards in front of the wrong bloke! He's a tough l'il tyke, though, isn't he? Reminds me of Al Pacino in that movie—what was it called?" After a moment's thought Colin laughed and said, "Scarface! that was it! Yeah—he's a Vietnamese *Scarface!*"

No one seemed to know for sure how the boy had gotten his scars. When we asked Kim about him, she told us that his mother claimed he fell off a motorcycle when he was a baby. A cyclo driver we'd become friendly with told us that the scars were the result of a bicycle accident. And a third source told us that the boy had hung out with a bad crowd of street kids when he was about six or seven years old. As a result of a confrontation with an older boy, he was supposedly slashed across his face to teach him a lesson.

The third version seemed the most believable, especially after meeting the little guy in person. But the reliability of the source was highly questionable—a local prostitute who didn't seem to like him very much. We never had the nerve to ask Scarface himself how he had gotten his scars, so their origin remained a mystery. With or without his scars, however, he was still a pushy little salesman when it came to marketing his goods and an ongoing nuisance during our stay in Saigon.

Since all the kids pretty much sold the same things, we soon learned that the issue wasn't *whether* we bought, but *from whom* we bought. By not buying anything, we stayed impartial. But as soon as we purchased something from one of them, the others viewed it as playing favorites. They thought: "we're all selling the same stuff, so why did you buy from her or him and not me?" If we bought something from one, the others moped around and feigned tears, or got angry and stamped around, shaking their fists at us while spewing forth a stream of invectives in Vietnamese until we bought something to calm them down. And nobody played that game better than "Scarface," as Colin had dubbed him. If you so much as hinted that you might buy something from him, and then bought something from one of the other kids, you were on his shit list. And somehow, over the next few days in Saigon, I made the top of his list.

After breakfast, we dashed past the kids waiting for us on the sidewalk and walked over to the Ben Thanh Market, a few short blocks from Pham Ngu Lao Street. It should have been an easy walk from Kim's Café but walking anywhere in Saigon wasn't easy. With a population of close to three million people, and an average density of 21,500 people per square kilometer, the traffic on the streets of Saigon was mind-boggling. The flow of bicycles, cyclos, and motorscooters was endless. And without the benefit of traffic lights to regulate the various vehicles coming at you from all sides, crossing the main avenues was treacherous. The easiest way to cross the streets without getting run over was to wade slowly into the traffic and let it flow around you. Throwing ourselves into the stream of traffic in front of us, we walked slowly through the intersection of Le Lai Street and Le Loi Boulevard until we reached the entrance to the market. Miraculously, we all made it across in one piece.

With all of that traffic on the streets of Saigon, it was hard to believe there was anyone left to fill the market. But it was packed—all eleven square kilometers of it. Once we were inside, the crowded aisles were an assault on the senses. Vietnamese in every shape and size wandered through the narrow aisles, chattering away as they did their shopping. Strong scents of fish, meats, spices, vegetables, and fruits drifted toward us from every direction. And every conceivable household, hardware, and clothing item used in Saigon was lined up on long metal tables as far as we could see. It was an amazing sight, and by the time we left, we felt we had seen at least half of the products and people in Saigon.

The same bustling atmosphere was prevalent wherever we went—crowded markets, congested streets, and a booming commercialism that started early in the morning and lasted well into the night. Saigon was a dynamic, energetic city, and wandering around the streets each day was a constant thrill. It was also exhausting. And by the end of each day's wanderings around the city, we were eager to return to Kim's Café for a cold drink and a chance to relax.

On our third evening in Saigon, tired from a full day of strolling around markets and museums, we went to Kim's for an early dinner. As soon as we sat down, one of the local girls came over to see if we wanted to buy her postcards. She was one of the original group of children who had approached us on our first morning in town, so I bought a pack of cards from her. Boy, was that a mistake. Somehow, Scarface found out and in his usual, tactful manner, came storming over to our table demanding an explanation.

He held out a stack of postcards identical to the ones I had just bought and seethed, "Why you no buy cards from me!"

Seeing the fire in Scarface's eyes, Colin whispered to me, "You're in for it now."

I didn't want to hurt the boy's feelings, so I tried to explain why I had bought the cards from the little girl. As gently as I could I said, "She showed me her cards before you came by the other day. If I need more cards I'll buy them from you next time, okay?"

"You buy cards now," he fumed.

"But I don't need any more cards right now. See?" I held up the cards I had just bought as proof that I was already well supplied.

Without blinking an eye, he let out a long, slow breath. Giving me one last chance to reconsider, he asked tentatively, "You no buy cards?"

"I don't need any more right now," I repeated patiently. "Next time, okay?"

To my surprise, instead of belting me, he rubbed his eyes as if he were going to cry. I hate when people cry. It always makes me feel sorry for them. Feeling guilty, I was just about to give in and buy another pack of the same damn cards when Colin beat me to it and said, "All right then lad, let's see what you've got."

After a cursory look at the cards, Colin bought a packet in order to appease Scarface, then sat back to finish his meal. Scarface glared at me with venom in his eyes and pointed to Colin. "He buy cards. I like." Then he pointed to Dan and said, "Him good too." Jabbing his finger towards me, he said slowly, and with considerable disdain, "You I no likc."

I pointed incredulously at Dan. "But . . . but *he* didn't buy anything from anyone," I protested. "Why do you like *him*?"

Unfortunately, Scarface wasn't one to explain himself. He squinted his eyes and wagged his finger slowly and menacingly at me and walked quietly away.

"What is that supposed to mean?" I asked Dan and Colin, nervously.

"I dunno, but it can't be good," Colin laughed. "If I were you, I'd watch my back from now on." With a slow nod of his head, he added, "No tellin' what Scar might do to ya' now. Good thing I bought the cards from 'im. I'd hate to have 'im mad at me. How 'bout you Dan?" Dan laughed and nodded his agreement with Colin.

"Well, that's great," I sighed. "It's just what I need—a pint-sized hoodlum who's out to get me. Why me?"

"Because *you* didn' buy his cards," Colin said, waving his postcards happily in my face.

Over the next few days, Scarface gave me the same angry glare and that same menacing wag of his finger, whenever he saw me. He also gave me the cold shoulder. Whenever we were at Kim's he would come over to our table and purposely avoid me, standing with his back to me while he spoke to Colin and Dan. If I tried to talk to him, he would tighten his lips and ignore me. Colin was loving it, and played it up whenever he could. Secure in the knowledge that he was Scar-face's buddy, he took incredible delight in egging him on. And just to make sure Scarface wouldn't forget to get even with me, Colin would point at me and say, "Him no good. He no buy postcards, right?" Colin was having a great time at my expense. Later that week, though, fate stepped in and evened things out.

Dan, Colin and I were walking up Pham Ngu Lao Street on our way back to the hotel one evening. It was dark and hard to see, but we could hear some people coming down the street in our direction. When they got closer, three local girls came into view. They were each dressed up in tight skirts and heels, and were walking a few feet ahead of another group of people. When the girls walked by, we glanced over our shoulders to look at them. As we turned back around we heard a soft thud, followed by a low moan on the ground beside us.

"I think I stepped on somethin'," Colin said with concern. He walked over to the curb to see what he had hit. Glancing down he saw a small, dark-haired boy on the ground by the curb. The boy was lying on his side, holding his foot. Colin bent down to help him up, but the boy waved him off angrily, clutching his ankle in pain near the unlit sidewalk.

When Colin saw who he had stepped on, he gasped and looked over at Dan and me. *"Bloody hell—it's Scar!"* Colin hollered, as he raced over to Dan and me with a look of terror on his face. "I stepped on Scarface!" he cried. "Let's get out of here!" Moving as fast as we could without drawing attention to ourselves, we hurried up the street, hidden by the shadows of the buildings.

When we reached the hotel, I laughed and said, "That's great!" Then added with delight, "Now *you're* on his shit list, too!"

Colin walked into the Prince Hotel, shaking his head uncertainly. "I'm not sure he knows it was me," he said hopefully, as he peered warily over his shoulder to make sure Scarface hadn't followed us. "But if he does, I'm fucked for sure!"

Fortunately for us, we would soon be putting some distance between ourselves and the wrath of Scarface since we had decided to leave Saigon later that week. Our plan was to head north up the coast, but we weren't exactly sure how to get there since we had heard that public transportation in Vietnam was a nightmare. A British girl who had taken some long trips on Vietnamese buses forewarned us against them. "The buses are so packed, that half the time you'll wind up standing for hours," she warned. "And the other times, when you do have a seat, they're so cramped that you'll wish you were standing. There's absolutely no leg room. And if you have your backpack with you, you'll be carrying it on your lap the whole time you're on the bus—if you're lucky enough to get it on the bus." Based on her glowing recommendation, as far as we were concerned, long-distance buses were out.

The 2,600 kilometer railway system was supposed to be more reliable than the buses, but were also reputed to be incredibly slow, sometimes averaging only fifteen kilometers an hour between cities along the coast. So, rather than deal with the hassles of broken-down, overcrowded buses, or an antiquated, slow train system, we took the easy way out. We recruited five other travelers and signed up for a ten day tour that had been organized by the Kim Café.

None of us was thrilled with the idea of an organized tour, each of us preferring independent travel where we could come and go as we pleased, but the group was small and we could change the itinerary if we wanted so it didn't really seem like a group tour. Plus, a private van and driver would be a welcome change from the hassles of public transportation. And, for less than fifty dollars a person, we would get a minivan, driver, and a daily itinerary of sights from Saigon up to Hué, where the tour would end. Since it sounded like a good deal, we decided to go for it.

The day before we were scheduled to leave, our newly-formed group sat around a popular backpacker hangout called the Sinh Café to plan our trip. A minivan was set to pick everyone up in front of Kim's Café at eight-thirty the following morning and we were reviewing the itinerary to figure out how much time we wanted to spend at each of the scheduled stops. Though we had arranged the trip through Kim, we had been spending a lot of our free time at the Sinh Café since it was just across the street from our hotel. It was also less crowded than Kim's. But best of all, Sinh didn't allow the local kids to bother the foreigners—which meant Scarface couldn't find us for awhile.

As luck would have it, though, Scarface spotted us at Sinh's Café on the afternoon of our last day in Saigon. Standing outside of the metal fence that separated the café from the street, he gave me his usual scowl. He was still on speaking terms with Colin and Dan, however, despite the fact Colin had run over him that night on the street.

Unfortunately, he still held his grudge for me, and glared mercilessly at me through the fence.

I did my best to ignore him and kept on talking as if he wasn't there. A few minutes later, Colin and Dan started to laugh. I glanced over at Scarface to see what he was up to behind my back. When I turned around, he looked at me innocently at first. Then he made a slashing gesture across his throat with his finger and smiled.

"*Oh Jee-sus!*" Colin laughed, "He's gonna do ya' in before ya' leave Saigon!"

"Yeah, well, you guys better hope he doesn't, or you'll be splitting the cost of the van over seven people instead of eight," I replied, uneasily.

I looked over at Scarface and decided it was time we made our peace. "Hey, you know what?" I asked casually. "I'm out of postcards. I can use some more if you've still got some." He studied me wordlessly for a few seconds, trying to determine if I was teasing him.

Unsure of my intent, he asked uncertainly, "You want buy postcards?"

"Sure. Let's see what you've got."

I looked through his selection of cards and handed him more than enough money for one of the packets. Hoping that this put an end to our dispute, I expected him to smile or to at least say something to let me know that we would once again be on speaking terms. But he just stood there, counting his money without even looking at me.

After stuffing the money in his pocket, he shook hands with Colin and Dan and then turned to leave. After a moment's hesitation, he turned back around and stuck his hand out to me. When I went to shake his hand he quickly pulled it away. Seeing the surprised look on my face, he laughed. I held my hand out and waited. Colin looked at Scarface and shook his head with mock disappointment. "Look at that," he told Scarface. "He bought your cards and you won't even shake hands with 'im. That's terrible, just terrible."

With a playful grin, Scarface looked at me and said, "Only kidding." He shook my hand, then turned quickly around and strode confidently down the street to Kim's Café.

As we watched Scarface walk off, Colin looked over at me and remarked, "I wouldn't lower my guard just yet. He may have made up with ya' just to make you think everythin's been set right. Then when you're not looking—phfftt!" He ran his finger across his throat the way Scarface had done earlier, and laughed. "Yup, he's a tricky one, that Scarface. I don't think any of us'll really be safe till we're on that van tomorrow and miles away from Kim's Café."

Before I fell asleep that night, I had visions of Scarface hanging onto the axle under the van as we drove away from Saigon, the way Robert DeNiro did when he followed Nick Nolte and Jessica Lange in the movie *Cape Fear*. And though I knew it was ludicrous to even think it, I made a mental note to check under the van the next morning. Just in case.

A Small Group of Tourists

Brothels and Boat Rides

Enroute to Hanoi

Don't turn a small problem into a big problem — say yes to your mother.
— Sally Berger

"Sam, could you turn up the air a bit? It's very hot back here."

Samantha gave her mother an exasperated look. "If I turn it up *too much* mother, I'll freeze up here." Despite herself, she raised the knob on the air-conditioner a token amount to keep her mother happy.

Colin, Dan and I shot quick glances at each other and smiled, each of us silently wondering if we wouldn't have been better off on a crowded, un-airconditioned, public bus with a hundred Vietnamese passengers, instead of traveling in a group with five other Westerners.

Other than the three of us, there were five other passengers in the van: Jose-Mari and Izaskun, a married couple from Spain; Susan and Samantha, a mother and daughter duo from England; and Calvin, a thirty-one year old American from Philadelphia, Pennsylvania.

The Spanish couple was in their late thirties. Quiet, soft-spoken and friendly, they were easy to get along with and pleasant to be around. They were on a one-month holiday from work and intended to travel around Vietnam for a few weeks before going to Paris on their way home. In addition to Spanish and French, Izaskun spoke excellent English. Jose-Mari could understand English but wasn't comfortable speaking it, so Izaskun wound up translating for him most of the time.

The mother-daughter combo was an entertaining addition to the group. With their constant, but good-natured bickering, they were more like sisters than mother and daughter. Samantha was a tall, independent woman in her early twenties who looked and acted much older than her age. She had graduated from university the year before and decided to take a year off to travel. During her travels, she fell in love with Southeast Asia and spent the past year living and working on a resort island in the south of Thailand.

Her mother, Susan, had recently arrived from England to visit her. Sam showed her around Thailand for a few weeks then arranged for them to take a short vacation in Vietnam. Having lived in Asia for a year, Sam was comfortable with foreign cultures and acted more like the mother than Susan, who seemed more than happy to leave the day-to-day travel decisions up to Sam.

The last member of our group was Calvin. He was easy enough to get along with, but was kind of an introvert and kept pretty much to himself. His father had fought in Vietnam, so he was much more knowledgeable about the war than the rest of us. Actually, his fascination with Vietnam almost bordered on excessive. In general, he was usually quiet and reserved, but whenever he spoke about the various battles and tactics used in Vietnam, he became very animated and took on an unsettled, faraway look in his eyes, which made me think he wished he had been there to take part in the action.

The unofficial leader of our group was Thang, our driver. Thang was also supposed to act as our guide, but his English was so limited that he wasn't much help in that department. Instead, whenever we stopped at one of our pre-determined sights along the way, each of us took turns reading from our various guidebooks to find out why we were stopping. Thang usually had no clue, and seemed as interested to learn about the places as we were and probably would have asked us questions if his English had been good enough.

Our first day on the road we drove to the Central Highlands and made it as far as Dalat, 300 kilometers northeast of Saigon. Dalat is located in the southern part of the Truong Son Mountain Range and is surrounded by evergreen forests, lakes and waterfalls. Because of its cool mountain climate and beautiful location, it's considered one of the nicest places in Vietnam and is visited by more than 300,000 domestic, Vietnamese tourists every year.

When we arrived in Dalat, it was Sam's turn to read. She took her guidebook from her daypack and read out loud: "The site of Dalat was 'discovered' in 1897 by Dr. Alexandre Yersin, a protégé of Louis Pasteur who was the first person to identify the plague bacillus. The city itself was established in 1912 and quickly became popular with Europeans as a cool retreat from the sweltering heat of the coastal plains and the Mekong Delta. In the local Lat language, Da Lat means the River of the Lat Tribe."

As soon as Sam had finished reading, her mother pointed to a busy market below a long flight of stairs and asked, "What's that over there, Sam?"

Sam rolled her eyes and sighed. "How do I know mother? Have I been to Dalat before?"

"Well, I thought you were reading the guidebook," her mother replied, innocently.

"I was, but I didn't *memorize* the book, mother." Sam passed the guidebook to her mother in the back of the van. "Here. You can read about Dalat for yourself," she said a bit impatiently. The rest of us laughed and pulled out our guidebooks to help Sam's mother find out what the marketplace was called.

Thang drove slowly past the locals strolling on the busy streets and pulled up in front of a pleasant looking hotel near the center of town. When the van came to a full stop, Dan and I hopped out so we could check out the rooms. As I closed the door, I heard Sam's mother say, "It's called the Central Market, Sam. It was built in 1958, and is—" Dan and I stifled a laugh as the door slid closed behind us, cutting off the rest of her lecture.

After the members of our little group checked into the hotel, they spent the rest of the day wandering around separately. And though the sights around Dalat were pretty spread out, we eventually ran into everyone as we walked around town, since the city center was fairly compact. We met Jose-Mari and Izaskun wandering around the little shops in the French District, stuffing their daypacks full of French breads, pastries and cakes. An hour later, we saw Calvin peering around huge, wicker baskets of vegetables in the Central Market. He was flitting around like he was on some sort of reconnaissance mission, darting in and out of the crowded stalls like a point-man scouting out enemy territory before his troops took over the village. We decided not to interrupt his daydreams, and went off to find something to eat.

After a late dinner at a small Chinese restaurant down the street from our hotel, we ran into Sam and her mother at a place called Café Tung, a *"former hangout of Saigonese intellectuals during the 1950's,"* according to my guidebook. The café was a cozy, little place, with a relaxed, subdued atmosphere, and served tea, hot cocoa, coffee and sodas to the accompaniment of mellow French music. It was an easy place to while away the night and we sat around drinking tea and coffee until it was time to close the place down.

Early the next morning, after a light breakfast of French rolls, cheese and coffee, we piled into the van to tour the sights around Dalat. Like dutiful tourists, we spent the whole day shuttling from one sight to another—lakes, waterfalls, flower gardens, valleys, and floating houses on stilts. Thang would stop the van and we would all scramble out into the hot, midday sun for a quick look around while someone read a brief description of the place from their guidebook. When everyone had seen enough, we would pile back into the cool, airconditioned van and drive on to the next place on the list until we had covered all the sights on our itinerary.

By the time we finished walking around the grounds of Emperor Bao Dai's Summer Palace later that afternoon, we were exhausted from a hard day of sightseeing. Tired and hungry, we returned to Dalat for a good dinner and a relaxing cup of coffee back at Café Tung. There wasn't a whole helluva lot going on in Dalat, so after another night of mellow conversation over coffee and tea, we each returned to our hotel rooms for a good night's sleep before leaving for Nha Trang early the next morning.

There is nothing more enticing, disenchanting, and enslaving
than the life at sea.

—Joseph Conrad, Lord Jim

"Hey Joe! You want take boat trip out to islands? Best price!"

We squinted up from our towels on Nha Trang Beach and saw a young boy standing in front of us, blocking our sun.

Shielding his eyes with the back of his hand, Dan looked up and asked, "How much?"

"Five US dollars for whole day. Price include lunch, snorkeling, everything. Best price—you want to go?"

Before we arrived in Nha Trang, some other travelers had told us that the boat trips offered by the locals were pretty good. We were interested in hearing what the boy had to say, but didn't want to rush into anything until we had a chance to check a few places out. "We'll let you know tomorrow," Colin said. "Where can we find you?"

The boy pointed past the coconut palms at the edge of the beach to one of the beachfront cafés and said, "You want to go, just wait at cafe there at ten o'clock tomorrow morning."

When we left the beach a few hours later, the decks of the cafés along the beachfront were crowded with Vietnamese teenagers. Thirsty from lying out in the sun all afternoon, we walked to the cafés to get a cold drink before returning to the hotel. Soon after we sat down, a Vietnamese woman, with leathery-brown, sun-tanned skin stopped by our table. In a harsh, raspy voice she said, "Today your first day in Nha Trang, right?"

"How can you tell?" I asked curiously.

"I haven't seen you before."

"You know all the foreigners who come to Nha Trang?"

"Most of them. They wanna take a boat ride they usually go with me, Mama Linh. My boy told me he spoke to you on the beach. He said maybe you wanna take a boat ride. I have a boat leaves every morning, if you interested."

I was surprised at how colloquial her English was. A lot of the older Vietnamese in the south had worked with the Americans during the Vietnam war and spoke English pretty well, especially the former South Vietnamese soldiers and officials. But none of the Vietnamese I had met in Saigon spoke half as naturally as Mama Linh. She used her 'wannas' and 'gonnas' like a native American. She had obviously spent a lot of time around American soldiers. And judging from her English, it sounded like they had all come from Brooklyn or the Bronx.

"How much?" I asked.

"How many people you got?"

"Well . . . if they're all interested in going, there would be eight of us."

Without a pause she said, "Eight people? Five dollars each person. That includes everything—boat trip, a fantastic, seafood lunch of fresh crabs and fish, drinks, snorkeling, swimming. Everything. I even drive you to the dock at Cau Da. It's the best price you gonna get, believe me. If you wanna go, just be here tomorrow morning around ten." Having said all she had come to say, she flashed a smile at us and walked off.

Not long after Mama Linh left, a second woman stopped by our table. She was about the same age as Mama Linh, but shorter and heavier, and with a softer edge to her voice. She introduced herself as Mama Hanh and asked curiously, "Mama Linh come by to see you yet?" When we nodded our heads, she chuckled.

With a sigh and a dismissive wave of her hand, she stood beside Colin and said, "Her boat is not good. Her food not good either. You have better time on my boat. Everything nicer and more clean on my boat. Ask anyone who knows Mama Hanh." Then, as quickly as she had come, she strode off toward two foreigners who were seated at the other end of the café. As she walked off, she called back over her shoulder, "If you want to go on my boat, be here at ten o'clock tomor-row morning."

After she left, the three of us looked quizzically at each other. "What do you think?" Dan asked, uncertainly. "Mama Linh or Mama Hanh?"

"It's hard to say," I replied. "Mama Linh's a little too street-tough for my liking. She was also selling us pretty hard, which always makes me suspicious. But on the other hand, I also get suspicious when someone tells me the other guy's no good, like Mama Hanh was doing."

"Phfffft! A boat's a boat," Colin blurted. "They're prob'ly both the same. Same boats, same crabs, same everythin'!"

After giving it some thought, Dan and I agreed that Colin was probably right. If the other members of our group were interested in going, we figured we would just go with Mama Linh and not make a big deal over a simple boat trip. Having made our decision, we finished our drinks and walked back to the hotel to shower up before going out to dinner.

Later that night, not long after Calvin and I had turned out the lights to go to sleep, we heard a faint knock on the door to our room. The rest of the group had gone upstairs to bed an hour before, so we couldn't imagine who was coming down to see us. My bed was closest to the door so I was elected to see who it was. I stepped out of bed in the dark room and stepped quickly across the cold tile floor. "Who is it?" I asked through the closed door. No answer, just more quick knocks. "Who is it?" I repeated, a little louder the second time. Still no answer. Though he couldn't see me in the dark, I glanced over at Calvin and shrugged. "Probably just someone knocking on the wrong door," I informed him, as I turned to go back to bed. More knocks. I spun around and swung the door open, hoping to catch whoever it was before they walked away.

Standing in the open doorway outside our room was a short, skinny, middle-aged Vietnamese man. When he saw me facing him he looked very surprised. He also looked very drunk. Muttering something in Vietnamese, he turned slowly around and staggered off.

Ten minutes later, there was another series of knocks on the door.

I crawled back out of bed. "Boy, this is going to be some night," I said wearily.

"It's probably that same guy again," Calvin replied.

I opened the door and stared down at two, short, Vietnamese women standing squarely in front of me. They each looked to be in their early twenties and were wearing tight shorts and low-cut shirts. One of them had long, black hair which fell straight back to her waist. The other one was shorter, with shoulder-length, dark hair and a heavier build. Neither of them was attractive. They looked up at me and giggled, covering their mouths with the back of their hands. With a playful smile, the one with the long hair leaned toward me and asked playfully, "You want us come inside?" When I didn't answer, she inched closer to the door. "Okay?" she asked, with a gleam in her dark eyes.

"Uh, well . . . actually . . . hold on a second, okay?" I mumbled. I closed the door a little and stepped back inside the room. "Calvin!" I hissed. "There are two girls out here who want to know if you want to sleep with them. You interested?" When he didn't answer, I thought he had fallen asleep. A few seconds later, I heard him answer "No." I laughed, suddenly realizing he had been thinking it over. I looked at the girls and shrugged. "Sorry, we're not interested." The one with the long hair put her foot by the door to keep it from closing. "We come inside, okay?" she whispered.

I could only think of one sure way to get rid of them, so I decided to give it a try. "Listen, we have two friends staying upstairs in room number three," I said. "They'd really love for you to visit them—I mean it. Room three. Just keep knocking until they open the door."

The girls giggled and walked quickly to the stairs at the other end of the lobby. When they reached the foot of the stairs, they turned and looked back at me. With an encouraging nod, I pointed up the stairs and called out, "That's right—room *three*."

When they were out of sight, I locked the door and went back to bed.

"How'd you get rid of them?" Calvin asked in the dark.

"I sent them up to Colin and Dan."

The following morning, Calvin and I went for breakfast at the garden restaurant beside the hotel. Jose-Mari and Izaskun were almost finished by the time we arrived but Samantha and her mother had just sat down to eat so we pulled up two chairs and joined them. Ten minutes later, Colin and Dan sauntered over to our table.

"How did you sleep?" I asked Dan, as he pulled up a chair next to mine.

"Not too bad," he replied, casually.

"Anyone bother you guys during the night?" I probed, eager to know what had happened with the girls I had sent up to their room.

"Nope. Slept like a baby," Dan said, happily. "Why do you ask?"

"*No one* came by your room last night?"

"Don't think so. Was someone supposed to?" he asked, innocently.

When I explained about the two women I had sent up to their room, Dan looked up with surprise and said, "You know . . . come to think of it, I thought I heard someone knocking on the door last night. But I was so tired, I wasn't sure if I was dreaming it or not. After awhile the knocking stopped and I must've fallen back asleep and forgotten about it." With a laugh, he said, "So *that's* what that was. You bastard!"

When we finished breakfast, we walked over to a tall, wooden hutch across the garden where a small monkey was chained to a post. The monkey watched us warily as we approached, racing nervously back and forth across the wooden beams of his hutch as we came nearer. When we got close enough to get a good look at him, we saw that he was cradling something small and white against his body. When we looked more closely, we could see that he was holding a small, white kitten that couldn't have been more than six or seven weeks old. As we continued our approach, the monkey jumped around nervously, shifting his grip on the little kitten to keep it close to his chest. Frightened by our presence, he grabbed the kitten around its neck and raced back and forth around the wooden platform to keep the kitten away from us.

As it got dragged around, the small kitten cried out and twisted its body to try and escape from the grip of its captor. But the monkey held it too tight for it to get away.

"Don't get too close," Izaskun cautioned. "He thinks we want to take it from him." With a worried look she sighed, "He squeezes the kitten so tight I am afraid he will hurt it."

When we stood still, the monkey eased its grip on the kitten and let it walk on the platform of the hutch. Whenever the kitten moved too far away, however, the monkey reached out and dragged it back in his arms, guarding it like a prized possession and never letting it out of his sight.

At first, I thought it was cute watching the monkey carry the kitten around. But then I felt sorry for it. The kitten wasn't a playmate. It was a play*thing*—a prisoner, unable to get away from the arms of its captor. Not wanting to get the kitten hurt by upsetting the monkey, we went back to our table and ordered some coffee while we waited for Thang to show up with the van.

When Thang pulled up in front of the hotel, we piled inside and drove over to the café near the beach to meet Mama Linh. At ten o'clock, right on schedule, she pulled up in an old, dilapidated pick-up truck. We followed her down the coast road to the dock at Cau Da and boarded a dark-brown, wooden boat that was so dingy and run-down looking that it made her truck look new.

In addition to our group and Mama Linh, there were four Viet-namese helpers on the boat—two middle-aged, skinny men, and two boys, each around ten years old. After we were seated onboard, Mama Linh walked back to her pick-up truck and barked a few orders to the young boys who were lounging around on deck. Like disciplined deckhands, they immediately jumped up and began unloading large coolers from the back of the pick-up to the deck of the boat.

From where we sat on Mama Linh's boat, we could hear loud music blasting from a portable cassette player a few boats away from us. Standing up, we looked down the dock and saw Mama Hanh and her crew loading their boat with coolers of beer, fruit, crabs, and kegs of tea. Seeing us watching them, one of Mama Hanh's workers grinned from ear-to-ear as he held up a bunch of ripened bananas in one hand, and a large sack of oranges in the other, to gloat over how much food they were placing on board. I looked at the dirty coolers on our boat to see if Mama Linh had brought any fruit along. Nothing. Not one damn banana.

I looked back at Mama Hanh's boat. Her nicely-dressed crew was happy and smiling as they loaded supplies from their truck to the boat in an efficient assembly-line over the heads of their passengers, each of whom sat comfortably on deck in nice, clean, lounge chairs, listening to music, eating bananas and oranges, and drinking iced-tea and beers.

I glanced back at our boat. The hard, wooden seats were wet from the coolers that had been placed on them before being dumped hap-hazardly on deck. Our workers looked like they had slept in their clothes for the past week, and I didn't see a cassette player or a radio in sight. We were sitting on hard, wet seats with nothing to eat or drink as our motley-looking crew shuffled wearily back and forth from the truck to the boat, trying unsuccessfully not to hit our heads with the heavy coolers, as they carried them on board. I sat next to Dan and frowned. "Something tells me we went with the wrong Mama," I said, dolefully. Dan looked at Mama Linh and her derelict-looking helpers and nodded his head in agreement.

Half an hour later, our boat was fully loaded and chugged noisily out of the harbor, leaving filmy gasoline swirls in its wake as we made our way into the clear, blue waters of the South China Sea. The sun was bright and hot above our old, wooden boat, its yellow-white flames bathing the deck with intensely hot, morning rays. To keep from getting sunburned as we moved out to sea, I sat beneath the wooden overhang of the engine room and read a classic book about Vietnam that Calvin lent me, titled 'The Quiet American,' by Graham Greene.

For the first hour or so, Mama Linh and Mama Hanh kept the same course, cruising out to sea in the direction of Bamboo Island. We could hear the music from their boat over the sputtering din of our engines, and every time I looked over at them I couldn't help but think how much better their boat was—which was exactly what they wanted us to think. But it was true. And I wasn't the only one noticing it.

Colin pointed across the waves to Mama Hanh's boat and laughed. "Lookit 'em over there—the whole lot of 'em are up and dancin'!"

When we looked across the glistening water, we saw the passengers on Mama Hanh's boat dancing with their crew, drinking beers, and singing along with the music. In contrast, our group was sitting around, quietly talking to one another, sunning themselves, and reading. Colin shook his head and smirked. "They're havin' a freakin' party over there and we're all sittin' around here like we're at a bloody funeral."

"You know they're just doing it to rub it in," Samantha said. "Just ignore them."

Thankfully, Mama Hanh's boat eventually took off in another direction and we cruised steadily along without any more distractions. When we reached a good swimming spot far off the coast of Nha Trang, Samantha, Calvin, and the two, young, Vietnamese boys dove off the back of the boat to swim and snorkel in the clean, cool water. The rest of us stayed on deck, talking and relaxing, while the crew prepared lunch in the galley, at the front of the boat.

Earlier that morning, I had watched one of the boys as he made our iced-tea and wasn't exactly thrilled with his training in hygiene. After dumping a large bucket of ice in a keg he unceremoniously stirred the tea with his dirty hands. I made a mental note to avoid the tea.

Having duly noted the lack of health standards among our crew, I made a point of keeping an eye on them as they prepared our lunch. I would have been better off not watching.

As I watched the crew prepare our meal, I noticed one of the men cut his finger as he sliced the vegetables. After pouring seawater over the cut to cleanse it, he wrapped a dirty piece of cloth around his finger to stop the bleeding. A few minutes later, he was handling the food again, dropping the crabs in the water and mixing the noodles and other food together from separate pots, all the while dragging his dirty bandage into the cooking pots. I made a mental note to avoid the food. When the meal had been served and Mama Linh asked me why I wasn't eating with everyone else, I lied and told her I was full from breakfast and wasn't hungry. Actually, I was starving.

The rest of the group seemed to be having a good time, however, eating and drinking and enjoying the sun out on the water. But by late afternoon, I'd had enough. It was sweltering hot in the middle of the sea, and I was hungry and thirsty. I couldn't wait to get back to the hotel. Stuck on the boat with nowhere to go, I felt trapped—like the kitten who couldn't get away from the monkey. And the more I thought about my plight, the more I thought about the kitten in the unrelenting hands of its captor.

When we finally returned to the dock at Cau Da at the end of the day, I was sick of the boat and relieved to be back on dry land. I was also famished and dying of thirst. As soon as Thang dropped us off at the hotel, I raced over to the outdoor café to get something to eat. As hungry as I was, though, I knew I wouldn't be able to eat a thing until I checked on the condition of the kitten. I walked slowly past the tables in the garden and stepped quietly over to the monkey's hutch, hoping the little kitten was still alive. As I inched my way around the side of the hutch, I spotted the back of the monkey's head. He was sitting in the corner of his hutch, in the same place we had left him. From where I stood though, I couldn't see if he was holding the kitten.

As I tip-toed carefully toward the front, I stepped on a twig and froze. The monkey immediately wheeled around and faced me. I held my breath and looked down at the monkey's hands. He was holding an orange. The kitten was gone. With a sigh of relief, I walked back to my seat and relaxed, happy with the knowledge that the monkey's little prisoner had somehow managed to escape.

It became necessary to destroy the town in order to save it.
— U.S. Army Major in Vietnam

Built along the banks of the narrow, slow-moving *Perfume River* which bisects the city, Hué's wide, tree-lined streets, small lakes, and canals give it a relaxing, easy-going atmosphere that makes it seem less like a former capital city and more like a laid-back, country town.

From 1802 until 1945, Hué had been the Imperial Capital and the religious, cultural, and educational center of a united Vietnam. Hué was also the site of the Citadel City, Vietnam's most famous structure—a Chinese-style fortress, fashioned after the Forbidden City in Beijing.

Built along the west bank of the *Perfume River*, the Citadel covered an area over five square kilometers in size and consisted of three enclosed cities: the Capital City, where most of the population lived; the Imperial City, where the emperor carried out his official functions; and the Forbidden Purple City, reserved for the private life of the emperor.

In its day, the Citadel had been one of the most magnificent royal courts in Asia. As a result of the Vietnam War, however, most of the Citadel had been destroyed—flattened by South Vietnamese and U.S. military efforts to reclaim Hué, after the North Vietnamese seized the city during the Tet Offensive of 1968.

While the country was celebrating the New Year on January 31 of 1968, the Vietcong initiated a massive offensive in over 100 cities and towns throughout Vietnam, capturing Hué in the process. The city stayed under Communist control for over 25 days until South Vietnamese and U.S. troops finally recaptured it. Unfortunately, the cost to take Hué back from the Vietcong was high, and the former center of Vietnamese culture and education became the site of one of the

bloodiest battles of the Vietnam War. The following account of the
battle is described in '*The Eyewitness History of the Vietnam War: 1961–
1975*,' by George Esper and The Associated Press:

> It took the equivalent of nearly two divisions of South Vietnamese and
> American troops to recapture Hué. In the process, much of the city had
> been leveled; some officials estimated nearly 70 percent of the homes
> and many historical treasures of the past had been destroyed. The hu-
> man toll had been tremendous. U.S. officials reported 142 U.S. Marines
> killed along with 384 South Vietnamese. North Vietnamese losses were
> estimated at 8,000 dead.
>
> An even more gruesome fate had been meted out to the civilians of Hué.
> In a massive political purge, the communists executed more than 2,800
> of the city's residents. Some were shot. Many others were buried alive.
> The victims included civil servants, teachers, government officials, mili-
> tary personnel, priests and any men who appeared to be of military age.
> It was a singularly brutal incident in the growing list of tragedies that
> marked the history of the Vietnam War.

More than twenty years after the war, even with most of the Citadel
destroyed, Hué is once again attracting tourists to its citadel com-
pound, royal tombs of the Nguyen emperors, pagodas, temples and
churches. But even without the Citadel and other sights, Hué was still
a pleasant place to visit. Whenever I walked through the Dong Ba
Market on the left bank of the city and watched the sampans floating
gently down the Perfume River past the ramparts of the Citadel, I felt
I was experiencing the Vietnam of a bygone era.

In the afternoons, I would sit and have lunch along the banks of
the river and watch the motorbikes, cyclos and bicycles roll slowly
along the peaceful, tree-lined streets. With a French baguette in one
hand, and a cold bottle of Coke in the other, I'd find myself wondering what life would have been like for the Vietnamese if the French
and the Americans hadn't come to their country. A quote by John
Kenneth Galbraith reflected my reveries when he wrote, "*If we were
not in Vietnam, all that part of the world would be enjoying the obscurity it
so richly deserves.*"

Hué was our last scheduled stop with Thang and the van. By the
end of our second day of sightseeing, we had seen the last of the
royal tombs and ancient pagodas on our scheduled itinerary. In late
afternoon, Thang dropped us back at the hotel and told us he planned

to leave for Saigon in the morning. He had been a good driver, as well as a friendly companion, and to show our appreciation, we each kicked in a couple of dollars and gave him a tip which was well deserved.

The following morning after breakfast, the eight members of our group met Thang in the courtyard outside our hotel to see him off and wish him a safe journey. When each of us had said our good-byes, Thang climbed in the van and drove slowly down the street on his long drive back to Saigon. With the departure of Thang and the van, our small group tour was officially over, and once again, we were back on our own.

The day after Thang left with the van, our little group went off in different directions. Jose-Mari and Izaskun planned to spend a few more days in Hué before traveling north. Samantha and her mother booked tickets on the evening train back to Saigon. And Colin, Dan, Calvin and I decided to travel north to Hanoi together. After wishing the former members of our group a safe and enjoyable journey, we went directly to the Hué railway station to purchase tickets for the overnight train to Hanoi.

To save money, they each bought "soft-seat" tickets—vinyl-covered seats that were one step up from the less comfortable benches in the "hard-seat" compartments. I didn't want to sleep sitting up, however, so I spent a few extra dollars for a "hard-sleeper" bed.

When we arrived at the station the following afternoon, a French couple told us they had heard the 3:30 P.M. train was delayed by at least an hour, maybe two. "The trains in Vietnam are always delayed," the French girl sighed complacently as she settled down to wait.

With nowhere else to go, we joined her and her companion on the two wooden benches in the small waiting room, resigned to wait at the station until the train showed up. Not long after we sat down, however, a Vietnamese train attendant stuck his head in the waiting room to tell us the train to Hanoi was pulling into the station. We stepped outside and saw a crowd of Vietnamese passengers rushing down the platform toward a long, green train that was braking into the station. Scrambling back into the waiting room, we grabbed our packs and ran down the platform behind the crowd of people ahead of us.

After finding my compartment, I chained my pack to my bed then walked through the train to the soft-seat carriages to see how Dan, Colin, and Calvin were making out. When I saw them crammed into their seats in the middle of a sea of black-haired heads, I knew I had made the right decision to buy a sleeper-ticket.

Unlike the hard-sleeper trains in China, which had padded mattresses, I soon discovered that the Vietnamese hard-sleepers were exactly that—hard. There were three berths on either side of the open-ended compartment, and each bed, if you could call them that, was nothing more than a wooden board, an inch thick, covered with a wafer-thin, straw mat.

Other than me, there was a young, British couple and three, Vietnamese men, who didn't speak any English, in my compartment. As soon as they walked in with their bags, the British couple and the Vietnamese men checked their tickets to see which beds they had been assigned. "Well, I guess these are ours," the Brit said to his girlfriend. He checked the numbers on their tickets against the berth numbers and threw their packs on the top and middle beds on the left side of the compartment. I had the top bunk across from the boyfriend.

For some reason, which wasn't quite apparent to either myself or the British couple, the Vietnamese men weren't happy with the sleeping arrangements. They stood in the center of the compartment and looked disappointedly at the vacant beds in front of them. One of the men, a short, chubby man who looked to be in his mid-thirties, tapped my bed and grunted to get my attention. Patting the three berths on the left side of the compartment, he barked, "Vietnam!" Pointing to the two beds below me he bellowed, "American!" With a vigorous nod of his large, round head, he glanced at the British couple and me with an ear-to-ear grin. The British guy and his girlfriend looked at each other and shrugged. It didn't make any difference to them which bunks they slept in, so they shifted their things to the two beds below mine and let the Vietnamese men have the three beds on the other side of the compartment.

Unlike top bunks on European trains, the upper bunks on Vietnamese trains were like small boxes. Located about two feet below the ceiling, there was virtually no room to move around. Sitting up was definitely out of the question. And because of the hard, wooden board below the thin, straw mat, even lying down was painful. When I lay on my side, my knee and ankle bones pressed against the hard board beneath me. Laying on my stomach was no better, since the board hurt my ribs. The only semi-comfortable position was to sleep flat on my back the whole night.

When I peered over the edge of my bunk, I could see that the Brits were also laying on their backs. The three Vietnamese—the chubby one in particular, with his abundant padding of fat—looked perfectly comfortable in any position. As I lay there on my back, sticking uncomfortably to the straw mat beneath me, it seemed impossible that I would ever find a comfortable enough position in which to sleep. With nothing else to do other than to accept my accommodations, I closed my eyes and listened to the snail-like pace of the train as it made its slow, but steady way north, towards Hanoi.

Sleep eventually won out over discomfort, however, and the next thing I knew, the morning sun was streaming through the windows of the compartment. When I looked down from my bunk, I saw Chubby sitting cross-legged on his bed, waiting for the train attendant to stop by and collect our breakfast tickets. Two minutes later, he was noisily slurping away at a small, tin canister filled with soupy rice and bits of chicken. It was a strange meal to eat first thing in the morning but I was very hungry, so I gave the attendant my breakfast ticket and slurped my soupy rice and chicken along with everyone else.

When I was done with breakfast, I grabbed my bottle of mineral water to go brush my teeth. Spotting the bottled water in my hand, Chubby picked up a small, plastic cup and reached his arm up to me on the top bunk. "Nnhh!" he grunted, loud enough for half the train to hear him.

The Brit and his girlfriend laughed at Chubby's forward manner. "I always thought Asians were supposed to be shy around foreigners," the British guy remarked.

"Yeah, me too," I laughed, as I bent down from my bunk to fill Chubby's cup with water. "Nnhh!" he grunted again, when his cup was full. I felt like I was feeding a baby gorilla. He stared at the water in his cup, then sipped it tentatively for a second or two before swallowing it down in one big gulp. After nodding his approval, he proceeded to lay down in his bunk to digest his breakfast.

When I returned from the washroom, I sat by the window and watched the countryside roll slowly by, surprised at how many people in the villages were up and about at six o'clock in the morning. All along the coast, men in small, wooden fishing boats were casting rope nets into the light green waters of the South China Sea. Further inland, cone-hatted women with baggy, black pants and light, cotton shirts strolled barefoot down narrow mud-embankments toward water-soaked rice paddies. Many other people were already busy at work in the rice paddies, holding shallow, straw baskets against their hips, as they stooped down in the long, neat rows of rice shoots that surrounded them.

It looked peaceful and serene from inside the train and I found myself almost envying their simple existence. But it wasn't as carefree as it seemed. With an estimated per capita income of two hundred dollars a year, Vietnam is considered one of the poorest countries in the world, with most Vietnamese struggling just to survive. By the looks of Chubby and his two friends, however, not everyone in the country was starving.

At 8:00 A.M., Dan stopped by my compartment. He looked exhausted from having sat up all night in the crowded and noisy soft-seat carriage. Standing in the doorway, his huge backpack towering over his straw hat, he said wearily, "We're supposed to arrive in Hanoi in about two minutes, so you'd better get ready."

I pulled my pack down from my bunk and heard Chubby grunt, "Nnhh!" to get my attention. With a big grin and a nod of his big, round head, he pointed outside the window and barked, "Hanoi!" I turned towards the window and looked out at a pleasant-looking skyline of low-rise buildings and shimmering lakes in the distance.

As the train slowed into the station, Chubby and his friends grabbed their little satchels and strolled briskly down the corridor to the exit doors at the front of the carriage. Not far behind them, Dan and I stepped eagerly off the train in Hanoi, the capital of the Socialist Republic of Vietnam.

An Inconsiderate Dane

Hanoi

Three Days in Laos

If an ass goes traveling, he'll not come home a horse.
— Thomas Fuller

Colin slid through the crowd of Vietnamese passengers ahead of us and waited outside the station while we made our way through the exits. When he saw us step out on the street, he waved his arms above the dark-haired, Vietnamese heads in front of him and shouted, "Come on! I've got two cyclos waitin' for us!" Just before we climbed into the cyclos, one of the drivers showed us the business card of a hotel called the *Dong Do*. It wasn't far, so we agreed to check it out before looking up any of the hotels listed in our guidebooks.

The cyclos in Hanoi were a bit wider than the ones down south, so squeezing two of us in each of them wasn't a problem—for us, anyway. I'm not sure the drivers felt the same way since they had twice as much weight to peddle around, plus the added weight of our backpacks. To deal with the load, each of the drivers gave their pedicabs a good shove and a running start before hopping onto their seats. When the cyclos got rolling, they were then able to peddle off without too much trouble.

As we cruised slowly through the streets of Hanoi, watching the people, scooters, and other cyclos flow around us, I studied my map and tried to get my bearings. When we had gone about a mile or so from the station, we peddled past a busy intersection and swung left down *Tong Duy Tan Street*, a narrow back-street lined with small pastry shops and food stalls. Our drivers negotiated their way past the bicycles and scooters that crowded both sides of the street and pulled slowly up in front of house number 27, the *Dong Do Hotel*.

The *Dong Do* was small but comfortable, and had a friendly, English-speaking staff. Across from the check-in counter was a small din-

ing area, behind which a narrow staircase led to the bedrooms upstairs. The rooms were sunny and clean and had bathrooms with hot
water showers—a welcome sight after our uncomfortable night on the
train. At five dollars a person, we doubted we would find a better place
for the money, so we thanked our drivers for the recommendation and
went downstairs to register.

When we had purchased our airline tickets in Bangkok three weeks
before, we had booked an onward flight from Hanoi to Laos. The
flight to Laos was almost a week away, so we decided to save our
sightseeing in Hanoi for the following week and head east toward the
Gulf of Tonkin so we could spend a few days at Halong Bay, an area
renowned for its fantastic limestone cliffs.

"Seems like a major pain in the ass to get up there," Dan commented, as he checked his guidebook for directions to Halong Bay.
"First we've got to take a train to Haiphong. Then we take a boat to
Bai Chay—wherever that is. Then, to get out to the limestone cliffs,
we have to take another boat. This whole thing is going to take a
couple of days, for sure."

"That's great," I said. "When we get back, we'll spend a few days
here in Hanoi and then it'll be time to fly on to Laos. The timing's
perfect."

Early the following morning, we boarded a local train for the five-
hour trip to Haiphong, Vietnam's third largest city and the main industrial center in northern Vietnam. Situated on the Cam River, Haiphong had been developed by the French into a thriving commercial
center through which most of the major export commodities from
Indochina—rice, rubber, and coal, once flowed. All that changed in
1946, however, when a French naval vessel captured a Vietnamese
pirate junk in the Gulf of Tonkin. When the Vietnamese let loose a
shot at the French vessel the French navy responded by bombarding
Haiphong, killing thousands of Vietnamese civilians in the process.
The Viet Minh War between France and Vietnam began a month
later, and lasted nine years, until 1954, when ten thousand French
troops surrendered to Viet Minh forces at Dien Bien Phu.

During the Vietnam War with America, Haiphong once again
came under attack when the United States mined and bombed Haiphong's harbor in its attempt to keep Soviet military supplies from
reaching North Vietnam. As a result of both the French and American

military actions in the area, the export door was finally closed and Haiphong soon became a run-down port with little traffic, dilapidated buildings and broken-down streets.

With little to interest travelers in the city, most people on their way to Halong Bay leave Haiphong soon after they arrive at the train station. Which is exactly what we did. Right after we arrived, we took a ferry to the Thuy Nguyen District on the north bank of the Cam River. When we set foot on the other side of the river, we boarded a crowded, uncomfortable local bus for the 55-kilometer, two-hour bus ride to *Bai Chay*—a small, waterfront town which is the main jumping off point for boats to Halong Bay.

After a whole day on trains, cyclos, ferries and buses, we eventually got to *Bai Chay* in late afternoon. Tired from a full day of traveling, we booked ourselves into the first decent hotel we looked at, the *Van Hai*, a low-budget hotel situated conveniently along the waterfront. After a quick shower and a change of clothes, we walked up the road from the hotel to a little, outdoor restaurant where we planned to relax over a good dinner and a few cold beers.

We had barely gotten ourselves seated when someone called out in a deep voice, "If you fellas are planning to hire a launch for a trip out to the bay, I've found someone with a boat that will take us out there for a good price. Think you'd be interested?"

We looked across the restaurant and saw a large, European man sitting with an attractive, blonde woman, a few tables down from us. Before we could answer, they stood up and carried their beers over to the balcony table where we sat overlooking the bay. "Mind if we join you?" he asked, as he pulled up two chairs beside us.

Our uninvited guest was a big man, in his late forties, with curly, brown hair and a deep tan that set off his light-blue eyes. His deep voice had a slight hint of an accent that sounded almost British, but wasn't. With a nod of his curly head, he introduced himself as "Teddy," and told us he was a writer from Denmark. His companion, Ülle, a tall, athletic-looking woman in her early thirties, was Teddy's wife, as well as his photographer.

They had come to Vietnam to do an article on some new species of mammal they'd heard had been spotted a few hundred miles south-west of Hanoi, close to the Laotian border. "If we can get a picture of it, we stand to make twenty, maybe thirty, thousand dollars selling

it to magazines—no problem," Teddy bragged, as he signaled our
waiter for a fresh round of beers.

"For *one* picture?" Colin asked, dubiously.

Teddy placed his beer down with a bang and leaned forward in his
seat. With a fiery look at Colin, he bellowed, "*Fucking right!* This is
a *new* goddamn species—never been photographed before. There's
only supposed to be about three hundred or so of 'em around." Leaning back in his chair he added, "It looks like a goat, but it's supposed
to be more closely related to the cow. Must be an ugly fucker. Once
all the goddamn paperwork is out of the way, we're going out to look
for it. If we can get it on film, the pictures will be worth a lot of
money, believe me."

If Colin still had any doubts about the value of the photos, he didn't
voice them. Instead, he sat quietly back and sipped his beer while
Teddy rambled on about the mysterious goat-cow and other species
of mammals that none of us had ever heard of before.

Though he was hard to take seriously, and more than a little obnoxious, Teddy was a very entertaining guy. With a captive audience to
listen to his adventures, he was also a willing storyteller. The more I
listened to him boast about his escapades, however, the harder I found
them to believe. But as hard as it was to believe his stories, it was even
harder to imagine that he was from Denmark. All of the Danish people
I had met were friendly and modest. Teddy was friendly enough, but
he was also loud and boastful. To his way of thinking, if he hadn't done
something or been somewhere then it obviously wasn't worth doing or
going to. And whenever someone else had an exploit to talk about, it
was a sure bet Teddy could top it with some hair-raising, life-threaten-
ing adventure that made the other person's story pale in comparison.

As the evening went on, the group of people around our table increased as other travelers wandered over to join our conversation. Before long, we had a small party going on, with stacks of beer bottles
piling steadily up in front of us. Popping the cap off another bottle of
beer, Teddy was just about to launch into another one of his exploits
when an Australian fellow chimed in about an earthquake in some
South American country he had visited a few years before. "I couldn't
believe it," he said enthusiastically, as he finished his story, "If I'd have
left one day later, I might never have made it out of there. That was
about as close to a national disaster as I'd like to get."

Teddy peered up from his bottle, anxious to regain the limelight. "Then it's a good thing you weren't in Israel with me during the Sinai War in '74. The place was a bloody mess. Bodies everywhere. Almost didn't get out of there in one piece."

I glanced curiously at Teddy. "I thought the Sinai War took place in '73?"

Teddy gazed nervously around the table before he replied. "Yeah, that's right. What did I say?" Before I could respond, he stood up and called over to the owner of the restaurant, "Where's our friend with the beers!" When the owner indicated he was out of beer, Teddy stood up and beckoned me to follow him. "Come on, we'll bring some back from the shop down the road."

As we walked down the dimly-lit, dirt road in front of the restaurant, I discovered that Teddy wasn't so obnoxious without an audience. While we strolled along, we actually had a pleasant conversation that showed he had a more serious, mature side—until we reached the little beer shop. The proprietor of the store didn't speak English, but that didn't stop Teddy from putting on a show.

He gave the small, Vietnamese shop owner a large grin and a friendly clap on the back that almost knocked the little man over. Then, bending down face-to-face with the little man, he barked, "Where's the beer?" When the man didn't respond, Teddy strolled around the shop to see for himself where the beer was stored. When he couldn't find any, he looked at the little shopkeeper and said impatiently, "Come on, we haven't got all night. Where d'ya store the beer?"

With a helpless expression, the little man looked at the big foreigner in front of him and tried to figure out what he wanted. Teddy turned to me with an exasperated look. "I've been buying beer here every night this week. You'd think the little bastard would know what I wanted by now." He shook his curly head and placed his thick arm around the shopkeeper's narrow shoulders. Recalling the Vietnamese word for beer, Teddy whispered, "*Bia.*" Then followed with, "Tám cái chai"—eight bottles.

With a vigorous nod of his head, the little man's face lit up as he raced off to get the beers. Teddy looked at me and rolled his eyes. "It's no wonder most of 'em got killed in the fucking war. They can't even remember where they store the beer!" When the shopkeeper returned, Teddy paid him for the beers and then pointed to me. "This here is an American. You'd better watch out for him. His people blew up half your fucking country." Seeing that the little man didn't understand a word he was saying, Teddy lifted his left hand over his head to mimic a plane dropping a bomb, then thundered, "*Nnnnyowwwwww . . . .BOOM!!!*"

I pulled his arm down and cried, "*Hey, cut it out—that's not funny!*" Fortunately, the shopkeeper had no idea what Teddy was talking about. He just stood there, smiling away at the big jerk who took up half his little shop, while nodding his head contentedly as we walked out with our beers.

It was hard to believe that even a loudmouth like Teddy could say something so stupid. But what bugged me even more than his attempt at bad humor, was how anyone who had traveled as much as he had, could behave so rudely in someone else's country. Despite his extensive travels, experiences, and interactions with different people and cultures, he hadn't learned a thing. Wherever he went, there he was. And when his travels were over, he returned home the same guy he had been when he went away.

The funny thing was that Teddy was actually a very nice guy. He was also interesting to talk to when he wasn't drinking or acting like a know-it-all. And though I was sure he had other good qualities, as well, his most redeeming quality, as far as I was concerned, was that he wasn't American. In a strange sort of way, it was comforting to know that not all the "Ugly Americans" traveling the world were from the States. But despite his personality deficiencies, Teddy was likeable enough to enlist a group of people—Colin, Dan, Calvin, and me, included—to split the cost of a boat to Halong Bay the following day.

When we left the hotel the next morning, the air was clear and warm as we walked along the waterfront to meet Teddy and his wife, a British friend of theirs, and three Israelis, at the jetty up the road. Still a bit hung over from the night before, none of us mumbled more than a few perfunctory words of greeting as we boarded the small, motorized, wooden launch behind Teddy and his group. Easing slowly away from the dock at Bai Chay into the calm turquoise waters of Halong Bay, our little boat cruised slowly past the coastal, coal-mining town of Hon Gai which loomed over Bai Chay from the other side of the narrow channel. As we glided effortlessly out into the wide-open waters before us, the scent of the sea and the lap of the waves lulled me into a blissful state of relaxation.

While we made our way out to sea, scattered streams of thin, white clouds trailed slowly above us in a light-blue sky, while exotic-looking junks with beautiful, fanned sails floated like butterflies along the horizon. The water was calm and peaceful and before long, we approached the first of the three thousand limestone cliffs that dotted the bay. Awed by the sight, we grabbed our cameras and began snapping away. In a short while, we were in the middle of a spectacular landscape of jagged, towering islands that rose straight from the sea. It was beautiful and surreal, and was almost like stepping into another world.

In Vietnamese, *Ha Long* means "Sea Dragon." According to Vietnamese legend, the islands were created by a giant dragon that lived in the mountains. As it made its way out to sea, its tail carved up the islands and created pockets of water between the peaks of the islands left standing behind it. Millions of years of wind and wave erosion formed massive caves and chambers in the limestone hills of the islands, producing exotic shapes and formations, many of which inspired such unusual names as *Isle de Suprise*, *Isle de Marveilles* (Isle of Marvels), and *Grotto of the Pious*.

Many of the larger islets had been used as hideouts by Chinese and Vietnamese pirates up until the end of the nineteenth century, and we spent the morning exploring their spectacular beaches, caverns, and grottos. As the day wore on, we went back to the boat and sailed lazily around the ragged peaks and limestone towers until it was time to head back to Bai Chay at the end of the day.

Before we went to Halong Bay, we had been told that the Vietnamese considered the limestone peaks to be the most beautiful natural wonder in Vietnam. Having seen them for myself, I couldn't have agreed more. It was one of the most spectacular natural sights I had ever seen and worth every minute of the tiring, daylong journey from Hanoi to get there. When we left the following morning, I hoped I'd have the chance to return again someday.

We arrived back in Hanoi early the next evening and re-booked ourselves into the *Dong Do Hotel* along with Teddy, Ülle, and a few other people whom we had met in Halong Bay. Tired out from our long day of traveling, we slept late the following morning. After a leisurely breakfast of eggs, croissants, and cheese, Dan, Colin, Calvin and I hired cyclos to ride us over to the Laotian Embassy across town so we could pick up our Laotian visas. From there, we rode over to the Vietnam Airlines Booking Office in the center of the city to confirm our flight reservations to Vientienne for later that week. With the last of our errands out of the way, we were totally free to spend the next few days exploring Hanoi before leaving Vietnam for Laos.